Global Politics of Defense Reform

Initiatives in Strategic Studies: Issues and Policies

James J. Wirtz
General Editor

Jeffrey A. Larsen
T. V. Paul
Brad Roberts
James M. Smith
Series Editors

INITIATIVES IN STRATEGIC STUDIES provides a bridge between the use of force or diplomacy and the achievement of political objectives. This series focuses on the topical and timeless issues relating to strategy, including the nexus of political, diplomatic, psychological, economic, cultural, historic and military affairs. It provides a link between the scholarly and policy communities by serving as the recognized forum for conceptually sophisticated analyses of timely and important strategic issues.

Nuclear Transformation: The New U.S. Nuclear Doctrine
Edited by James J. Wirtz and Jeffrey A. Larsen

Proliferation of Weapons of Mass Destruction in the Middle East: Directions and Policy Options in the New Century
Edited by James A. Russell

The Last Battle of the Cold War: The Deployment and Negotiated Elimination of Intermediate Range Nuclear Forces in Europe
Maynard W. Glitman

Critical Issues Facing the Middle East: Security, Politics and Economics
Edited by James A. Russell

Militarization and War
Julian Schofield

Global Politics of Defense Reform
Edited by Thomas Bruneau and Harold Trinkunas

Global Politics of Defense Reform

Edited by

Thomas Bruneau
and
Harold Trinkunas

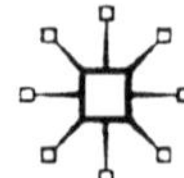

GLOBAL POLITICS OF DEFENSE REFORM

First published in 2008 by
PALGRAVE MACMILLAN™
175 Fifth Avenue, New York, N.Y. 10010 and
Houndmills, Basingstoke, Hampshire, England RG21 6XS
Companies and representatives throughout the world.

PALGRAVE MACMILLAN is the global academic imprint of the Palgrave Macmillan division of St. Martin's Press, LLC and of Palgrave Macmillan Ltd. Macmillan® is a registered trademark in the United States, United Kingdom and other countries. Palgrave is a registered trademark in the European Union and other countries.

ISBN-13: 978–0–230–60444–5
ISBN-10: 0–230–60444–7

Library of Congress Cataloging-in-Publication Data

Global politics of defense reform / edited by Thomas Bruneau and Harold Trinkunas.
p. cm.—(Initiatives in strategic studies: issues and policies series)
Includes bibliographical references and index.
ISBN 0–230–60444–7
1. Civil-military relations. 2. Armed Forces—Reorganization. 3. National security—International cooperation. I. Bruneau, Thomas C. II. Trinkunas, Harold A.

JF195.G56 2008
322'.5—dc22 2007027020

A catalogue record for this book is available from the British Library.

Design by Newgen Imaging Systems (P) Ltd., Chennai, India.

First edition: March 2008

10 9 8 7 6 5 4 3 2 1

Printed in the United States of America.

Contents

Acknowledgments

This volume would not have been possible without the support of the Center for Civil-Military Relations in Monterey, California. By sponsoring the initial conference in September 2005, the Center has provided the environment and resources needed to sustain this project through to its conclusion, and this would not have been possible without the support of its director, Richard Hoffman. We would also like to acknowledge the constant effort of our copyeditor, Elizabeth Skinner, who worked diligently to ensure that our contributors' efforts and thoughts were presented as clearly as possible. We would also like to thank Cristiana Matei for her research assistance on international democracy support programs that is found in chapter 3. Finally, we would both like to thank our families for their support.

About the Contributors

Rajesh Basrur is Visiting Research Fellow at the S. Rajaratnam School of International Studies at Nanyang Technological University, Singapore. He also directs the Centre for Global Studies in Mumbai, India. His publications include *Minimum Deterrence and India's Nuclear Security* (Stanford University Press, 2006) and *South Asia's Cold War* (Routledge, forthcoming).

Thomas Bruneau is Distinguished Professor of National Security Affairs at the Naval Postgraduate School. He received his Ph.D. in Political Science from the University of California, Berkeley. He recently coedited *Who Guards the Guardians and How* (University of Texas Press, 2006) and *Reforming Intelligence: Obstacles to Democratic Control and Effectiveness* (University of Texas Press, 2007).

Anne Clunan is an Assistant Professor of National Security Affairs at the Naval Postgraduate School in Monterey, California. She received her Ph.D. in Political Science from the University of California, Berkeley. She has recently authored articles on terrorism financing and coedited a volume on biological weapons attribution.

Michael Malley is assistant professor of comparative politics in the Department of National Security Affairs at the Naval Postgraduate School in Monterey, California. Dr. Malley's research is focused on issues of state formation, state failure and survival, and regime change in Southeast Asia. He has particular expertise in the area of center-local relations, decentralization policy, and provincial politics and political economy in Indonesia. He earned his doctorate in political science at the University of Wisconsin-Madison.

Liviu Muresan is the founder and the Executive President of the EURISC Foundation—European Institute for Risk, Security and Communication Management (1995). He is an Associate Professor with the Academy of Economic Studies, Bucharest where he got his Ph.D. in Economics (1978).He has published numerous articles and books on the issues of international security. He has held several positions in the government of Romania. He was Director of the Romanian Agency for setting up the regional SECI Center for Combating Transborder Organized Crime, the Deputy Director of the National Defence College, and he was the first civilian appointed in command position in the Romanian Army (1993–1994).

David Pion-Berlin is a Professor of political science at the University of California, Riverside. He has written extensively on Latin America, particularly on civil-military relations, military political thought, human rights, and Argentina. He is the author or editor of numerous volumes, including *Transforming Latin America: the International and Domestic Origins of Change* (coauthored with Craig Arceneaux) 2005, and *Civil-Military Relations in Latin America: New Analytical Perspectives* (2001).

Douglas Porch is Professor and Chair of the Department of National Security Affairs at the Naval Postgraduate School in Monterey, California. He has written extensively on military history. His latest book, *The Path to Victory. The Mediterranean Theater in World War II,* published by Farrar, Straus, Giroux in May 2004, was a selection of the Military History Book Club, the History Book Club, and the Book of the Month Club, and received the Award for Excellence in U.S. Army Historical Writing from The Army Historical Foundation.

Marcos Robledo has been chief advisor to the Minister of Defense of Chile, and since March 2006, serves as advisor on foreign and defense policy to the Presidency of Chile. He is a journalist, and he has lectured international relations at the Political Science Institute of the Catholic University of Chile. He received an M.A. in National Security Affairs from the Naval Postgraduate School in Monterey, California. He has published extensively.

Jim Schweiter is an attorney currently practicing with the law firm of McKenna, Long & Aldridge, LLP. He previously served as counsel, general counsel, and minority staff director of the Committee on Armed Services, U.S. House of Representatives, and as Deputy Assistant Secretary of Defense for Manpower and Reserve Affairs.

Harold Trinkunas is Associate Professor of National Security Affairs at the Naval Postgraduate School in Monterey, California. He received his Ph.D. in Political Science from Stanford University. He recently authored *Crafting Civilian Control of the Armed Forces: Venezuela in Comparative Perspective* (University of North Carolina Press, 2005) and *Terrorism Financing and State Responses* (Stanford University Press, 2007), coedited with Jeanne Giraldo.

Kim Wincup has more than thirty years of experience in a variety of positions in the U.S. government in both the executive and legislative branches, as well as in government-related activities in the private sector. This service includes working in the U.S. Congress as Staff Director of two congressional committees, and holding two presidential appointments in the Department of Defense. In 1992, he was appointed Assistant Secretary of the Air Force (Acquisition) and served as Service Acquisition Executive responsible for the management and oversight of the U.S. Air Force's acquisition program.

James Wirtz is a Professor in the Department of National Security Affairs, Naval Postgraduate School, Monterey, California. He is the author or editor of numerous publications on intelligence, deterrence, the Vietnam War, and military innovation and strategy. He received his Ph.D. from Columbia University in 1989.

Toshi Yoshihara is an associate professor in the Strategy and Policy Department at the Naval War College, Newport, Rhode Island. Previously, he served as a visiting professor in the Strategy Department at the Air War College, Montgomery, Alabama. He received his Ph.D. from the Fletcher School of Law and Diplomacy at Tufts University.

Marian Zulean is an adviser with the National Security Department, Office of the Romanian President and Associate Professor at the University of Bucharest and SNSPA. Among his latest international publications are: "Civil-Military Cultural Gap in Romania," in G. Caforio and G. Kummel, eds., *Military Missions and their Implications Reconsidered: The Aftermath of September 11th*, (Greenwich, CT: JAI Press, 2005); "Reforming the Security Sectors in SEE: Lessons Learned and Their Relevance for a Wider Black Sea Area Policy," *Connections* 3,4 (December 2004); "Security Sector Reform in Romania," in E. Cole, Th. Donais, and Ph. Fluri, eds., *Defence and Security Sector Governance and Reform in South East Europe Self-Assessment Studies: Regional Perspectives* (Nomos, 2004). He has a Ph.D. in (Military) Sociology from Bucharest and holds a Master in International Affairs, University of Pittsburgh.

Part I

Global Trends: Implications for Defense Reform

1

Global Trends and Their Impact on Civil-Military Relations

Thomas Bruneau and Harold Trinkunas

It is increasingly clear that since the end of the Cold War a number of important global trends have become self-perpetuating, far beyond the ability of any one state to control. The current worldwide struggle against transnational terrorism since 9/11, the spread of democracy, the globalization of commerce and communications, and the implications of new technologies all have affected military organizations and their civilian counterparts profoundly. Leaders have reacted to these events with a reexamination of defense policies, military roles and missions, and the development of new capabilities to meet emerging threats. In the United States, the George W. Bush administration has issued a series of security policies intended to produce a military and intelligence transformation, and a whole new field of endeavor, homeland security, in reaction to the failures of both pre-9/11 policy and the hunt for weapons of mass destruction in Iraq. European countries continue to debate whether they can afford to fund militaries that can match the pace of technological development in the United States, even as NATO takes on greater out-of-area missions in the Balkans and Afghanistan. Countries from El Salvador to Mongolia to Romania have discovered peacekeeping as a new mission, which has its own set of increasingly more difficult challenges, as recent operations in East Timor, Congo, and Lebanon demonstrate. Even traditionally inward-looking Brazil is now leading a major peacekeeping mission in perpetually unstable

Haiti. Moreover, the post-Soviet world offers a multitude of ways in which defense and security institutions still influence political outcomes, ranging from their laissez-faire attitude during the Orange Revolution in Ukraine to their virtual takeover of the new Russian state. This flurry of defense reform nevertheless has yet to be addressed in any systematic and integrated fashion in the contemporary literature on civil-military relations.

This volume highlights the impact of global trends on defense reform and civil-military relations, including phenomena such as globalization and economic liberalization that are not usually associated with these matters. Until now, most analyses of civil-military relations have focused on the domestic level to develop explanations of the kinds and degrees of change taking place. They have generally assumed that efforts to change defense establishments are driven by either domestic political calculations or rational technical assessments of changes in the security environment. The two exceptions to this point of view have been analyses of the efforts by former Warsaw Pact states to join NATO, where alliance membership brings significant payoffs to local politicians; and work by scholars such as Michael Desch that relates changes in the structure of the international system with the stability of domestic civil-military relations.[1] In the present volume we examine specific cases of defense reform as a means to analyze changes in the nature of civil-military relations in recent decades. We are convinced that the success or failure of defense reform policies cannot be understood without examining the interaction between reform and civil-military relations. Until recently, most scholars of civil-military relations focused almost exclusively on questions of oversight and control, but in this project, we reconceive civil-military relations as a trinity that balances democratic oversight and control of military affairs, efficiency in defense spending, and the effectiveness of military forces.

Defense reform is a particularly useful policy locus from which to examine the relationship between the global trends we identify in this volume and civil-military relations. In general, defense reforms are intended to bring about changes in the military establishment, to achieve greater oversight and control, greater effectiveness, and/or greater efficiencies in spending. For this reason, reform efforts represent opportunities to instigate rapid shifts in civil-military relations. Many studies of defense reform tend to be purely technical in nature, however, focusing either on responses to a changing security environment or, in the case of NATO aspirants, on checklists of entry requirements met and unmet. If this literature considers the politics of reform, it tends to examine single cases using a domestic level of analysis.[2] These approaches do not lend themselves well to understanding why defense reforms occur or how they might succeed. By focusing attention on the international dimension, we are better able to explain the timing, speed, and sequence of defense reforms, as well as the reasons behind their success or failure. We also find that reform efforts are rarely responses purely to changes in the security environment, but are often driven by the impact of global trends on particular states. One of the most interesting findings is the extent to which states are able to modulate the effect of globalization, which we explain as the product of differences among states with regard to their relative power, internal structural capacity, and regime type.

In this introduction, we describe a framework with which to analyze the international dimensions of defense reform and civil-military relations. In the first section of the Introduction, we look at current global trends that have had a substantial impact on civil-military relations. In the second part, we deepen our reconceptualization of civil-military relations as a trinity of elements. In the final section, we discuss the rationale behind the book's structure and our selection of case studies.

THE IMPACT OF GLOBAL TRENDS ON DEFENSE REFORM AND CIVIL-MILITARY RELATIONS

Globalization has become a catchall phrase for any transnational trend that is beyond the control of any one state actor. So many different effects are subsumed under this heading that it finally loses its analytical worth. In this volume we focus on four specific tendencies that have had a clear effect on civil-military relations: democratization; the transnationalization of new norms and ideas; the diffusion of economic liberalism; and the military implications of the spread of new technologies, sometimes referred to as the revolution in military affairs (RMA) in U.S. defense literature. While each of these phenomena has been associated with globalization in its broadest aspect, we find it analytically useful to examine each one somewhat independently. As our case studies suggest, individual countries are not equally vulnerable to all of these global trends. In fact, much to our surprise, globalization and democratization turned out to be much more important factors in explaining defense reform than economic liberalization and technological change. In addition, there are interesting interactions among the variables that help to explain the particular shape that defense reforms take in each case, with its consequent impact on civil-military relations.

We chose to narrow our inquiry to these concepts because they seemed theoretically to have the greatest influence on changes to three dimensions of civil-military relations—civilian control, defense efficiency, and military effectiveness. Globalization has created a world of "softened sovereignty" wherein states are much less capable than ever before at shielding their institutions and citizens from the transnational diffusion of norms, ideas, practices, legal understandings and knowledge that alters how these perceive themselves. We find that this is even true of the core "hard" institutions of the state, such as the security services and the armed forces. Democratization, by altering the nature of a regime and the selection mechanism for state leaders, makes possible rapid shifts in the degree of civilian control over defense policy, although it is quite clear that this does not always occur in every case. We also posited that economic liberalization, which reduces the role of the state in economic decisions, opens economies to the international market, and changes ideas about the relative importance of security, has an impact on concepts of defense efficiency. The RMA is only one example of how rapid technological advances have forced changes on states and their armed forces, yet as this volume will suggest, this trend turns out to be most relevant to great powers. Mid-ranking and regional powers have generally abandoned the competition with leading powers altogether and have repurposed their armed forces for nontraditional missions such as peacekeeping.

Perhaps the most mature of the global trends we analyze is democratization, beginning its most recent wave with the Portuguese revolution in 1974. Democratization has placed control over military and security forces in the hands of elected officials in more countries than ever before. There is already an extensive literature on civil-military relations in emerging democracies, much of which is quite sophisticated, but which focuses mainly on the developing world.[3] This limits the scope of analysis on the one hand, since the cases these studies examine do not provide adequate insight into many of the civil-military issues important to defense establishments in advanced industrial democracies, such as budgeting and program oversight, technology development, personnel management, and acquisitions policies. Studies of civil-military relations in developed countries such as the United States, on the other hand, take civilian supremacy largely as a given and focus purely on the internal dynamics of defense policy.[4] They therefore do not address one of the most central questions facing emerging democracies: that of asserting control over the armed forces, nor do they describe the mechanisms used by developed countries to foster democracy and civilian control of the armed forces in other parts of the world.

The domestic focus of most democratization and civil-military relations literature is at odds with the reality that the international community has deliberately created a large number of programs and institutions to promote democratization. We argue that democracy promotion by leading powers such as the United States and the European Union has propagated a particular liberal understanding of civil-military relations that, in most parts of the world, has clearly privileged civilian control over the other two elements of democratic civil-military relations, efficiency, and effectiveness. Only those countries that have become members of NATO since the end of the Cold War, or belong to a club of aspirants such as the Partnership for Peace, have balanced the impetus toward greater civilian control against requirements for military effectiveness. The case studies in this volume also suggest, however, that in the face of greater transnational threats, other new democracies have begun to promote effectiveness and efficiency in their security sectors.

The global diffusion of norms and ideas has had an impact on civil-military relations that reaches far beyond that of democratization, yet there have been only limited studies on the spread of new norms of military professionalism. These typically look at either state-society relations in developed countries or the consequences of legal battles over the punishment of the perpetrators of past state terrorism.[5] One new area that deserves more study is how globalization fosters changes in military norms today, including both the growing influence of nongovernmental organizations and global news channels, and traditional military-to-military training, education programs, and professional exchanges.

In this volume, we focus on three aspects of the spread of norms: the reduction of barriers to their dissemination throughout the international system; the speed with which new norms propagate; and the diffusion of authority beyond state actors when it comes to the norms governing the organization and use of military forces. As Anne Clunan points out in chapter two, non-state actors are developing a much greater ability to propagate new views on the use of the armed forces in ways that states find hard to resist. Norms on human rights, prisoner abuse, and land mines are only some of the more prominent examples of this trend. Human rights campaigners now find it much easier to organize across state boundaries to pressure governments and militaries. Chilean civil-military relations, as Marcos Robledo documents in chapter five, came under strain during the 1998 crisis precipitated by the detention of former dictator, Augusto Pinochet, in London on charges of complicity in human rights abuses during his tenure in power. The spread of economic liberalization and its impact on defense is rarely studied, but it is an important constraint on defense reform and civil-military relations, both in terms of its impact on the availability of resources for reform and on the ideas and attitudes that reformers develop toward defense. International financial institutions such as the World Bank and International Monetary Fund, which dominate the market for development advice and monies, typically advocate freeing markets and reducing the size of government, including the military, in developing countries. Defense spending is rapidly becoming a residual in the economic calculations of most countries competing to attract international trade, investment, and assistance. Paradoxically, developed Western democracies conduct two thirds of the world's defense spending, thus rejecting the very policies that they advocate in the developing world. A related debate, in both developed and developing countries that are currently engaged in conflicts, asks whether defense spending is better used to address the social causes of conflicts or to find military solutions. This divergence in attitudes toward defense spending has significant implications for how quickly or thoroughly defense reform is carried out across the range of cases considered in this volume. Defense efficiency is all too often understood solely as a budget-driven downsizing of the armed forces, with little attention to retaining, let along obtaining, needed military capabilities. We see this phenomenon most clearly in a case such as Indonesia, but we can see some of this logic emerging even in the case of the United States during the 1990s.

Finally, the development of new military and civilian technologies, that is, RMA, and their diffusion to new actors, is forcing defense reform in some of the leading powers in the international system.[6] During the 1990s, RMA was a voguish way to describe some pressing realities: The pace of military technological development is highly variable across even the developed countries, technological change may be creating barriers to interoperability even among allies, and the military lead achieved by the United States and a few key allies looms so large that it calls into question the relevance of conventional military establishments, roles, and missions in both developed and developing countries During the George W. Bush administration, military transformation has become the buzzword for a program that seeks to change radically the way in which military forces do business through technology, while at the same time making them cheaper and more subject to civilian direction. Initially, it was thought that the RMA would give the United States and a few key allies with the economic wherewithal to achieve these capabilities, a devastating offensive dominance.[7] Other states would either have to learn to cooperate within an international system in which the RMA buttressed U.S. hegemony, or become so-called pariah states, such as North Korea and Cuba. It was also supposed to radically alter civil-military relations, at least according to proponents of military transformation, by allowing leaders simultaneously to increase oversight and control of military operations at all levels and improve the effectiveness of military force, while at the same time reducing the cost of defense.

The reality of the RMA and its present-day manifestation, however, is that it turns out to be relevant in a much more limited range of cases than its theorists had first believed. While important for assessing the balance of power between the leading states in the international system, such as China and the United States, the ideological underpinnings of the assumptions behind military transformation have been shaken by the outcomes we are witnessing in Iraq and Afghanistan. Internal security and stabilization and reconstruction campaigns remain largely impervious to technological solutions, as chapters six and nine document in the cases of Colombia and India. The Indian case also suggests the extent to which states can sidestep the implications of the RMA by choosing alternatives, such as the nuclear weapon/ballistic missile revolution. Threats from non-state actors, such as global terrorist networks, that conduct asymmetric campaigns often using civilian technologies such as the transportation infrastructure, bring a whole new set of issues to the table. Liberal democracies, which have traditionally excluded the military from internal security operations to protect civil rights and preserve civil supremacy, have had difficulty coping with devastating attacks that can be conducted from within, and the Indian and Colombian cases also provide evidence of this challenge.

GLOBAL TRENDS AND DEFENSE REFORM: EXPLAINING THE IMPACT ON CIVIL-MILITARY RELATIONS

How do we then develop an integrated understanding of how these global trends affect defense reform? How can we tell if defense reform has actually been accomplished? Do we know whether the effect of the defense reform is positive or negative? This volume demonstrates that any type of defense reform will inevitably be reflected in the structure of a given state's civil-military relations, which our authors analyze according to the new methodology presented here. We begin by disaggregating the relatively vague term of democratic civil-military relations into a trinity. The first element is civilian control of the armed forces and other security structures, including police and intelligence services, with particular emphasis on the degree to which officials have institutionalized oversight mechanisms and the means to develop a community of civilian defense professionals. The second element is military effectiveness, here understood as the ability of defense and security forces to successfully carry out the roles and missions assigned to them by elected leaders. Roles and missions can range from traditional territorial defense to humanitarian assistance, peacekeeping, counterterrorism, and intelligence gathering. The third element of democratic civil-military relations, defense efficiency, seeks to determine whether military and security establishments can accomplish their assigned roles and missions at an acceptable cost to society. In order to determine efficiency, civilian and military leaders must agree beforehand on roles and missions; otherwise, there is nothing to measure efficiency against.

The dependent variable in this book is the nature of civil-military relations. Clarity in defining the dependent variable obviously is necessary to establish meaningful comparisons between cases. We are poorly served by what passes for the conceptualization of civil-military relations in the literature today.[8] Indeed, not only is the definition of civil-military relations inconsistent, but the trend in Europe has been to use the term security sector reform (SSR), a broader concept that in our opinion captures an additional and useful dimension of the civil-military relationship.[9] The definition and understanding are important not only for purposes of systematic analysis, but also because there remains a certain bias in much of the literature that associates the concept with powerful historical and regional baggage. Whereas civil-military relations in the United

States is associated with the tensions of directing an armed force in a democracy, in many parts of the world it was traditionally associated with military coups and military rule. Today, in the era of consolidating Third Wave democracies, it is incumbent on us to break down these barriers and refine the concept for comparative purposes, so that we can deduce general propositions with some predictive value. This book is the first systematic attempt to analyze the impact of external independent variables (trends in globalization) on the dependent variable of civil-military relations.

Civil-Military Relations in Historical Perspective

The classic literature on civil-military relations is closely associated with the major works of Samuel Huntington and Morris Janowitz.[10] For all intents and purposes, these authors focused on the more established democracies, especially the United States, and were chiefly concerned with the issue of reconciling a military strong enough to do what civilian leaders want it to do, with a military subordinate enough to do only what civilians authorize it to do.[11] This conceptualization, dominated exclusively by U.S. authors, assumed the democratic context, and thus is associated with the Cold War military standoff between the West and the East.

Since the beginning of the Third Wave of democratization started on 25 April 1974 in Lisbon, the nature of the civil-military problem shifted. Even though neither Portugal nor Spain, whose transition began upon the death of General Francisco Franco in late 1975, were pure military dictatorships, their militaries played key roles in the transitions to democracy.[12] This was even more the case as the Third Wave spread to include military regimes in Latin America, Asia, and sub-Saharan Africa. Even the transitional governments of the former Marxist-dominated Soviet bloc, while never under military tutelage, had to come to terms with their armed forces once the Wall came down. In Romania for example, the army was a central actor in the transition from the dictatorship of Nicolae Ceausescu and his nefarious Securitate to a democracy. Therefore, many analyses of democratic transitions and consolidation since 1974 included a focus on civil-military relations. The major contribution by Juan J. Linz and Alfred Stepan on southern Europe, South America and post-Communist Europe includes different military groups as a central variable under the category of actors.[13] Major analysts of transitions and consolidation, such as Adam Przeworski and Philippe Schmitter, call explicit attention to the "military variable" (although they never fully address it).[14] There also are some excellent case studies of civil-military relations in the context of transitions and consolidation, or, in the case of Venezuela, deconsolidation.[15] These works all evaluate the role of the military, including in some cases the police and intelligence agencies, in democratic consolidation. Most of these authors also take into account the institutions whereby civilian control is implemented, some of which include oversight. What these works demonstrate is that, in contrast to their authoritarian pasts, whether military- or civilian-dominated, the emerging democracies of South America, Romania, and elsewhere emphasize democratic security over national security. In other words, these new regimes focus on how to control the armed forces that in many cases were themselves previously in control of—or even constituted—the government.

Civil-Military Relations in the Twenty-First Century

We have found from our experience of working directly with consolidating democracies, that the narrow analytical focus on civilian control, as described above, is not adequate either empirically or, for the purpose of developing comparisons, conceptually. At the end of the Cold War, not only governments themselves, but also donor states and leading international organizations such as the prolific Geneva-based Centre for the Democratic Control of Armed Forces, stayed focused overwhelmingly on issues of control. Yet in reality, very few transitional countries abolished their armed forces; at a minimum militaries were redirected toward humanitarian assistance such as disaster relief, or to back up the police in domestic upheavals and riots. As peacekeeping became increasingly critical in the former Yugoslavia, several parts of Africa, East Timor, and elsewhere, more and more countries opted to become peacekeepers, primarily under the auspices of the United Nations. In short, the issue has become less that of control, and more seeking to have effective militaries to implement a wide variety of roles and missions.

The demands of peacekeeping require governments to pay attention to military capabilities and costs on a globally comparative level. Attacks by international terrorists in Bali, Nairobi, the United States, Madrid, London, and Moscow, and the launch of Washington's "global war on terrorism," also led militaries everywhere to become involved in fighting terrorism to a greater or lesser extent. Under these circumstances, civil-military relations came to include not only the armed forces, but also police and intelligence services. In the real world, leaders are paying attention to both matters of control and outcomes: They must provide not only for democratic security, but also national security and defense, while simultaneously protecting democratic liberties. This volume brings these new priorities into the spotlight. In this conceptualization, while civilian control is considered a fundamental aspect of democratic consolidation, it is not assumed to exist in any particular case. Our authors pay close attention to the development and management of the institutions whereby *both* control and effectiveness are achieved and maintained, at a cost that is as low as possible without jeopardizing results.

To capture the priorities and requirements of democratic consolidation and reform, we analyze civil-military relations according to the three dimensions of control, efficiency, and effectiveness, because each of the elements is in tension with the others.[16] It is interesting to note that some U.S. and NATO Partnership for Peace policy documents give attention to all three, as we illustrate in the third chapter on the impact of democratization.[17] This, however, still is not the case in many of the programs funded by the U.S. government through its international military education and training programs, the U.S. State Department and Agency for International Development, other governments interested in democratization such as in the European Union, or in the literature produced by important research centers.

The first leg of the triangle is indeed democratic civilian control. It must be emphasized, as there is so much confusion and ignorance in this area, that civilian control does not exist unless it is grounded in and exercised through institutions ranging from organic laws that deal with the Ministry of Defense or oversight committees, to budget processes and civilian control of officer promotions. If these institutions are not in place and functioning, democratic civilian control is only a façade. While the range of such institutions varies from country to country, they would normally include a civilian-led ministry of defense with a professional staff; one or more committees in the legislature that deal with policies, budgets, and oversight; and a well-defined mechanism for civilians to exert authority in determining roles and missions, and monitor such personnel matters as recruitment, education, training, promotion, and retirement.

The second leg of the triangle is effectiveness in the implementation or achievement of the roles and missions assigned to the armed forces. There are a few basic requirements to consider in the conceptualization of this leg. First of all, there is a very wide spectrum of potential roles and missions for the armed forces, including disaster relief, support of the police, intelligence collection, peace support operations, counterterrorism, counterinsurgency, and waging war, to name a few. Second, the roles and missions cannot be effectively implemented or achieved without sufficient resources, including money, equipment, and training. Third, no imaginable role or mission in the modern world can be achieved by only one service in the armed forces or one agency, such as a Ministry of Defense or joint General Staff, without the involvement of other services and agencies. Thus "jointness" and interagency coordination are necessary. Fourth, to make things even more complicated, there are the paradoxes of evaluating effectiveness in the context of deterrence, wherein wars are avoided precisely because a country is perceived not to be vulnerable; or, under the umbrella of effective intelligence organizations, where bad things do not happen because intelligence prevented them from happening, without the knowledge of anyone but those directly involved. Finally, most of the imaginable military roles and missions will be carried out within a web of coalitions or alliances. This point is obvious in the real world, where we see NATO, various multilateral coalitions, and the United Nations undertake difficult missions, but again not adequately accounted for in the literature. Mongolia, for example, maintained its identity as a nation by linking closely with the USSR through most of the twentieth century; since 1990, it is doing the same through alliances with the United States, Japan, South Korea, and Europe. The effectiveness of its military in its roles and missions in peace support operations or intelligence, for example, can only be understood in light of the larger strategy of alliance formation. In short, although there are complicated methodological issues and nuances involved in evaluating effectiveness, analysts must grapple with them to begin to understand what the armed forces and other security forces do in the contemporary world. The least likely role for most armed forces today, ironically, is to fight conventional wars.

The third leg of the triangle is efficiency in the use of resources to fulfill assigned roles and missions. This dimension is of course complicated by the wide variety of these goals and the difficulty in establishing measures of effectiveness for any one, let alone a combination of them. What most often happens is that budget planners allocate a certain percentage of GDP or the national budget to the armed forces, who are then expected to achieve a (probably random) set of goals or priorities. In most instances there is no defining document, such as a national security strategy, that clearly lists objectives and establishes preferences for one set of goals over another. There is no document for at least two reasons. First, incumbent presidents and prime ministers are loath to develop and prioritize national security strategies, because their opponents will point out the discrepancies between the intended goals and the actual achievements. Thus it is understandable that very few democratically elected governments develop such strategies. The United States only began to do so because the U.S. Congress passed a law called the Goldwater-Nichols Defense Reorganization Act in 1986 that requires the executive to do so. Second, following from the comments above on effectiveness, an interagency process is necessary not only to define but also to assess priorities. Very few countries have such a mechanism that is anything more than formal. To begin to assess efficiency, a country must make the effort to establish both a robust interagency process and reliable budget oversight, as has been accomplished by some of the newest NATO members.

It should be obvious that the three elements of civil-military relations, as conceptualized in this book, must be assessed as indispensable parts of a whole. Each of the three is necessary for democratic reform, but individually none is sufficient to accomplish it. Civilian control, for instance, is irrelevant unless the armed forces can effectively fulfill their roles and missions. Both control and effectiveness must be implemented at an affordable cost or they will vitiate other national priorities. This interdependency makes it difficult to provide absolute measurements of change in any one dependent variable. For this reason, the contributors to this volume have focused on relative changes in the dependent variable, and especially on the direction of the change.

We also suggest that there are likely to be practical trade-offs among the three dimensions of civil-military relations. Some military experts argue that increased civilian control reduces effectiveness, although we are convinced, based upon examples such as Colombia and Chile, that democratic civilian control does not necessarily have this result given that the least likely contemporary role is massed combat against an equal adversary. Another possible source of tension is in the trade-off between efficiency and effectiveness, where cost-cutting drives may leave armed forces less able to perform their declared missions. There is also evidence for the proposition that technological change both limits civilian control, and can increase it to the detriment of overall effectiveness. These tensions are included as areas of inquiry for our authors.

A Final Word on Case Selection and the Structure of the Volume

We posit that major global trends are having a significant impact on civil-military relations in many democratic societies. We focus on cases of defense reform because they offer the opportunity to observe rapid changes in the dependent variable, civil-military relations. As the cases in this volume suggest, however, not all states are equally open or vulnerable to these global trends. Possible factors that help explain the differing ability of states to mediate the impact of globalization include military power, the strength of governing institutions, economic development, and the threat environment (both internal and external). We have chosen our seven case studies of defense reform (Chile, Colombia, India, Indonesia, Romania, Taiwan, and the United States) because they exhibit substantial variation in the dependent variable of civil-military relations, but also allow us to examine the ways in which domestic factors have moderated the effects of democratization, liberalization, globalization, and the RMA.

Some of the contributors focus on how the changing international security environment influences the ways in which defense establishments react to global trends. As James Wirtz discusses in chapter four, the success or failure of democratization and economic liberalization affects the power of states and the threat perceptions they derive from their relative status. Globalization and the RMA bring new threats to the forefront, and complicate the employment of military force in the pursuit of state objectives.

In this project, we find that democratization and globalization have an outsized impact on the processes of defense reform compared to economic liberalization and technological change. All the countries examined in this volume had to react to or address the impact of the Third Wave of democratization and of the accelerating pace of diffusion of new norms affecting the organization and employment of military force on their civil-military relations. In both cases, these global trends truly determined the timing of defense reform efforts. Economic liberalization was not a factor precipitating defense reform in any of the cases presented in this volume, although it sometimes served as an important constraint on the resources available to politicians to conduct defense reform. An example of this distinction can be seen later in the volume in the Indonesian case, where democratization rather than economic reform precipitated defense reform. The RMA, although clearly relevant to those aspiring great powers studied in this volume, was simply not relevant to most of the cases in this volume, particularly those countries that had made the choice not to compete with the leading powers.

Even democratization and globalization did not have the same impact across all states because some are simply such powerful actors in the international system that they can limit the impact of globalization on their defense systems. The United States and India are clear examples of such states. Our authors' findings suggest that great powers are still able to take or leave globalization. Because they are chiefly interested in managing emerging security threats, military effectiveness, both their own and that of their adversaries, becomes one of the most important dimensions of civil-military relations.

Other countries are particularly vulnerable to global trends because they have relatively weak governing structures and are dependent on others for development assistance, financial stability, or military aid. We chose to examine how this vulnerability affects Colombia and Indonesia. In the Colombia case, foreign aid provides a large proportion of the national defense budget so that the state has no choice but to follow U.S. preferences when it comes to defense reform. Indonesia showcases the radical transformation a confluence of global factors such as globalization and democratization can have on a defense establishment. In each case, nevertheless, we see that internal factors are still relevant to explain when and how states are able to resist, divert, or even use global trends to their own domestic ends.

In this volume, we also find it useful to contrast those cases where countries belong to formal international alliances, such as Romania, with those that do not, such as Chile. It is also important to compare countries like Taiwan, which faces significant external threats from a large, powerful neighbor, with ones like Colombia, where the danger to state security is almost entirely internal. In each case, the comparison allows us to contrast different incentive structures for civilians and the military as they think about defense policy.

It is clear that the cases we chose do not draw ready comparisons, so in the concluding chapter we group them into four general categories: Great powers versus minor powers; strong states versus weak states; alliance members versus non-alliance members; and those facing internal versus external threats. By doing so, we hope to offer a more meaningful basis for comparison among what would otherwise be a very far-ranging set of cases. This also allows us to draw out some commonalities among states in terms of how global trends condition their defense reform processes and civil-military relations.

Notes

1. Michael Desch, *Civilian Control of the Military: The Changing Security Environment* (Baltimore, MD: Johns Hopkins University Press, 1999).
2. Istvan Gyarmadi and Theodor Winkler, *Post–Cold War Defense Reform: Lessons Learned in Europe and the United States* (Dulles: Brassey's Inc., 2002); Dmitri Keridis and Charles Perry, *Defense Reform, Modernization and Military Cooperation in Southeastern Europe* (Dulles: Brassey's Inc., 2004).
3. Wendy Hunter, *Eroding Military Influence in Brazil: Politicians Against Soldiers* (Chapel Hill, NC: University of North Carolina Press, 1997); David Pion-Berlin, ed. *Civil-Military Relations in Latin America: New Analytical Perspectives* (Chapel Hill, NC: University of North Carolina Press, 2001); Harold Trinkunas, *Crafting Civilian Control of the Armed Forces in Venezuela: A Comparative Perspective* (Chapel Hill, NC: University of North Carolina Press, 2005); Thomas Bruneau and Scott Tollefson, *Who Guards the Guardians and How: Democratic Civil-Military Relations* (Austin, TX: University of Texas Press, 2006).
4. Peter D. Feaver, *Armed Servants: Agency, Oversight, and Çivil-Military Relations* (Cambridge, MA: Harvard University Press, 2003).
5. For the former, see *The Postmodern Military: Armed Forces after the Cold War*, Charles Moskos, James Williams, and D. Segal, eds. (New York: Oxford University Press, 2000). On the latter, see *Societies of Fear: The Legacy of Civil War, Violence and Terror in Latin America*, Kees Koonings and Dirk Krujit, eds. (New York: Palgrave, 1999). For older literature on how militaries in developed countries influence the military establishments of developing countries, see Frederick Nunn, *Yesterday's Soldiers: European Military Professionalism in South America, 1890–1940* (Lincoln: University of Nebraska Press, 1983).
6. Colin S. Gray, *Strategy for Chaos: Revolutions in Military Affairs and the Evidence of History* (London: Frank Cass, 2002).
7. Jeffrey Cooper, "The Revolution in Military Affairs," paper presented at conference Global Determinants of Defense Reform, Monterey, California, September 2005.
8. See, for example, Peter D. Feaver, "Civil-Military Relations," *Annual Review of Political Science* 2 (1999): 211–241, in which he documents how the dependent variable in this literature ranges from coups to military influence, civil-military friction, military compliance, and delegation and monitoring.

9. For example, Timothy Edmunds, "Security Sector Reform: Concepts and implementation," paper presented at the Geneva Center for the Democratic Control of Armed Forces Workshop, Geneva, 22–23 November 2001.
10. Samuel P. Huntington, *The Soldier and the State: The Theory and Politics of Civil-Military Relations* (Cambridge, MA: Harvard University Press, 1957); and Morris Janowitz, *The Professional Soldier: A Social and Political Portrait* (New York and Glencoe: Free Press, 1960).
11. Peter D. Feaver, "The Civil-Military Problematique: Huntington, Janowitz, and the Question of Civilian Control," *Armed Forces & Society* (Winter 1996): 149–177.
12. Thomas Bruneau and Alex MacLeod, *Politics in Contemporary Portugal: Parties and the Consolidation of Democracy* (Boulder, CO: Lynne Rienner Publishers, 1986); Felipe Agüero, *Soldiers, Civilians and Democracy: Post-Franco Spain in Comparative Perspective* (Baltimore, MD: Johns Hopkins University Press, 1995).
13. Juan J. Linz and Alfred Stepan, *Problems of Democratic Transition and Consolidation: Southern Europe, South America, and Post communist Europe* (Baltimore, MD: Johns Hopkins University Press, 1996).
14. Adam Przeworski, *Democracy and the Market: Political and Economic Reforms in Eastern Europe and Latin America* (New York: Cambridge University Press, 1991); and Philippe Schmitter, "The Consolidation of Political Democracies: Processes, Rhythms, Sequences, and Types," in G. Pridham, ed., *Transitions to Democracy* (Dartmouth, MA: Aldershot, 1995), 535–569.
15. *Democratic Control of the Military in Postcommunist Europe: Guarding the Guards*, Andrew Cottey, Timothy Edmunds, and Anthony Forster, eds. (New York: Palgrave, 2002); David Pion-Berlin, *Through Corridors of Power: Institutions and Civil-Military Relations in Argentina* (University Park: Pennsylvania State University Press, 1997); Alfred Stepan, *Rethinking Military Politics: Brazil and the Southern Cone* (Princeton, NJ: Princeton University Press, 1988); Trinkunas, *Crafting Civilian Control of the Armed Forces in Venezuela*.
16. Bruneau and Tollefson, *Who Guards the Guardians and How*.
17. See, for example, the new and important emphasis in the U.S. Quadrennial Defense Review Results, 2 March 2006 on "enhancing partner capacity." This is the most explicit statement available on the (re)discovery of effectiveness in defense reform.

2

Globalization and the Impact of Norms on Defense Restructuring

Anne Clunan

Introduction

One of the aphorisms of U.S. national security policy during the Cold War was that politics stops at the water's edge. When facing a difficult international environment, the many actors within the state pulled together and acted as one. Globalization and its proponents contest this aphorism at every level: They challenge the notion of distinct spheres of national and international policy; the idea of a state as a unitary actor; the idea that politics is a domestic affair even in the face of a national threat such as the Cold War; and, in the extreme, that state decision makers exercise control over their nation's security. While there is much debate about what globalization is, those who see it as a prevalent influence in the world insist that there are global forces, decentralized and beyond any one state's control, that significantly affect how states organize and behave both domestically and externally, as well as their ability to do so effectively and autonomously. Here I investigate the logics that drive many of the globalists' claims, particularly with regard to the diffusion of knowledge and ideas. I focus on the mechanisms and processes that are purportedly at work, with an eye to generating propositions about how such mechanisms might affect the ways and means by which, and the reasons why, states restructure their military forces. This chapter does not offer any general empirical conclusions; rather, the purpose is to think about what we should expect to see if globalists' claims are correct.

Globalization and Its Discontents: Sweeping a Conceptual Minefield

Before proceeding to a discussion of the logics underpinning much globalist literature, some attention must be paid to the plethora of competing claims about what globalization is and is not. To some extent, this is a dialogue—often among the deaf—between globalists and skeptics of globalization. The arguments are instructive, as they provide a basis for judging what the significance of globalization is for defense restructuring. If globalization does not matter, or only matters in some minor areas, then we should shift our attention from the impact of globalization on defense restructuring to the impact of other states and of domestic politics on how governments reform their militaries. I am personally agnostic in this debate, and any emphasis on the globalists' side is a result of the questions that this project seeks to address: What are the global determinants of defense restructuring, and what are their consequences?

At root, globalization refers to the speed, quantity, and cheapness of global flows of labor, capital, production, knowledge and ideas.[1] The politically critical corollary is the diffusion of authority over people, ideas, knowledge and technologies, capital, productive processes (whether of services or goods), and their respective transportation networks.[2] This redistribution of authority highlights why globalists claim that globalization directly challenges the capacity of nation-states to offer their traditional services, including the provision of security. In a globalized world, at the extreme, security and defense become just one set of services alongside financial management, risk management, communications—all services that arguably were once within the firm control of the state.[3] Entities that are more effective and efficient than states, or more normatively compelling, will win adherents to their way of defining and providing these services. States themselves increasingly rely on sub-state actors domestically and abroad to fill the gaps in what they can supply on their own.[4] The erosion of state authority and state sovereignty ensure that the increasing demands and challenges arising out of globalized flows will decrease governments' ability to master and meet them without significant non-state assistance. That assistance in turn leads to a further decline in state authority and sovereignty.

Skeptics respond that the erosion of states' capacity and authority to govern and to provide services is overblown. They insist that the state has never had full command over the provision of these goods in the first place.[5] They suggest instead that states are able innovators, adapting to environmental challenges in unique ways while retaining control over actors and processes.[6] At a minimum, it is only small, weak states that are susceptible to the pressures of globalization, while strong states are able to resist and largely control their own fates in this world.[7] In the area of national security, democratic states—despite their openness—are no more at a disadvantage responding to global pressures in a globalized world than nondemocratic states. When it comes to national security, maintain the skeptics, it is still correct to argue that politics stops at the water's edge. States retain the capacity to redefine issues as national security concerns, which increases the state's authority and capacity for control.[8]

At the root of the disagreement between globalists and skeptics is whether we should consider the state to be the primary actor in world politics. This question guides the way I frame the discussion of mechanisms of globalization. On the one hand, there are a multitude of non- and sub-state actors who supply knowledge, ideas, and technologies to states and other non-state actors through various paths of diffusion. On the other hand, there are states that demand ideas, technologies, and knowledge for the purposes of success, survival, or normative status. A key question is whether this supply and demand leads to states becoming more similar in how they reform their militaries, or to important national variation in defense restructuring. In more theoretical terms, we want to know if the main mechanisms at work are diffusion and isomorphism or syncretism. Which mechanisms are most prevalent and important should shed light on which actors significantly shape defense reform. They should also help us determine whether globalists or skeptics offer a more useful basis for understanding the factors that influence military restructuring.

Both issues—who the important actors are, and what the important mechanisms are—directly and indirectly affect the three dimensions of military restructuring, civilian control, military effectiveness, and defense efficiency, that animate this project. They shape the prospects for and nature of civilian control of the military (e.g., debates about command responsibility at the Guantánamo Bay and Abu Ghraib prisons, or about political control of war plans) and defense reform (e.g., the entire notion of military transformation and the revolution in military affairs). The identity of the actors in globalization and the nature of its mechanisms also shape military effectiveness, defined as the ability of civilians and the military legitimately and effectively to fulfill the missions and roles elaborated in defense reforms, such as nation building, preventive war, peacekeeping/humanitarian operations, or coercive counterproliferation. They similarly affect defense efficiency, the determination of what costs are deemed too high for the achievement of those missions and roles. Economic costs of war and reconstruction, human costs in casualties, and the societal and legitimacy costs associated with shameful episodes such as the abuses at Guantánamo and Abu Ghraib come to mind. These issues are taken up in turn below, starting with the overarching causes of globalization.

Globalization's Causes

When we consider the significance of globalization, several factors leap to mind, chief among them technology, ideas about how things should work (for example, free-market economics), and power. Technology is clearly and intrinsically linked to both the spread and effect of globalization. Information and transportation technologies, ranging from the Internet to global air travel, are often seen as the root cause of globalization and its impact. The death of distance, the shrinking of physical spaces, the elimination of a world of places and its replacement by a world of flows, are all common consequences attributed to technological innovations.[9] In this sense, Marshall McLuhan's idea that the medium is the message rings true: The technological media (Internet, airplane) are the political message: decentralized, privatized, and individually empowering. Technologies diffuse throughout the globe and their ubiquity is thus a consequence of globalization. But technologies are very much viewed as a cause of globalization. Information technologies such as the Internet and cell phones are difficult to control centrally, and are indivisible—if you want to take down a cellular network in order to prevent its use by terrorists, your own forces will be unable to communicate. Such technologies therefore facilitate the rapid and inexpensive spread of knowledge, information, and ideas to a variety of non-state actors. The same is true of transportation and delivery technologies. They allow the rapid and inexpensive spread of physical goods and people, be those goods flowers or missiles and those people tourists or terrorists. In both cases, this rapid movement of ideas, goods, and persons is often seen as a potential source of power. Not surprisingly, technological innovation is seen as the fundamental global determinant shaping how and why militaries should be reformed. New roles, ranging from counterdrug to counterterrorism to counterproliferation to counterepidemic, appear in military portfolios. New missions, such as information dominance, are added to the list of areas in which militaries need to maintain the technological and operational edge over traditional state actors.

While McLuhan argued that the technological medium is the message, others point to the content that is being so easily diffused.[10] Here the central focus is on ideas, under which I class knowledge, information, and norms. Knowledge is one of the most critical power resources for any actor. Knowledge of how to build computers, Internet routers, and packet switches means that a power resource that was once largely in the hands of U.S. scientists is now globally available. Knowledge, in other words, is what produces technologies. The spread of knowledge is therefore a more fundamental cause of globalization and a more important power resource than the technologies themselves.[11] In the case of information technologies, knowledge and hardware mutually reinforce a diffusion of power away from state-sponsored research labs to non-state and sub-state actors.

Knowledge is an important cause of globalization in another sense. The dissemination of particular kinds of knowledge can change what is considered relevant to national and international security. Scientific knowledge produces new insight into the ways issues such as environmental degradation, public health, and poverty link with national security. New global standards develop from the transnational transmission of this knowledge. Developed Western countries, to take one minor example, require their militaries to leave a small environmental footprint, and in some cases to undertake environmental cleanup and remediation. This puts an additional role in the militaries' portfolio, with its attendant consequences for budgets, financing, planning, and oversight. Advances in science also are reflected in the controversy over the use of weapons systems that are viewed as environmentally unsound, such as depleted uranium shells, Agent Orange, and napalm; and the World Health Organization's request for an advisory ruling by the International Court of Justice on whether nuclear weapons could legally be used because of their environmental consequences. The creation of categories of environmental security in the early 1990s, and the United Nations' adoption of the idea of human security at the turn of the century, resulted directly from better environmental science.[12] Canada has taken the notion of human security the farthest, establishing a Human Security Agenda for its foreign policy, which includes protection of civilians, peace support operations, governance and accountability, public safety, and conflict prevention.[13] Scientific inquiries into the propensity for inequality, demographics, and resource scarcity to produce violence are now a central part of the debate about the root causes of terrorism, and therefore of the debate about how to achieve national security.[14] The spread of scientific knowledge can directly affect all three dimensions of defense reform: The ability of civilians and officers to control and agree on what missions and roles are appropriate, and the military's ability legitimately to fulfill those roles and missions in as cost-efficient a manner as possible.

Another subset of ideas is information. One aspect of the importance of information, its rapid spread through communications technology, has already been mentioned above. Non-state as well as state actors now can spread information or disinformation worldwide within minutes. Two related aspects are important to stress. The use of the Internet by terrorist organizations and antigovernment or antiestablishment movements is well known. The transmission of information about their goals, successes, and methods is a potent source of power for them in terms of securing adherents, clarifying their cause, justifying their methods, highlighting the sins of their opponents, and, in general, securing their desired outcomes. This information often poses a challenge to militaries seeking to meet security challenges from such movements, and can lead to the creation of new military missions such as counterterrorism, counterinformation operations and cyber warfare.

The second aspect is the growth of a twenty-four hour news cycle. This has changed both the public environment in which militaries and their civilian leaders must respond to information relayed over news wires, and the organizational demands of creating and managing the "information battlespace." It is not merely that the media report news constantly to fill air time, it is what issues they report on, be they humanitarian crises, environmental fallout, genocide, human rights violations by military personnel, insufficient force protection measures resulting in military casualties, or collateral damage leading to civilian deaths and suffering. This information shapes public opinion, which in turn shapes the pressures civilian leaders face in establishing and defending particular roles and missions and omitting others. The public outrage over televised photographs of U.S. military practices at Abu Ghraib prison and the subsequent revisions in military practices are excellent examples of the impact of information and public opinion. Both have the potential to influence military effectiveness and defense efficiency by altering the roles and missions assigned to the military. When journalists report directly from the battlefield, government officials lose some of their ability to ensure control over and credibility of propaganda campaigns. Access to direct information shapes the public's perception of the societal costs entailed in particular military roles and missions, as well as the legitimacy of the armed forces themselves.

The third subset of ideas is norms. Norms are widely shared beliefs that define how an issue is viewed, who can act on that issue and how they should act. Norms define war, for example, as a legally regulated activity governed by morality as well as necessity. Norms also determine who can conduct war and by what means. Only states can designate certain individuals to be military personnel, who in turn have the authority to do what others cannot legally do—kill other people. Military personnel have this authority only under limited conditions—on the battlefield. And even on the battlefield certain acts are agreed to be criminal, and certain technologies are not value-neutral but immoral. A central theme in the constructivist literature is how the global diffusion of norms shapes both what states do domestically and what they want.[15] When we apply this logic to defense restructuring, norms (be they laws of war, democratic governance, or unregulated markets) are argued to influence to one degree or another how states build and organize their militaries (and thereby the variable of civilian control of the military), At a more basic level, constructivists suggest norms shape how leaders define the national interests those militaries are to secure and defend (which directly shapes the definition of military effectiveness and defense efficiency). One prominent norm, democracy, is the subject of a separate chapter in this book, so I will not dwell on it. Instead I will focus on other norms that may shape defense restructuring with respect to missions (such as humanitarian missions, nation building, peacekeeping), actors (such as the role of lawyers in the military, and the military in traditionally civilian roles), and means (such as weapons systems, airpower, interrogation, training, and planning).

POWER IN A GLOBALIZED WORLD

As should be evident from the globalists' claim that state sovereignty is eroding, power is at the heart of the debate about globalization: What is power, who has it, who is losing it, and whether the nature of power has fundamentally changed as a result of globalization. One of the arguments put forward in the literature on norms is that legitimacy is a key source of power, and that the sets of ideas that constitute a proto-norm are a power resource when they become so widely adopted and institutionalized that they define what is appropriate and what is not.[16] Norms, in this view, confer authority, both to wage war and to limit the conduct of war. Norms define the purposes for which militaries can be legitimately used, and the particular methods that militaries can legitimately employ.

Norms or other kinds of ideas about how to make things work are clearly not the only source of power in a globalized world. Many scholars argue that ideas are only an instrument that the powerful use to legitimate their dominance. This is of course the premise of Marxism and realism, and of critical theorists who note that the ideological structures of liberalism and democracy serve to reinforce the power of those states or economic actors already possessing preponderant political, physical, or economic power.[17] The realist tradition of power politics applies the same logic: Ideas and norms are only the window dressing used to cover the pursuit of naked interests and the reality that material power determines outcomes.[18] To the extent that realists accept that ideas matter, it is in the form of knowledge.[19] The powerful seek to control the creation and development of knowledge and its physical manifestation in technologies; they will organize and use their military capabilities to deny these power resources to others.[20] The powerful dominate the process of knowledge accumulation and technological development, and their normative ideas reinforce the political subordination of the weak.[21]

From this perspective, power is a material good, and we should expect different actors to have different interests that are served by the diffusion of knowledge, ideas, and technologies. Powerful actors will allow globalization to proceed so long as it serves their interests, and will have the capacity to rein it in when it ceases to. The globalization of norms of military professionalism, in this narrative, would serve to reinforce the position of the industrialized states, by perhaps imposing more expensive forms of military organization and maintenance, as well as reducing uncertainty when facing a future opponent in a crisis or in battle. In a similar vein, new ideas about the expanded missions of militaries, including peacekeeping and humanitarian intervention, are a means of creating a global division of military labor, with lesser states geared for lesser roles, while powerful states would concentrate on core war fighting missions. The creation and diffusion of a new military role of counterterrorism serves to reduce a state's uncertainty about who it will face in a military setting, as it empowers the state to eliminate non-state actors. This in turn reinforces the power of all states, but also the position of the most powerful state, as it will not need to pursue non-state actors that threaten its security on its own.

In this world, the spread of scientific knowledge and technology is controlled by states, and they disseminate it to their allies but deny it to their adversaries. Alternatively, powerful forces within states seek to exploit these new ideas about missions to further increase their own power. Latin American militaries have exploited global interest in humanitarian intervention to secure increased budgets for peacekeeping forces.[22] A related argument is that globalization is designed to empower economic actors. They will support the proliferation of missions, roles, and ideas that require states to further rely on their services.[23] Such functionalist propositions are amenable to empirical evaluation, which I do not undertake here, though I offer some illustrative examples below.

PROCESSES AND MECHANISMS OF GLOBALIZATION

Two overarching logics, diffusion and isomorphism, inform the literature on why and how ideas spread and become globally adopted. Both logics make implicit assumptions about who are the key agents in the process of globalization. In the diffusion story it is usually normatively driven non-state or sub-state actors who are the key vectors, who then "capture" states. They are the "pushers" of norms. Keck and Sikkink demonstrate how human rights activists and nongovernmental organizations cooperated across borders to convince the U.S. government to pressure Latin American regimes to reform.[24] Adler shows how an epistemic community of scientists and nuclear strategy experts convinced U.S. policymakers of the logic of arms control.[25] The diffusion mechanism is generally begun when non-state actors take it upon themselves, wittingly or unwittingly, to promote ideas, information, norms, and knowledge processes to other influential non-state, sub-state and state actors. These key recipients then in turn attempt to socialize other states. In some cases, scholars discuss norm or policy "entrepreneurs," who consciously seek to promote a particular set of ideas to change the behavior, and ultimately the interests, of important actors such as states and corporations.[26] In other instances, we can speak of epistemic communities of scientists and experts who promote, for example, a particular conception of security such as nuclear arms control, and the relevant military organizational changes in missions, weapons-system design and development, organization and training required to meet the emerging new goal.[27] With regard to military reform, actors promote and diffuse particular ideas, knowledge, and norms that then shape how states transform their militaries. Why states adopt these norms is politically important, but usually based on a logic of persuasion: They are persuaded that doing so will serve their interests. The main alternative logic is that of consequences: States are afraid of the consequences of not adopting the norms, especially when powerful states are pushing the norms, and so they rationally choose compliance if the costs of doing so are less than the costs of nonadoption. This latter method shades into one form of isomorphism, coercive isomorphism.

Isomorphism means similarity or homogeneity in process or structure between organizations.[28] In contrast with diffusion, isomorphism is more centered on demand, usually driven by states who are the "demanders" or "consumers" of norms. For example, the post-Communist countries demand the norms of democratic civilian control over the armed forces in order to achieve entry into NATO and the European Union. There are four basic explanations for why states want to adopt certain ideas, norms, practices, and knowledge processes.[29] The first is an essentially rational process of *competitive isomorphism*, whereby states engage in simple, or trial and error, adaptation to environmental stimuli.[30] The second is *mimetic isomorphism*. States respond to uncertainty about how to behave in a particular environment or when their goals are ambiguous by modeling themselves on other states. The third explanation is *coercive isomorphism*, where states adopt a particular practice or idea because of the threat of punishment or the denial of benefits from more powerful actors. This is the familiar story of realism: The powerful force their norms and rules on the less powerful; the weak rationally adopt these rules because they have little choice.[31] The fourth process is *normative isomorphism*, in which states adopt a practice or norm because that norm constitutes a part of what it means to be a state at that particular point in history.[32] These adaptive functions are closely related to the process of normative supply, but the emphasis lies on states as consumers of norms. States are viewed as social actors that respond to societal pressures of normative conformity. The supply of ideas, norms, practices, and knowledge is largely assumed in such an analysis, with the emphasis on why states want to adopt them.

Diffusion and isomorphism are not mutually exclusive; indeed they are temporally complementary, but their proponents tend to emphasize the power of different actors and different variables. The term diffusion is commonly applied by authors employing the logic of isomorphism, so for clarity I use diffusion here to refer solely to the supply-side stories.

Normative Influences on Defense Restructuring

States have adopted three important sets of norms that inform their decisions on defense restructuring. The first are norms regarding how militaries should be constituted, whether as professional, all-volunteer corps rather than conscript armies, or as citizen-armies rather than professionals.[33] The second set regards the purposes of the military instrument, and the creation of new military missions and roles.[34] The third concerns ideas about the appropriateness of particular weapons systems or military practices.[35] The first and second set of norms relate to the variable of civilian control of the military—indeed, the norm of civilian control is a key element of the global diffusion of democratization, as discussed in chapter three. National debates over whether and to what degree the military should be organized as subordinate to civilians, and what are appropriate missions for "democratic" militaries, are subject to normative pressures to conform to "international democratic practice," and include the question of whether militaries are involved in domestic policing or not. The second and third set of norms relate to the variable of military effectiveness, as they directly concern the roles, missions, and purpose of the military instrument, and what practices and weapons militaries can legally use to achieve assigned roles and missions. These two sets of norms also are especially important for the third element of the structural trinity motivating this volume, defense efficiency. This variable is heavily dependent on domestic and international public opinion about the legitimacy of particular missions, weapons systems, and military practices. The degree to which media and nongovernmental actors shape perceptions of legitimacy impacts civilian and military leaders' control over both military effectiveness and defense efficiency. As will be discussed below, such trends existed before the information age; however, diffusion processes and their consequences for civilian control, military effectiveness, and defense efficiency are arguably much more pronounced since the advent of high-speed electronic communications.

The Constitution and Organization of the Military and the Implications for Civilian Control

Janice Thomson outlines how a particular norm, that of the subordination of citizens to their state, led the United States to reject the common practice of using mercenaries in the organization and constitution of its armed forces in the late eighteenth century.[36] The United States at the time was a weak state, and it initially acted under pressure from the powerful United Kingdom. As such, the choice to rely on conscription of citizens instead of recruitment of professionals is simply a story of coercion rather than isomorphism, as the United Kingdom had not banned the practice of mercenaries outright. This adopted norm, however, fitted neatly into emerging new norms about state sovereignty, and a state's control over its citizens as well as their obligations to the state. The new norm, which asserted that the leadership of the state controlled all military forces as well as the use of force by its nationals, was transmitted when one of the most powerful states in the system, the United Kingdom, in 1816 banned all natural born subjects from acting as mercenaries. The ban was extended to all British colonial subjects in 1870. By the end of the nineteenth century all states in the international system but two had banned the practice.[37] Thomson suggests that a process of normative isomorphism generated the diffusion and adoption of this norm, as states came to redefine what it meant to be sovereign. A new obligation of sovereignty was to prevent the privatization of violence by one's nationals; in other words, to establish governmental, though not necessarily civilian, control over the use of force. Here states had an individual as well as social incentive to adopt the norm, as this is what sovereigns "do."

The spread of this antimercenary norm set the stage for the development of what Charles Moskos terms the modern and late modern forms of military organization, in which citizen-soldiers are the mainstay of the military force.[38] The central normative structure underpinning this way of organizing the military is the sovereign nation-state. In his view, the end of the Cold War and the demise of the threat of interstate war greatly accelerated the shift from this normative structure of world politics to a postmodern world, and to a postmodern form of military organization. The postmodern military form reflects the decreased distinction between civilians and soldiers both in the functions they perform and their increased interaction, and a diminished assumption that the lives, rules, and behavior of soldiers are separate from civilian life. Norms concerning gender equality, homosexuality, and economic rationality have reduced the distinction between civilian and military, and have altered the form of military organization. Militaries are now more reflective of broader cultural and economic norms.[39]

The information revolution has also decreased the specialization of the individual soldier, and made military specializations less distinct from civilian ones.[40] Peter Singer writes about how the diffusion of the "privatization revolution" has essentially reversed the trend that Thomson outlined, and contributed to the creation of a global industry of private warriors. This significantly reduces the control exercised by state authorities over the use of force, and blurs the distinction between public civilian control over the military and private civilian provision of military services. This ideological diffusion of economic liberalism, writes Singer, "provided the logic, legitimacy, and models for the entrance of markets into formerly state domains."[41] The growing influence of global markets and the global supply of mercenary labor and arms, the information revolution and its diffusion of power to civilian actors, all have made private military companies viable options. The demand has come from failed states and the increase in intrastate war, where private armies battle over the remains of nations. Even developed countries are relying on private military companies to provide a wide array of services in combat and noncombat situations.

Military restructuring has as much to do now with outsourcing as with redefining what militaries do. This in turn profoundly complicates the questions of civilian control over the military and private contractors employed by the military, as the United States discovered when private contractors were alleged to have tortured and killed detainees in U.S. custody in Iraq and Afghanistan. More generally, norms of economic and technical rationality embodied in "privatization" have in whole or part replaced norms of social solidarity, central to civilian control and military effectiveness.[42] The normative diffusion of privatization has not only eroded civilians' ability to control the military; it also has altered the menu of purposes, roles, and missions the military is to address.

The Purposes of the Military as an Instrument, and New Roles and Missions

A second set of arguments about diffusion relates to norms concerning the purposes of the military. According to this point of view, these norms have begun to shift from the defense of the nation to missions that are not traditionally military.[43] Broader international norms of humanitarianism—"separating belligerents, resettling of refugees, delivering of food and medical supplies, providing security for humanitarian organizations," as well as a focus on domestic unrest and terrorism—have replaced "war fighting or war deterrence" rooted in ideals of duty and service to country.[44] In these accounts, the primary cause is the broad shift to postindustrial societies and away from a focus on purely national forms of organization and allegiance. Empirically, the most widespread finding is that the purposes to which militaries are put have in fact changed. The end of the Cold War removed the existential threat to nation-states that called for a traditional form of military organization and traditional military purpose.[45]

Two of the most prominent changes in the purposes for which militaries are used have been the emergence of peacekeeping in the twentieth century, and its later reincarnation as peacemaking and nation-building in the 1990s and early twentieth century. The perceived increase in the number of intrastate conflicts is the primary cause of this shift, at the same time that the level of interstate war has dropped sharply. A normative cause of this shift was the increased legitimacy of the norm of self-determination after 1945. The United Nations and the international community were willing to keep peace between warring communities if they were invited to.

That invitation was deemed no longer necessary in the post–Cold War era, as the related notions of "robust peacekeeping," "failed states" that were places of perpetual war, "contingent sovereignty," and "the responsibility to protect" gained hold.[46] Here the humanitarian impulse was a primary cause. In the conflicts since 1945 civilians accounted for 90 percent of the total casualties, as compared to 5 percent in World War I and 50 percent in World War II.[47] Globalized media spread the images from these wars, prompting an expansion of military missions to embrace intervention in internal conflicts from Somalia to Bosnia to Kosovo and East Timor.

Martha Finnemore suggests that a key cause of this shift has been changes in collective understanding of who is "human," and the framing of human rights violations as threats to regional peace and security.[48] She notes that the purposes for which militaries would intervene has shifted over time from traditional political-military concerns regarding the balance of power and spheres of influence to humanitarian disasters. Security has now become coupled with human rights, and that coupling is institutionalized in the United Nations as well as in the foreign policies of major states.[49] These new military roles can range from peacekeeping requiring the consent of the conflicting parties, to interventions in failing states that "involve a wide range of nonmilitary components involving reconstruction and social services...aimed at overhauling war-torn societies and remaking them in accordance with the normatively preferred liberal democratic model."[50] In a word, powerful developed countries and non-state actors have diffused global norms regarding human rights and appropriate forms of governance. These norms have generated a new military mission of nation building, or in military parlance, postconflict stabilization and reconstruction. Developing states have absorbed these norms for a variety of reasons. Coercive isomorphism is part of the explanation, but rational competitive isomorphism is clearly at work, according to Claudio Fuentes and Felipe Agüero.[51] They maintain that domestic military elites exploit these international norms in order to increase their bureaucratic influence and resources at home.

Weapons and Military Practices: Implications for Military Effectiveness and Defense Efficiency

There is a growing literature on how non-state actors and epistemic communities generate ideas and norms about how and whether weapons systems and military tactics can be used, which has important consequences for defense restructuring. Emanuel Adler's work discusses how an epistemic community of scientists and experts at MIT and Harvard formulated the idea of strategic arms control as a necessary corollary to the doctrine of mutual assured destruction. This group sold the idea within the U.S. government and to Soviet peers, who in turn diffused the idea in the Kremlin and Soviet military. This diffusion fundamentally shaped how both countries structured their nuclear forces, designed and developed their nuclear weapons systems, and why they refrained from building defensive weapons systems.[52] Richard Price has documented how norm entrepreneurs created a chemical weapons taboo, and how this taboo altered the way militaries planned, trained, and equipped their forces.[53] Price also shows how a nongovernmental organization (NGO), the International Campaign to Ban Landmines, successfully used the Internet to rally popular support for a total ban on the production, stockpiling, and use of antipersonnel mines.[54] Within five years of its founding, this NGO, with the active support of Canada, got 144 states to ratify the 1997 Landmine Ban Treaty, which entered into force in 1999. The ban means that signatory states will have to restructure their militaries to do without mines, and that even nonsignatory states will need to redesign and retrain for deployments with states party to the treaty.

Similarly, James Ron has focused on how particular norms have affected the choice of tactics security forces can adopt, in particular interrogation techniques in the Israeli military.[55] In the United States, official documents regarding the application of the Geneva Conventions and the norms of POW status to the Taliban and Al Qaeda—designated "enemy combatants" as distinct from soldiers—reflect a sharp internal debate over the role of such norms and military practices.[56] Contrary to the expectations of power analysis, important groups in the military and the State Department argued against loosening or changing the standards for military treatment of terrorists. This debate suggests that along with the growth in new missions, states will have to grapple with whether and how to change military practices in conducting those missions, and civilian accountability and oversight of those practices. This process of defense restructuring will be subject to intense public and media scrutiny, as the international and domestic furor over the U.S. detention of prisoners at Guantánamo Bay, Cuba, and the treatment of prisoners at Iraq's Abu Ghraib prison suggests.

On the other side of the spectrum, states promote the adoption of particular norms, ideas, and knowledge systems through the diffusion of norms concerning democratic civilian control of the military, and the proper education and training of professional military personnel. Such efforts are amply demonstrated by the work of institutions such as the sponsor of this project, the Center for Civil-Military Relations, or through the work of NATO's Partnership for Peace. Such a pattern, when accompanied by threats or inducements, would reflect the logic of coercive isomorphism. Normative isomorphism would be operative in cases in which states, wishing to become part of a particular community of nations such as the European Union or NATO, adopt these countries' norms regarding civil-military relations and defense missions, planning, and training.

GLOBALIZATION OF NORMS AND THEIR IMPACT ON DEFENSE RESTRUCTURING

The foregoing has focused on the supply of norms and their potential impact on how militaries should be controlled and organized, emerging roles and missions, and the legitimacy of armed forces. With regard to civilian control of the military, powerful state and sub-state actors may push weaker states to adopt norms such as democratic civilian control and military professionalism, as chapter three demonstrates. The remaining question is why weaker states adopt these norms. On the demand side, the logics of isomorphism suggest several reasons why states might pursue the trinity of goals that motivate this volume: civilian control of the military, military effectiveness, and defense efficiency.

Civilian Control of the Armed Forces

According to the coercive logic of isomorphism, the ability of norm pushers to manipulate states with material incentives and penalties determines the extent of norm adoption. Weaker states therefore should restructure their militaries to be subordinate to democratic civilian control when the norm pushers threaten to withhold important material incentives, such as membership in NATO or the European Union; military, technical, and/or economic assistance; or political support for the negotiating regime. Similarly, states will adopt norms if the norm diffusers are able to penalize states for non-adoption, either through some form of material sanction or through reputation-tarnishing. The logic of normative isomorphism, by contrast, says that states will adopt norms of democratic civilian control because this is what it means to be a "democracy" or a "normal country." An array of norms may affect civilian control of the military beyond simply a norm of democratic civilian control advocated by the U.S. government. In Chile, for example, human rights norms prohibiting torture, and the arrest of General Augusto Pinochet in London, prompted Chilean society to rethink the meaning of democracy, civilian control over the military, and the rule of law. In 2005 the Chilean Supreme Court stripped the former head of state of immunity from prosecution and found him subject to prosecution for human rights violations as well as other charges.[57] A normative isomorphic explanation would emphasize that Chileans measured their country against the standards of the community of democratic states, and adopted its norms. States seek to define themselves by adopting the standards and norms of the high prestige members of their social milieu. Here the main impetus is not material pressure from external actors, but rather concerns for conformity with societal standards; in this case, the society in question is the group of democratic states.

The logic of competitive isomorphism is essentially an account of rational and efficient adaptation to the external environment, while mimetic isomorphism bases such adaptation on legitimacy rather than efficiency. Competitive isomorphism rests on the assumption that actors are choosing strategies based on the material success of those strategies in other situations. This would seem to generate two straightforward rationalist propositions. The first is that democratic civilian control is simply an optimally functional solution for organizing the military to achieve national security and foreign policy goals. States, through a process of trial-and-error, have learned that such a method of organizing armed forces produces the best method of ensuring territorial integrity and political autonomy from other states. Other newer or weaker states merely emulate the practice of successful states. Whether democratic civilian control over the armed forces is in fact an optimal solution is open to empirical cross-national and historical evaluation of the "success" of democratically and non-democratically controlled militaries. The second rationalist explanation based on competitive isomorphism is that democratic civilian control is merely one option among many that states will try out as they seek to adapt to their external environment. They will emulate the success of others, and if others have more success using other models of control over the armed forces, then the attachment to the norm of democratic civilian control will decline.

The logic of mimetic competition is that actors emulate those who are seen as more *legitimate*, not only as more materially successful.[58] The emphasis, therefore, is not solely on success defined as technical efficiency. This leads to a third proposition: States should seek to emulate highly visible states that are perceived as legitimate even if they are not especially effective or efficient.

Military Effectiveness: Military Capacity to Carry out Roles and Missions

The variable of military effectiveness is clearly related to the question of success in achieving national security goals. Military effectiveness has been defined in this volume as the ability of the armed forces to carry out the roles and missions that civilian authorities assign to them. There are two dimensions to this definition. The first is why civilian authorities come up with the roles and missions that they do. The second is whether militaries can carry out these assignments. As we will see, the question of capacity is intertwined with the question of defense efficiency.

The main contribution of a focus on globalization is to understand why new roles and missions arise. As the discussion of norm diffusion highlighted, new roles and missions are often pushed by norm entrepreneurs and are not always a direct reflection of objective challenges posed by the international environment. An instrumental argument derived from the logic of two-level games suggests that civilian and military leaders may exploit the existence of global norms regarding humanitarian intervention to develop new roles and missions that will increase their domestic power and authority.[59] A rationalist proposition suggested by competitive isomorphism is that the external environment presents states with particular challenges. States will adopt roles and missions to meet these challenges, and will emulate states that seem to be successful at doing so. Thus, if peacekeeping is a new mission required by the environment, states will emulate highly visible successful and legitimate peacekeeping states, such as Canada.

The difficulty with this logic is that it assumes that all actors similarly interpret the external environment. Yet as state behavior regarding the issues of peacekeeping, transnational terrorism or proliferation illustrates, that assumption is not true. This is the added value of analyzing the supply of norms—to learn what roles and missions are being pushed as "legitimate" and important. But the supply of these norms may not in fact be what brings civilian leaders to set certain roles and missions before the military. Empirical analysis is necessary to establish whether states are more motivated by domestic political and security issues than by external environmental conditions when they define the military's roles and missions. For many states, internal stability may dominate how they define what the purposes of the military instrument are. Isomorphic logics can establish what we should expect if global norms are in fact shaping roles and missions. A global norm of military professionalism, for example, would lead civilian leaders to task the military with a mission of professionalization. Pressure from states such as the United States and other permanent members of the UN Security Council could lead civilian leaders to take on new security roles that include counterproliferation, in line with the Proliferation Security Initiative, UN Security Council Resolution 1540 and the other nonproliferation regimes. We might nevertheless expect domestic leaders to meld domestic traditions with selective international norms, to produce more syncretic forms of norm adoption.[60]

Defense Efficiency: Legitimacy and Military Capacity

The second part of military effectiveness is the capacity for militaries to carry out roles and missions. But the question of military capacity cannot be separated from the third variable under study here, defense efficiency. Defense efficiency concerns the ability to achieve military effectiveness at acceptable social, political, and economic costs. It is therefore tightly bound in the notion of legitimacy that will almost always come from a combination of domestic and global forces. Domestic politics and resources are likely to be highly significant in determining the military's capacity, as well as societal estimates of the costs associated with its roles and missions. It is in the realm of legitimacy that the syncretic blending of global and local norms is most likely to be relevant.[61]

The existence of global norms or standards can substantially impact the legitimacy of particular military operations or military roles. If a country seeks to become part of a particular international club or organization, it is likely that its military effectiveness and its defense efficiency will be shaped by global norms. Here the logics of normative and mimetic isomorphism are at play. If the global standard for military modernization is widely seen to be the U.S. armed forces, then this will legitimate military restructuring programs that seek to increase the role of information technology and information dominance even in countries whose likely peer competitors do not include the United States.[62] This can increase the costs that a society is willing to bear to achieve military effectiveness.

Broadly speaking, global norms either facilitate or inhibit military capacity. To the extent that militaries are tasked with new roles and missions that are concordant with global norms, we should expect external factors to have a null or positive effect on military capacity. Latin American militaries can decrease the domestic political costs of increasing their organizational mandates and budgets by exploiting global norms.[63] States or international organizations are likely to supply technical assistance and financing to help militaries take on globally sanctioned roles. When adopted roles and missions run counter to global norms, the reverse should hold and military capacity should be negatively affected.

Global humanitarian norms can dramatically alter defense efficiency and military capacity by shaping the legitimacy of certain civilian-mandated military missions. The George W. Bush administration's counterproliferation and counterterrorism policies have generated new military roles as nation-builders, jailers, and interrogators. The military's capacity to carry out these functions has been dramatically shaped by the global prohibition of torture, the requirements of the laws of war, and norms regarding due process. These norms have shaped how publics both domestically and internationally view the actions of the U.S. military, made it much more costly for civilian leaders to mandate particular military roles, and ultimately impeded the ability of the military to carry out both those and other missions. Citizens in democracies are likely to punish civilian and military leaders for contravening global norms of human rights.

Conclusion

Globalization has increased the power of non-state actors in the private sector, academia, and the NGO community to influence how states control, use, and evaluate their military forces. Though the foregoing leaves many questions unanswered, the examples above suggest that the impact of norms on military reform is not a new phenomenon or one peculiar to the information age. Nevertheless, the confluence of particular ideas, such as those regarding the purposes of military force, and the information spread through globalized media, play a mutually reinforcing role in determining the rapidity and intensity with which military reform is demanded. Norm diffusers are more easily able to demand that states change the ends to which militaries are put and the means they use when images of prisoner abuse or genocide or starvation are continually in the news. Technology and rapid access to information make it easier for norm entrepreneurs to mobilize, organize, and pressure states, as the case of the International Campaign to Ban Landmines suggests. Societal norms about the acceptability of the use of force and rejection of military casualties directly affect military effectiveness and civilian leaders' ability to use the military instrument. The legitimacy or lack thereof associated with new missions, weapons systems, and tactics shapes defense efficiency. The power of non-state actors to shape what constitutes a security threat or a prohibited military practice appears to have grown. The expansion of military missions into the realms of humanitarian intervention and nation building suggests that the military will more regularly find itself in the news and subject to the scrutiny of norm entrepreneurs. This in turn generates the potential for an unending process of defense restructuring, and for civilian control of the military to be increasingly subject to public pressure.

Notes

1. David Held and Anthony McGrew, "The Great Globalization Debate: An Introduction," in David Held and Anthony McGrew, eds., *The Global Transformations Reader* 2nd ed. (Cambridge and Oxford: Polity Press/ Blackwell Publishing, 2000), 1–50; Robert O. Keohane and Joseph S. Nye, Jr., "Globalization: What's New? What's Not? (And So What?)," *Foreign Policy* 118 (Spring 2000): 104–119; Paul Romer, "Increasing Returns and Long-Run Growth," *Journal of Political Economy* 94, 5 (October 1986): 1002–1037; and Paul Romer, "Endogenous Technological Change," *Journal of Political Economy* 98, 5, pt. 2 (October 1990), S71–S102.
2. Susan Strange, *The Retreat of the State: The Diffusion of Power in the World Economy* (Cambridge: Cambridge University Press, 1996); James N. Rosenau, *Distant Proximities* (Princeton, NJ: Princeton University Press, 2003).
3. Strange, *The Retreat of the State.*
4. Keohane and Nye, "Globalization," 104–119; Anne-Marie Slaughter, *A New World Order* (Princeton, NJ: Princeton University Press, 2004).
5. Stephen D. Krasner, *Sovereignty: Organized Hypocrisy* (Princeton, NJ: Princeton University Press, 1999).
6. Stephan Haggard and Robert R. Kaufman, "Institutions and Economic Adjustment," in Stephan Haggard and Robert R. Kaufman, eds., *The Politics of Economic Adjustment* (Princeton, NJ: Princeton University Press, 1992), 3–40; Peter A. Hall, *Governing the Economy: The Politics of State Intervention in Britain and France* (Cambridge, UK: Polity Press, 1986); Richard Samuels, *The Business of the Japanese State* (Ithaca, NY: Cornell University Press, 1987); Kathleen Thelen, *How Institutions Evolve: The Political Economy of Skills in Germany, Britain, the United States and Japan* (Cambridge: Cambridge University Press, 2004); John Zysman, *Governments, Markets and Growth* (Ithaca, NY: Cornell University Press, 1983); and John Zysman, *Political Strategies for Industrial Order: State, Market, and Industry in France* (Berkeley: University of California Press, 1977).
7. Peter J. Katzenstein, *Small States in World Markets: Industrial Policy in Europe* (Ithaca, NY: Cornell University Press, 1985).
8. Stephen D. Krasner, *Defending the National Interest: Raw Materials Investments and U.S. Foreign Policy* (Princeton, NJ: Princeton University Press, 1978).

9. See Manuel Castells, *The Information Age: Economy, Society, and Culture: The Rise of the Network Society* (Oxford: Blackwell Publishing, 1996); Frances Cairncross, *The Death of Distance* (Cambridge, MA: Harvard Business School Press, 1997); Kenichi Ohmae, *The Borderless World: Power and Strategy in the Interlinked Economy* (New York: HarperBusiness, New York 1991/1999); and Kenichi Ohmae, *Evolving Global Economy: Making Sense of the New World Order* (Cambridge, MA: Harvard Business School Press, 1995).
10. Marshall McLuhan, *Gutenberg Galaxy: The Making of Typographic Man* (Toronto: University of Toronto Press, 1965); and McLuhan, *The Medium Is the Message* (New York: Bantam, 1967).
11. Romer, "Increasing Returns and Long-Run Growth" and Romer, "Endogenous Technological Change."
12. On environmental security, see Jon Barnett, "Security and Climate Change," Tyndall Centre Working Paper No. 7, University of Canterbury, New Zealand, 2001: 1–17; Thomas Homer-Dixon, "On the Threshold: Environmental Changes as Causes of Acute Conflict," *International Security* 16, 2 (1991): 76–116; Marc A. Levy, "Is the Environment a National Security Issue?" *International Security* 20, 2 (1995): 35–62; and Karen T. Litfin, "Environmental Security in the Coming Century," in T.V. Paul and John Hall, eds., *International Order and the Future of World Politics* (Cambridge: Cambridge University Press, 1999), 328–351. On human security, see United Nations Development Programme, *Human Development Report, 1994: New Dimensions of Human Security* (New York: Oxford University Press, 1994); Roland Paris, "Human Security: Paradigm Shift or Hot Air?" *International Security* 26, 2 (Fall 2001): 87–102; Gary King and Christopher J.L. Murray, "Rethinking Human Security," *Political Science Quarterly* 116, 4 (2002): 585–610.
13. Walter Dorn, "Human Security: An Overview," Pearson Peacekeeping Centre, Royal Military College of Canada, 2001, available at http://www.rmc.ca/academic/gradrech/dorn24_e.html; accessed 21 October 2005.
14. Nazli Choucri, *Population Dynamics and International Violence: Propositions, Insights, and Evidence* (Lexington, MA: DC Heath/ Lexington Books 1974); Thomas Homer-Dixon, *Environment, Scarcity, and Violence* (Princeton, NJ: Princeton University Press, 1999).
15. Martha Finnemore, "Norms, Culture, and World Politics: Insights from Sociology's Institutionalism," *International Organization* 50, 2 (Spring 1996): 325–347; Peter J. Katzenstein, ed., *The Culture of National Security: Norms and Identity in World Politics* (New York: Columbia University Press, 1996); John Gerard Ruggie, "What Makes the World Hang Together? Neo-Utilitarianism and the Social Constructivist Challenge," *International Organization* 52, 4 (1998): 855–885.; Margaret E. Keck and Kathryn Sikkink, *Activists beyond Borders: Advocacy Networks in International Politics* (Ithaca, NY: Cornell University Press,

1998); Richard Price, "A Genealogy of the Chemical Weapons Taboo," *International Organization* 49, 1 (Winter 1995): 73–103; and Price, "Reversing the Gun Sights: Transnational Civil Society Targets Land Mines," *International Organization* 52, 3 (Summer 1998): 613–644; and Nina Tannenwald, Stigmatizing the Bomb: Origins of the Nuclear Taboo," *International Security* 29, 4 (Spring 2005): 5–49.

16. Peter Berger and Thomas Luckmann, *The Social Construction of Reality* (New York: Anchor Books, 1966); John W. Meyer and Brian Rowan, "Institutional Organizations: Formal Structure as Myth and Ceremony," *American Journal of Sociology* 83 (1977): 340–363; James G. March and Johan P. Olsen, "The Institutional Dynamics of International Political Orders," *International Organization* 52, 4 (1998): 943–969; and Martha Finnemore and Kathryn Sikkink, "International Norm Dynamics and Political Change," *International Organization* 52, 4 (Autumn 1998): 887–917.
17. Robert W. Cox, "Social Forces, States and World Orders: Beyond International Relations Theory," in Robert O. Keohane, ed., *Neorealism and Its Critics* (New York: Columbia University Press, 1986), 204–254; Antonio Gramsci, *Selections from the Prison Notebooks*, ed. and trans. Quintin Hoare and Geoffrey Nowell Smith (New York: Columbia University Press, 1992); and Strange, *The Retreat of the State.*
18. Kenneth Waltz, *Theory of International Politics* (Reading, MA: Addison-Wesley, 1979); Hans Morgenthau, *Politics among Nations* (New York: Alfred Knopf, 1949); and John Mearsheimer, *Tragedy of Great Power Politics* (New York: W.W. Norton, 2002).
19. Michael Borrus and John Zysman, "Industrial Competitiveness and American National Security," in Wayne Sandholtz et al., eds., *The Highest Stakes* (New York and Oxford: Oxford University Press, 1992), 7–52.
20. Barry R. Posen, "Command of the Commons: The Military Foundation of U.S. Hegemony," *International Security* 28, 1 (2003): 5–46.
21. See the following works by Michel Foucault, *The Archaeology of Knowledge* (New York: Harper & Row, 1976); *Discipline and Punish* (New York: Vintage Books, 1979); *Politics, Philosophy, Culture* (New York: Routledge, 1990); and *Power/Knowledge* (New York: Pantheon Books, 1980). Also see Gramsci, *Selections from the Prison Notebooks.*
22. Claudio Fuentes and Felipe Agüero, "Importing Globalization: Military Discourse and Practice in Argentina and Chile," paper presented at the International Studies Association Annual Convention, New Orleans, 24–28 March 2002.
23. Strange, *The Retreat of the State.*
24. Keck and Sikkink, *Activists beyond Borders.*
25. Emanuel Adler, "The Emergence of Cooperation: National Epistemic Communities and the International Evolution of the Idea of Nuclear Arms Control," *International Organization* 46 (1992): 101–145.

26. Finnemore and Sikkink, "International Norm Dynamics and Political Change."
27. On epistemic communities, see John Gerard Ruggie, "International Responses to Technology: Concepts and Trends," *International Organization* 29, 3 (Summer 1975): 557–583; and Peter M. Haas, "Epistemic Communities and International Policy Coordination: Introduction," *International Organization* 46, 1 (1992): 1–35. On nuclear arms control, see Adler, "Emergence of Cooperation." On weapons design and development, see Lynn Eden, *Whole World on Fire: Organizations, Knowledge, and Nuclear Weapons Devastation* (Ithaca, NY: Cornell University Press, 2003).
28. Paul J. DiMaggio and Walter W. Powell, "The Iron Cage Revisited: Institutional Isomophism and Collective Rationality," in Walter W. Powell and Paul J. DiMaggio, eds., *The New Institutionalism in Organizational Analysis* (Chicago: University of Chicago Press, 1991), 66.
29. Ibid., 67–74.
30. Ibid., 69–70. For environmental fitness arguments that stress rational or competitive adaptation to environments rather than symbolic fitness, see Jeffrey Peffer and Gerald R. Salancik, *The External Control of Organizations* (New York: Harper & Row, 1978); Richard R. Nelson and Sidney G. Winter, *An Evolutionary Theory of Economic Change* (Cambridge, MA: Harvard University Press, 1982); Robert Axelrod, *The Evolution of Cooperation* (New York: Basic Books, 1984); Waltz, *Theory of International Politics*; Douglass C. North, *Structure and Change in Economic History* (New York: W.W. Norton, 1981); Joseph S. Nye, Jr., "Nuclear Learning and U.S.-Soviet Security Regimes," *International Organization* 41 (Summer 1987): 371–402; Elinor Ostrom, *Governing the Commons: The Evolution of Institutions for Collective Action* (New York: Cambridge University Press, 1990); and Philip E. Tetlock, "Learning in U.S. and Soviet Foreign Policy: In Search of an Elusive Concept," in George W. Breslauer and Philip E. Tetlock, eds., *Learning in U.S. and Soviet Foreign Policy* (Boulder, CO: Westview, 1991), 20–61.
31. Robert Gilpin, *War and Change in World Politics* (Cambridge: Cambridge University Press, 1981).
32. John W. Meyer, "The World Polity and the Authority of the Nation State," in George M. Thomas, John W. Meyer, Francisco O. Ramirez, and John Boli, eds., *Institutional Structure: Constituting State, Society and the Individual* (Beverly Hills: Sage, 1987), 41–70; Mark C. Suchman and Dana P. Eyre, "Military Procurement as Rational Myth: Notes on the Social Construction of Weapons Proliferation," *Sociological Forum* 7, 1 (March 1992): 137–161; Finnemore, "Norms, Culture, and World Politics"; Tannenwald, "Stigmatizing the Bomb"; Robert Jackson, *Quasi-States: Sovereignty, International Relations and the Third World* (Cambridge: Cambridge University Press, 2004).

33. Janice E. Thomson, "State Practices, International Norms, and the Decline of Mercenarism," *International Studies Quarterly* 34, 1 (March 1990): 23–47; Peter W. Singer, *Corporate Warriors: The Rise of the Privatized Military Industry* (Ithaca, NY: Cornell University Press 2003).
34. On the purpose of the military, see Martha Finnemore, *The Purpose of Intervention* (Ithaca, NY: Cornell University Press, 2004). On the emergence of new roles and missions, see Adler "The Emergence of Cooperation"; and Christopher Dandeker, "New Times for the Military: Some Sociological Remarks on the Changing Role and Structure of the Armed Forces of the Advanced Societies," *British Journal of Sociology* 45, 4 (December 1994): 637–654.
35. Adler "The Emergence of Cooperation"; Price, "A Genealogy of the Chemical Weapons Taboo"; and Price, "Reversing the Gun Sights," 613–644; Tannenwald, "Stigmatizing the Bomb."
36. Thomson, "State Practices, International Norms, and the Decline of Mercenarism."
37. Ibid., 39–40.
38. Charles C. Moskos, "Toward a Postmodern Military: The United States as a Paradigm," in Charles C. Moskos, John Allen Williams, and David R. Segal, eds., *The Postmodern Military: Armed Forces after the Cold War* (Oxford: Oxford University Press, 2000), 14.
39. Charles C. Moskos, John Allen Williams, and David R. Segal, "Armed Forces after the Cold War," in Moskos, Williams, and Segal, eds., *The Postmodern Military*, 1–13. On homosexuals in the military, see Elizabeth Kier, "Homosexuals in the U.S. Military: Open Integration and Combat Effectiveness," *International Security* 23, 2 (Autumn 1998): 5–39; and Aaron Belkin, "Don't Ask, Don't Tell: Is the Gay Ban Based on Military Necessity?" *Parameters* 33 (Summer 2003): 108–119.
40. John Allen Williams, "The Postmodern Military Reconsidered," in Moskos, Williams, Segal, eds., *The Postmodern Military*, 265–279.
41. Singer, *Corporate Warriors*, 49.
42. For a discussion of technical rationality, see Max Weber, *The Theory of Social and Economic Organization* (New York: Free Press, 1947/1964); on norms of social solidarity, see Charles C. Moskos, "From Institution to Occupation: Trends in Military Organization," *Armed Forces and Society* 4, 1 (Winter 1977): 41–49; and David R. Segal and Mady Wechsler Segal, "Change in Military Organization," *Annual Review of Sociology* 9 (1983): 151–170.
43. Williams, "The Postmodern Military Reconsidered," 265–279.
44. Moskos, Williams, and Segal, "Armed Forces after the Cold War," 3.
45. Williams, "The Postmodern Military Reconsidered," 265–279.

46. See United Nations, "A More Secure World: Our Shared Responsibility," Report of the High-Level Panel on Threats, Challenges and Change to the Secretary General, UNGA A/59/565, 2 December 2004, 66; and Kofi Annan, "In Larger Freedom: Towards Development, Security and Human Rights for All," Report of the Secretary-General, UNGA A/59/2005, 21 March 2005, 34–35.
47. Holsti, *Taming the Sovereigns*, 284–285.
48. Finnemore, *The Purpose of Intervention.*
49. Ibid. 135–136; Michael N. Barnett and Martha Finnemore, "The Politics, Power, and Pathologies of International Organizations," *International Organization* 53, 4 (Autumn 1999): 699–732; Audie Klotz, "Norms Reconstituting Interests: Global Racial Equality and U.S. Sanctions against South Africa," *International Organization* 49 (Summer 1995): 451–478.
50. Finnemore, *The Purpose of Intervention*, 136.
51. Fuentes and Agüero, "Importing Globalization."
52. Adler, "The Emergence of Cooperation."
53. Price, "A Genealogy of the Chemical Weapons Taboo," 73–103.
54. See the following articles by Richard Price: "Genealogy of the Chemical Weapons Taboo"; "Reversing the Gun Sights," 613–644; and "Emerging Customary Norms and Anti-personnel Landmines," in Christian Reus-Smit, ed., *The Politics of International Law* (Cambridge: Cambridge University Press, 2004), 106–130.
55. James Ron, "Varying Methods of State Violence," *International Organization* 51, 2 (Spring 1997): 275–300.
56. For these memos, see Karen J. Greenberg, and Joshua L. Dratel, eds., *The Torture Papers. The Road to Abu Ghraib* (New York: Cambridge University Press, 2005).
57. Anne L. Clunan, "Man vs. the State: The Shifting Boundary of Sovereign Authority," paper presented to the 2005 Annual Meeting of the American Political Science Association, Washington, DC, 31 August–5 September 2005.
58. DiMaggio and Powell, "The Iron Cage Revisited," 151–152.
59. For an explanation of two-level games, see Robert Putnam, "Diplomacy and Domestic Politics: The Logic of Two-level Games," *International Organization* 42, 3 (Summer 1988): 427–460. On the application of two-level game logic in humanitarian intervention, see Fuentes and Agüero, "Importing Globalization."
60. Gerald Berk and Dennis Galvan, "A Field Guide to Creative Syncretism or How and When People Remake Institutions," paper prepared for presentation at the 100th Annual Meeting of the American Political Science Association, Chicago, 2–5 September 2004.
61. Ibid.

62. Chris C. Demchak, "Creating the Enemy: Worldwide Diffusion of an Electronic Military," in Emily Goldman and Leslie C. Eliason, eds., *The Diffusion of Military Knowledge from the Napoleonic Era to the Information Age* (Palo Alto: Stanford University Press 2003), 307–347.
63. Fuentes and Agüero, "Importing Globalization."

3

International Democracy Promotion and Its Impact on Civil-Military Relations

Thomas Bruneau and Harold Trinkunas

Introduction

It has become common to think of democratization as a global phenomenon. The designation "Third Wave of democracy" makes it clear that observers believe the group of democracies that emerged in the wake of Portugal's transition in 1974 had an impact on one another, at least in terms of timing and proximity. The puzzle is that most of the literature on democratic transitions views the phenomenon of democratic transitions as inextricably linked to local circumstances, political leaders, and strategic decisions.[1] To the extent that theorists have identified global linkages to explain the latest wave of democratization, explanations attribute it to either imitation effects on a regional level or a shift in the global zeitgeist that favors democracy.[2] This theoretical perspective appears to be at odds with the reality of myriad major efforts by the United States, European countries, and international organizations to promote democratization through political and economic incentives such as foreign aid, accession to regional treaty organizations such as NATO and the European Union, and most recently, a new "Wilsonianism" in U.S. foreign policy that associates at least minimal democratization with the maintenance of state sovereignty and legitimacy.[3] Democratization as a global trend with an impact on security issues has only been seriously explored by the proponents of "democratic peace theory," who argue that insofar as democracies do not fight each other, waves of democratization tend to reduce the likelihood of international conflict.[4] Critics such as Jack Snyder counter by pointing out that emerging democracies are conflict prone, while others point to emerging but poorly understood transnational threats that target democratic societies.[5]

The Third Wave of democratization has been accompanied by an unprecedented shift in civil-military relations that has placed more power and instruments of control in the hands of elected leaders than at any other time in history. Pure military dictatorships have become rare, as are military coups d'etat. Such is the global compulsion toward maintaining at least the appearance of democracy that the traditional military dictatorship has been largely replaced by the emergence of qualified semi-democracies with civilian leaders clearly in charge despite their reliance on armed force to rule.[6] Tellingly, scholars of democratic civil-military relations have rarely, and not even systematically, examined the impact of democratization as a global trend on civil-military relations. Even more than democratization, civil-military relations have been treated as a product of domestic political interaction on which international forces have little influence. Practically the only argument of any currency that takes seriously the impact of global forces is that which points to the nefarious influence of U.S. military training, particularly in Latin America; as this chapter will point out, however, much U.S. and other international assistance actually has focused on improving civilian control of the military since the 1980s.[7]

Once we take democratization seriously as a global phenomenon with an impact on civil-military relations, we are led to explore an important set of new phenomena. First, the empowering of civilian political leaders, who often have little or no background on security issues and may be suspicious of the armed forces, is likely to alter the ways states approach security issues. In particular, this change in authority and control over budgets and resources produces shifts in national defense strategies, military capabilities, and defense spending, with their consequent impact on neighboring states' threat perceptions.[8] Similarly, to the extent democracies are indeed unlikely to fight each other, as seems the case among the members of well-established security communities such as NATO, the European Union and Mercosur, democratization is likely to foster a search for new roles and missions for the armed forces. For example, the emergence of South America as a major source of peacekeeping forces gives additional international status and credibility to Mercosur partners and associates Chile, Brazil, Uruguay, and Argentina. Most importantly, the United States and Europe have launched and sustained a major effort to export their characteristically liberal understanding of civil-military relations to new democracies around the world. Although largely uncoordinated, the emphasis on civilian control is remarkably consistent, but it has not previously been systematically studied.

We examine the impact of global democratization trends on civil-military relations by focusing on the linkages that have allowed the United States and Europe to transmit their civil-military doctrine and practices to emerging democracies. Democracy promotion by these leading powers has structured the globalization of a particular "liberal" understanding of civil-military relations that, in most parts of the world, has clearly privileged civilian control over the other two elements of democratic civil-military relations, military effectiveness and defense efficiency.[9] Interestingly, the almost exclusive focus on civilian control is tempered in very particular circumstances by the traditional security requirements produced by either the international environment, such as the Cold War, or by alliance structures such as NATO and the Partnership for Peace (PfP). The privileging of civilian control in other parts of the world has led many countries to place too little emphasis on developing effective and efficient defense establishments. In our conclusion, we suggest that we may begin to see a shift in emphasis within new democracies toward defense efficiency and effectiveness, yet the shift is likely to be uneven and chaotic in many states, particularly the vast majority that lack explicit national security strategies or defense planning processes.

The chapter first examines the development of democracy promotion programs by the United States and Europe from the beginning of the Third Wave, and their impact on civil-military relations in emerging democracies. We analyze the circumstances under which global democracy promotion has tended to focus almost exclusively on issues of civilian control. We then turn to the impact of democracy promotion on defense efficiency and military effectiveness in emerging democracies. The chapter concludes with our conjectures on how emerging transnational threats are affecting the current configuration of civil-military relations in new democracies, and how this may be forcing a shift toward greater attention to the output, in terms of security, of the defense sector in these countries.

Democracy Promotion and the Spread of Civilian Control of the Armed Force

In the contemporary era, after the imposition of democracy by the democratic victors of World War II in Germany, Italy, and Japan, and more recently on a small scale in Grenada and Panama, the beginning of explicit democracy building programs is synonymous with the advent of the so-called Third Wave of democratization. As Samuel Huntington has suggested, the current spread of democracy, the Third Wave, began on 25 April 1974 with the military coup in Portugal that became a revolution, and ultimately opened the way to democratization, not only in Portugal but also in Spain, Greece, and then in South America.[10]

While the rhetoric of U.S. foreign policy may long have enshrined the promotion of democracy as a mission, the United States did not begin to think seriously about what tools it needed to carry out such a mission until it began to react to democratization in southern Europe. The democracy promotion model established at the beginning of the Third Wave in revolutionary Portugal in the mid- and late-1970s is essentially the same as is followed today, but with unprecedented growth and institutionalization of the actors, instruments, and resources involved. This model is far more complex than what is proposed by analyses in the scholarly literature on international determinants of democratization, which in our view, are too general.[11] By focusing on democratic zeitgeists or contagion effects, these theories overlook the specific diplomatic instruments and bargaining strategies employed by states and international institutions to foster particular kinds of democracy. Aside from the reports of those directly involved, we can only imagine what kinds of promises and threats are made along the way, including military diplomacy, utilizing demarches, "non-papers," cajoling, and other informal instruments of power. Similarly, arguments about democratic contagion effects are generally structural, and they do not account for the strategic behavior of a wide variety of external actors in transition processes, which seems strange because democratization theory does a good job of explaining the impact of this type of activity by domestic actors.[12] What is lacking in the contagion analysis is a description of the explicit mechanisms that promote democratic civil-military relations. We are unlikely to acquire detailed knowledge of the diplomatic strategies major powers use in specific instances, but we can begin to get a sense of the general approach by focusing on their democracy promotion programs and the resources they commit to them.[13]

The Origins of Contemporary Democracy Promotion: The Portuguese Revolution 1974

The 1974 Portuguese revolution galvanized the international promotion of democracy and set the current pattern for external actors to support Third Wave democracies. It must be stated up front and forcefully, however, that the coup of 25 April 1974 that began the revolution took place with no foreign involvement, and, for that matter, no foreign awareness. Once begun, the archaic political structure of the Salazar dictatorship, based fundamentally on repression, collapsed and opened the way for a political radicalization that was stoked by the Portuguese Communist Party (PCP) and other rapidly forming parties and movements to its left. The Soviet Union and its surrogates quickly became deeply involved, Portugal underwent revolutionary changes, its colonies were given independence, and Portuguese foreign policy shifted far to the left. In this era, when Richard Nixon was president of the United States and Henry Kissinger secretary of state or national security advisor, Washington was extremely concerned by radical changes in a NATO ally that provided important military bases for defense against the Soviet Union, as well as out-of-area operations such as during the October 1973 Arab-Israeli war.[14] Initially, the United States was unwilling to accept a major political upheaval in Portugal, even though the changes taking place had already escaped beyond its control. This virtual paralysis in U.S. policy opened the way for European political involvement, thereby initiating a pattern that has been frequently repeated since 1974.[15]

The Europeans, chiefly the Germans and Norwegians through their leadership of the Socialist International, moved into the vacuum to encourage a democratic direction for Portugal.[16] They did this initially by providing resources to strengthen the nascent democratic forces in Portugal, which were very weak and extremely fragmented. The instruments they utilized were basically the *stiftungen* (foundations) of the three major German political parties, the Konrad Adenauer, Friedrich Ebert, and Friedrich Naumann foundations, and the national (in Germany and Belgium) as well as international offices of the labor unions. These groups encouraged Portuguese would-be or proto-democratic politicians, union leaders, journalists, and agricultural cooperative leaders to build democratic institutions.[17]

As the Europeans helped put content into the basic and preliminary institutions of Portuguese democracy, the United States and other major economic powers would begin to shape the overall development of Portugal. That is, they provided economic support to ensure that Portugal would develop as a pluralist democracy and not a Communist dictatorship. As Portugal was the first transition of the Third Wave, democratic contagion effects were not relevant. Indeed, the contagion effect would have been more likely to push for a return to fascist dictatorship given the concern the United States and Spain had regarding the radicalization of the Portuguese Revolution.[18]

The above analysis is more or less generally accepted among scholars, although there is little literature explicitly describing developments in Portugal. What is less well understood is the military dimension of Portuguese democratization. A sector of the young officers who had led the coup in 1974 intended that the new regime would institutionalize a predominant role for the armed forces in government. The counterstrategy developed by the United States, Germany, and NATO itself sought to wean the officers out of politics and into more purely professional activities, largely through their inclusion in NATO missions. What was most important is that the United States, Germany, and others had the institutional framework of NATO within which to develop and implement their strategy. Furthermore, the NATO allies could provide powerful incentives to Portuguese officers through their ability to provide modern training and equipment. This was the first time that these strategies, actors, and instruments were used to promote a democratic transition and later democratic consolidation.

There are several lessons from Portugal at the beginning of the Third Wave. First is the need for external actors to be flexible when supporting democratization. Nobody, not the Portuguese themselves (with the possible exception of the 200 young officers who were the instigators), the United States, or NATO, was prepared for the coup that became a revolution. Once it began, the Europeans, especially the Germans, used their foundations and other organizations to influence developments and put Portugal on a democratic path. Second, the role of external security considerations in shaping defense reform appears to be significant. The military dimension of democratization in Portugal took place in the context of the Cold War, when base access and NATO unity were critically important for U.S. and European national security. Third, once the value of foundations, labor organizations, and the like were proven in Portugal, they were then repeatedly called on throughout the Third Wave of democratization. The common dominator in these programs is the promotion of political learning, whereby individuals and groups in the Third Wave democracies can understand how their predecessors created and managed their democratic institutions.

CONTEMPORARY DEMOCRACY PROMOTION PROGRAMS AND CIVIL-MILITARY RELATIONS

The historical evolution of the Third Wave from southern Europe to South America and beyond was not directly caused by specific programs implemented by major powers, but rather by an interaction of domestic and international factors. Once a given transition began, however, whether for endogenous reasons or in reaction to an external shock, and certainly as countries seemed to be consolidating new regimes, democratizers could benefit from a myriad of programs to support this consolidation. In an early monograph, Larry Diamond surveyed the remarkable variety of actors and programs engaged in democracy promotion.[19] Democracy promotion has now become big business, and the United States has a wide array of programs at its disposal. Following the lead of Germany and its foundations, Congress created the National Endowment for Democracy (NED) in 1984. NED supports, at least in part, a series of other organizations including the National Democratic Institute and the International Republican Institute, foundations associated with the two major U.S. political parties. USAID, through its Office of Democracy and Governance, helps its field missions design and implement democracy strategies, provides technical and intellectual leadership in the field of democracy development, and manages some USAID programs directly. In Fiscal Year 2006, the Agency's basic Democracy and Governance programs cost about $37 million. The USAID Office of Transitional Initiatives also supports democratizers during the very initial stages of regime change. In terms of funding, the Geneva Centre for the Democratic Control of Armed Forces, for example, had a 2005 budget of $11 million, and the U.S. International Military Education and Training 2005 budget was just short of $100 million. Private and international initiatives have also gained prominence. Billionaire George Soros established the Open Society Institute, just one of the most famous of the private foundations that support one or another element of democracy; the United Nations Foundation, funded by American media tycoon Ted Turner, has also become engaged in this field. Other prominent actors include the United Nations Development Program, the European Union, and the Organization of American States. These programs deal to a large extent with the basic elements of democracy such as the media, nongovernmental organizations, electoral systems, and political parties.[20]

It is nevertheless remarkable that despite all the work to promote democratic civil-military relations, there has been virtually no systematic assessment of the roles external actors have played in shaping civil-military relations in the Third Wave. To highlight this lack, it is worth noting that the highly regarded Freedom House index, which rates democracies globally, does not include a variable dealing with security, defense, and the relations between military and civilians.[21] The few academic studies of democratic civil-military relations rarely include a reference to the impact of external assistance programs. Felipe Agüero's 1995 monograph on civil-military relations during Spain's transition to democracy, for example, only briefly discusses the influence of NATO accession on the domestic interplay between military and civilian actors, despite the fact that accession to NATO and the European Union caused major public debates before, during and after Spain's democratic transition, and according to Agüero, assisted the transition.[22] There is, in short, no literature that deals with civil-military relations in which the effect of foreign programs and relationships is systematically analyzed.

Coupled with the failure to assess the impact of external actors is an absence of any systematic survey of the programs that promote democratic civil-military relations themselves. Jay Cope's short monograph on the International Military Education and Training program (IMET), and an even shorter survey by Hans Born of programs that deal more or less with oversight in the security sector, are the only such published studies we know of.[23] It is shocking that even in the case of the U.S. government there is no comprehensive listing of the programs that provide support for defense reform, civilian oversight of the security sector, and civil-military relations. This is despite the fact that they are funded, directly or indirectly, by the U.S. government, and are thus obliged to follow its reporting and auditing requirements. There have been only two systematic attempts to survey the programs funded by the United States: A limited inventory conducted by the Naval Postgraduate School (NPS) in October 2002; and a more comprehensive survey mandated by and conducted for the powerful office of the Undersecretary of Defense for Policy in 2003, the results of which will not be released.

What became obvious from the NPS assessment of a large number of government programs that support democratic civil-military relations through training or education is that every component of the U.S. military education and training endeavor includes some form of international outreach. There is a glaring problem with these diverse programs, however, for they fail to make any explicit linkage with, or even demonstrate a clear concept of, how they support democratic civil-military relations, let alone democratic consolidation. In short, the programs that support democratic civil-military relations are not integrated into the larger field of democracy building.[24] Similarly, Hans Born finds that while there are many organizations supporting security sector reform and democratization processes, "civil-military relations are apparently not a central issue of parliamentary assistance programmes. Mostly military different [*sic*] institutions, such as the NATO or national defence ministries, carry out the assistance programmes for promoting democratic civil-military relations but they are not so much regarded as being central to parliamentary assistance programmes." He continues, "It seems that assistance programmes for democratic civil-military relations and for parliaments are taking place but on different tracks, carried out by different aid providers."[25] Clearly the fragmentation of democratic civil-military relations efforts pertains in both U.S. and European programs.

In the United States, besides the much larger programs supported by foreign military sales and financing, there are two main categories of programs that are oriented specifically toward improving democratic civil-military relations. The first include those funded by the International Military Education and Training program (IMET); the second are the regional centers designed to promote democratic civil-military relations and security. The IMET program was begun in 1976, and was revised in 1991 after the end of the Cold War. Explicit objectives of the IMET programs include fostering civilian control of the military, promoting human rights, and helping resolve civil-military conflicts. The 2006 IMET budget was slightly less than $100 million, and supports a wide variety of democracy promotion organizations that are designed to provide education and training in the United States and abroad.

The Department of Defense undertook its own initiative in this area beginning in 1992, and has created five regional centers that seek specifically to promote democratic civil-military relations (security assistance is included in the Department of State appropriation). The first, the George C. Marshall Center in Germany, was created in 1992, and its mission statement captures the overall sense of the other four: "The mission of the Marshall Center is to create a more stable security environment by advancing democratic institutions and relationships, especially in the field of defense; promoting active, peaceful security cooperation; and enhancing enduring partnerships among the nations of North America, Europe and Eurasia." In addition to the Marshall Center, the Department of Defense has founded and generously funds the Africa Center for Strategic Studies, the Asia-Pacific Center for Security Studies, the Center for Hemispheric Defense Studies (for Latin America), and the newest, founded in 2000, the Near East and South Asia Center. The budget for these regional centers easily rivals the total size of the IMET budget. Thus, with nearly $200 million per year committed to democratic civil-military relations promotion, the effort of the U.S. government easily exceeds that of other countries that also have programs, such as the Geneva Centre for the Democratic Control of Armed Forces, and smaller organizations in Canada and Great Britain.[26]

The content of the different IMET and regional center programs puts the emphasis overwhelmingly on civilian control. Defense efficiency (using limited resources rationally and with the least possible waste) comes in as a very distant second. They give minimal attention to the promotion of effectiveness in the implementation of military roles and missions (getting the assigned job done with the resources and within the time allotted). The only programs where effectiveness is included as a key element are those of NATO, the PfP, and in peacekeeping and counterterrorism education and training. This highlights an important dichotomy among programs that promote democratic civil-military relations: There are those that promote both military effectiveness and defense efficiency on an equal basis with civilian control, for new NATO and PfP countries; and there are those that focus solely on civilian control. This is all the stranger when we discover that the U.S. Department of Defense guidance to combatant commanders on security assistance emphasizes all three elements of the defense trinity. It should be noted that in the nondemocratic regimes of the original PfP members, civilians did control the armed forces; they just were not democratically elected civilians.[27]

Since the end of the Cold War, the PfP, which serves as both a pathway into NATO and a way to engage countries that are not members of NATO, has reinforced and made very clear the importance of all aspects of the trinity of civil-military relations. Point 1 of the *Partnership Action Plan on Defence Institution Building* states: "The Member states of the Euro-Atlantic Partnership Council reaffirm their conviction that effective and efficient state defense institutions under civilian and democratic control are fundamental to stability in the Euro-Atlantic area and essential for international security cooperation. They agree to establish a Partnership Action Plan to support and sustain further development of such institutions across the Euro-Atlantic Area."[28] In short, the PfP plan essentially commits the NATO allies to help the new democracies develop control, effectiveness, and efficiency, goals also promoted in the programs sponsored by the NATO School at Supreme Headquarters in Belgium, the PfP Training and Education Centers, and the Military Assistance Program. The fact that these elements are essentially prerequisites for NATO accession acts as a carrot and a stick for both civilian and military leaders in the new democracies, much as did the offer of NATO assistance to Spain and Portugal in the 1970s and 1980s.

By contrast, programs to promote democratic civil-military relations in Africa, Asia, and Latin America focus almost exclusively on civilian control of the military. There is no overarching directive framework for the regions similar to NATO and PfP, but rather a fragmented menu of programs. Most of the work sponsored by the four DoD regional centers (excluding the Marshall Center), IMET institutions, the U.S. National Endowment for Democracy, and the Geneva Center for the Democratic Control of Armed Forces also deals only with the civilian-control element of the defense trinity. This is perhaps not surprising given that the previous nondemocratic regimes in these three regions were dominated by the armed forces, and we therefore should not minimize the achievement that consolidating civilian control represents. The lack of attention to effectiveness and efficiency of the armed forces, however, not only puts national security at risk, it also endangers what is likely a tenuous bond of trust between civilians, the new democratic regime, and the armed forces.

Explaining Variation in Democratic Civil-Military Relations Promotion Programs

The split impact of democratization programs on military effectiveness and defense efficiency is striking when we compare the cases of Central Europe with those in Latin America, Africa, and Asia. In this section we examine the interests of donor and recipient countries in improving each of these aspects of democratic civil-military relations.

In Central Europe, democratization produced governments that focused on all elements of democratic civil-military relations because they were eager to accede to NATO and the European Union. It is true that these alliance structures had strict requirements for civilian control of the military, but they also expect aspirants to achieve significant military capabilities compatible with the overall alliance strategy. This provided democratizers with an incentive to take the dimensions of civil-military relations other than control seriously. It also helped democratic politicians justify continuing investment in the military at a time when the likelihood of interstate war in Europe was declining rapidly.

In the rest of the world, by contrast, politicians—and donor countries—had few incentives to maintain significant military capabilities, except in localized instances where interstate conflict was a real possibility, or to achieve particular defense outcomes. For politicians, promoting military effectiveness meant strengthening the very forces that could potentially overthrow them. It also meant committing a significant amount of resources, energy, and government attention to the problem of defense reform.[29] For the armed services, the possibility of reform under civilian rule opened the door to a frightening world in which none of their traditional missions would remain sacred. Given the perceived lack of an external threat, particularly in Latin America, there was the possibility of being reduced to a mere constabulary force.[30] Similarly, civilians did not necessarily have the time or the interest, except in some situations in Asia where the external threat was high, to formulate national strategies and policies. This led them to neglect the definition of clear roles and missions for their armed forces, or to relate the development of certain capabilities and effectiveness with particular national objectives.

The main concern of donor countries with interests in these parts of the world was to prevent local armed forces from abusing their own populations or overthrowing their governments. Beyond that, donors had little interest in military effectiveness, at least until the 9/11 attacks on the United States forced them to reexamine the need for capable regional military partners. Even then, international donors, to the extent that they promoted military effectiveness, were interested in niche capabilities such as counterdrug or peacekeeping operations, none of which justified maintenance of the kinds of conventional defense establishments that fit with the traditions and self-image of the military establishments of these regions.

Of the explanations for why military effectiveness receives such minimal attention in new democracies, probably the most important factor is the motivation of civilian leaders, now that the armed forces are generally under control, to promote a capable military. At a minimum, better forces would cost more money, and there is no obvious electoral gain from pushing for an increased level of effectiveness. Even in the NATO and PfP regions, where there are incentives in the form of accession to regional alliance structures, it is difficult for elected politicians to sustain programs and obtain the resources required for building effectiveness. Outside of this region, achieving a capable military is rare, even in high threat situations. The case of Colombia, where there is a well-recognized threat, is illustrative. The Colombian military has so far resisted establishing the necessary reforms and institutions to build effectiveness, while civilian politicians do not want to commit the required political capital and energy, even though they are the recipients of massive U.S. military aid to do just that.[31] In short, civilians and officers in most of the world's newer democracies have few incentives to focus on their deficiencies when it come to achieving effectiveness in military roles and missions. This may be why these countries rarely formulate national security strategies. To the best of our knowledge, only Colombia, at the behest of Washington that is financing much of the government's fight against insurgencies, and Chile, where it was part of the consolidation agenda, have well-developed national security strategies.

Outside the NATO/PfP region, politicians in aid-recipient countries actually have had more incentive to reduce than to promote efficiency. One of the few scholars to have taken the impact of democratization on military budgets seriously is Wendy Hunter, who demonstrates that politicians will naturally seek to reduce defense budgets in order to satisfy the demands of important constituents and stakeholders.[32] Some of the literature on the Argentine transition to democracy suggests that an important objective of the civilian governments after 1983 was to eliminate border disputes and foster democratization in neighboring states, so as to undercut the rationale for a large military force.[33] Overall, the evidence seems to suggest that democratization as an international phenomenon has led politicians to focus on defense reduction as part of an overall drive to free resources to meet the demands of other constituencies, and not incidentally reduce the ability of the armed forces to threaten the security of new regimes.

Defense efficiency, understood as the ability to field military capabilities sufficient to satisfy assigned roles and missions at the lowest cost, has been part of the international democratization agenda of donor countries only to a limited extent. The International Monetary Fund and World Bank appear to have goals congruent with those of politicians in donor countries, to the extent that they consider defense spending superfluous. Defense efficiency has been promoted by the major donor countries mostly as an aspect of effectiveness. Codified national security objectives, in the form of either Defense White Books (popular with European donors) or National Security Strategies (popular with the U.S. defense establishment), are seen as a precursor to the rationalization of defense capabilities. Promoters of democratization in the United States and Europe have pushed for transparency in defense spending as part of the overall drive to reduce interstate tensions, reduce corruption, and increase citizen access to defense data in new democracies.[34] Argentina and Chile are engaged in a sustained project to produce an accounting of their defense expenditures in a common format with such goals in mind. Nevertheless, outside of Europe and NATO, the purpose of defense efficiency at best is to rationalize budget reductions.

These findings reemphasize the gap between those democratizing states that participate in one set of alliance structures and those that do not. New NATO and PfP countries consider defense efficiency to be important because it allows their governments to realign their defense capabilities to meet alliance standards more rapidly. It also helps establish the credibility of new NATO partners among those of longer standing. In less conflict-ridden regions of the world, however, any focus on defense efficiency is undermined by a failure to agree on what the roles and missions of the armed forces should be. The United States maintains that the role of the military in Africa and Latin America essentially should be to carry out internal security functions associated with counterdrug operations and counterterrorism, as well as some level of peacekeeping or peacemaking. This limited inventory of roles and missions often does not square with what military leaders would prefer, or for that matter with the civilian leaders in at least the Southern Cone countries, who want even fewer roles for the armed forces. The lack of clarity over what roles and missions should be, and how to implement changes, means that governments have no clear idea of what defense "product" they are paying for. In the absence of concrete defense outputs, it is difficult to make a case for robust defense budgets in democratizing states.

Conclusion

There are large gaps in the literature on the impact of international factors on democratic consolidation. To begin with, few scholars include external factors in their analyses of democratic consolidation. Those studies that do examine the impact of democracy promotion programs focus on the basic components of democracy such as electoral systems, political parties, the media, and the like, and exclude elements of national security and defense, including civil-military relations. There also is scant analysis of international programs that support civil-military relations within the context of democratic consolidation. For that matter, there are barely any surveys on the spectrum and scope of these programs. From our research, we find the overwhelming emphasis of these programs is on democratic civilian control. The only region where this is not the case lies under the NATO and PfP umbrella, where there is an explicit framework for membership that emphasizes effectiveness. In the rest of the world, there is an almost total absence of attention to the institutional and other requirements for military effectiveness, and a very powerful set of disincentives for this circumstance to change.

There are, however, two current global trends that may encourage attention to defense efficiency and effectiveness in the developing (non-NATO/PfP) world: Peacekeeping and counterterrorism. Peacekeeping has become a major industry since the end of the Cold War, with the number of both missions and personnel expanding substantially. Currently, 110 countries indicate they engage in peace keeping and there are 77,000 military and police forces deployed. Increasingly, these missions deviate from traditional peacekeeping into peace enforcement operations in hostile environments. The demands on the professionalism and skill of peacekeeping troops have grown, and the eagerness of countries to participate has increased as well. This can be explained in part by the attractiveness of UN reimbursements for peacekeeping troops, the enhanced international image garnered by those countries that are major peacekeeper providers, and the desirability of new professional roles for militaries in democratizing states. One of the side effects is renewed attention to issues of effectiveness and efficiency as new peacekeeping providers interact with more established and professional armed forces in these types of operations, creating a demand within democratizing states for defense reform.

Counterterrorism operations may also provide an impetus for better military effectiveness, particularly in those countries that have been the targets of terrorist attacks. Here, the momentum for defense reform may still be slowed by domestic arguments over the role of the armed forces in internal conflict, threats to civil liberties and preference for police-led counterterrorism activities. There is also the danger that international donor countries, particularly the United States, may emphasize military effectiveness at the cost of promoting civilian control of the armed forces. The United States and the European Union are clearly at odds over whether military or police forces are the best instruments for counterterrorism policies, and this divergence may be reflected in their programs that target democratizing states. It is too soon to tell whether there will be significant future tradeoffs in these areas.

Finally, there is one very old motivator that may still foster pockets of defense effectiveness and efficiency outside of existing alliance structures or new missions such as peacekeeping and counterterrorism: The balance of power. There are parts of the world, particularly in East Asia, South Asia, and the Middle East, where traditional security concerns lead civilian and military leader to share a preference for defense efficiency and military effectiveness. In these cases, however, democratization as a global trend has not necessarily been the prime motivator of defense reform, as some of the cases examined in this volume illustrate.

Notes

1. Guillermo O'Donnell and Philippe Schmitter, *Transitions from Authoritarian Rule: Tentative Conclusions about Uncertain Democracies* (Baltimore, MD: Johns Hopkins University Press, 1986).
2. Laurence Whitehead, ed. *The International Dimensions of Democratization: Europe and the Americas, Expanded Edition* (Oxford: Oxford University Press, 2001).
3. Thomas Carothers, *Aiding Democracy Abroad: The Learning Curve* (Washington, DC: Carnegie Endowment for International Peace, 1999); and Carothers, "Promoting Democracy and Fighting Terror," *Foreign Affairs* 82, 1 (January/February 2003), available at http://www.foreignaffairs.org/20030101faessay10224-p10/thomas-carothers/promoting-democracy-and-fighting-terror.html.
4. Michael W. Doyle, *Ways of War and Peace* (New York: W.W. Norton, 1997).

5. Jack L. *Snyder, From Voting to Violence: Democratization and Nationalist Conflict* (New York: W.W. Norton, 2000); Jeanne Giraldo and Harold Trinkunas, "Terrorism Financing and State Responses in Comparative Perspective," paper prepared for 101st American Political Science Association conference, Washington DC, 1–4 September 2005.
6. Steven Levitsky and Lucan Way, "Autocracy by Democratic Rules: The Dynamics of Competitive Authoritarianism in the Post–Cold War Era," paper prepared for the conference Mapping the Great Zone: Clientelism and the Boundary between Democratic and Democratizing, Columbia University, 4–5 April 2003.
7. Adam Isacson and Joy Olson, "Just the Facts: A Civilian's Guide to U.S. Defense and Security Assistance to Latin America and the Caribbean," Washington, DC: Latin America Working Group, 1999.
8. Michael Barletta and Harold Trinkunas, "Regime Type and Regional Security in Latin America: Toward a 'Balance of Identity' Theory," in Michel Fortmann, T.V. Paul, and James J. Wirtz, eds., *Balance of Power* (Stanford: Stanford University Press, 2004), 334–359.
9. Joseph Nye, "Epilogue: The Liberal Tradition," in Larry Diamond and Marc Plattner, eds., *Civil-Military Relations and Democracy* (Baltimore, MD: Johns Hopkins University Press, 1996).
10. Samuel Huntington, *The Third Wave of Democracy* (Norman, OK: University of Oklahoma Press, 1991).
11. Whitehead, *The International Dimensions of Democratization*; Juan J. Linz and Alfred Stepan, *Problems of Democratic Transition and Consolidation* (Baltimore, MD: Johns Hopkins University Press, 1996).
12. O'Donnell and Schmitter, *Transitions from Authoritarian Rule.*
13. Peter J. Schraeder, ed., *Exporting Democracy: Rhetoric vs. Reality* (Boulder, CO: Lynne Rienner Publishers, 2002).
14. George McGovern, "Revolution into Democracy: Portugal after the Coup," report to the Committee on Foreign Relations, United States Senate, August 1976, 103–109.
15. Thomas Bruneau, "Patterns of Politics in Portugal Since the Revolution," in Jorge Braga de Macedo and Simon Serfaty, eds., *Portugal Since the Revolution: Economic and Political Perspectives* (Boulder, CO: Westview Press, 1981).
16. McGovern, "Revolution into Democracy," 72–75.
17. From field interviews conducted by author Bruneau between 1975 and 1981.
18. Interviews conducted by Bruneau in Lisbon, Brussels, and Washington, DC between 1977 and 1978.
19. Larry Diamond, "Promoting Democracy in the 1990s: Actors and Instruments, Issues and Imperatives," report to the Carnegie Commission on Preventing Deadly Conflict, December 1995 (New York: Carnegie Corporation of New York, December 1995).
20. Ibid.

21. Freedom House is an NGO founded in the 1940s by Eleanor Roosevelt and others to promote global democracy, primarily through a number of highly regarded annual publications that measure specific trends, such as freedom of the press. See http://www.freedomhouse.org; accessed 6 March 2006. Note also that the authoritative *Bertelsmann Transformation Index 2006: Toward Democracy and a Market Economy* (Gutersloh: Verlag Bertelsmann Stiftung, 2006) does not include security or civil-military relations in its very comprehensive approach to democracy.
22. Felipe Agüero, *Soldiers, Civilians and Democracy* (Baltimore, MD: Johns Hopkins University Press 1995), 203–206.
23. Jay Cope, "International Military Education and Training: An Assessment," Institute for National Strategic Studies, National Defense University, Washington, DC. McNair Paper 44, October 1995; Hans Born, "Representative Democracy and the Role of Parliaments: An Inventory of Democracy Assistance Programs," Geneva: Geneva Center for the Democratic Control of Armed Forces, 2002.
24. C.J. LaCivita and John Christiansen, "Enhancing International Education Support to Security Cooperation," Volumes I–III, Naval Postgraduate School, Monterey, California. 16 April 2003.
25. Born, "Representative Democracy and the Role of Parliaments," 12 and 15–16.
26. Diamond, "Promoting Democracy in the 1990s."
27. The Partnership for Peace was created in 1994 as a way to bring the newly independent states of Eastern Europe and the former Soviet Union into a cooperative alliance with NATO short of full membership. There are twenty current members, including Ireland, Switzerland, and Sweden. For a list, see http://www.nato.int/pfp/sig-cntr.htm; accessed 7 March 2006.
28. "Partnership Action Plan on Defence Institution Building," NATO, 7 June 2004. See the NATO online Library of Basic Texts: http://www.nato.int/docu/basics.htm#II-D; accessed 7 March 2006.
29. Harold Trinkunas, *Crafting Civilian Control of the Military in Venezuela: A Comparative Perspective* (Chapel Hill: University of North Carolina Press, 2005).
30. David Pion-Berlin, *Through Corridors of Power* (University Park: Penn State University Press, 1997).
31. Richard Goetze and Thomas Bruneau, "Report on CCMR Project Colombia," Monterey, CA: Center for Civil-Military Relations, July 2005; *Fuerzas Militares para la Guerra: La agenda pendiente de la reforma militar* (Bogota: Fundacion Seguridad & Democracia, 2003).
32. Wendy Hunter, *Eroding Military Influence in Brazil: Politicians against Soldiers* (Chapel Hill, NC: University of North Carolina Press, 1997).

33. Barletta and Trinkunas, "Regime Type and Regional Security in Latin America," 334–359.
34. Jeanne Giraldo, "Defense Budgets, Democratic Civilian Control, and Effective Governance," in Thomas Bruneau and Scott Tollefson, eds., *Who Guards the Guardians and How: Democratic Civil-Military Relations* (Austin, TX: University of Texas Press, 2006), 178–207.

4

Changing International Threat Perceptions

James Wirtz

Introduction

The U.S. government, to say nothing of a bevy of American scholars and observers housed in universities, think tanks, and consulting firms, spend much time writing and speaking about actual and potential threats to national and international security. The George W. Bush administration, much like its Democratic predecessor, also has issued several white papers that describe the threats faced by the United States and proposed policies to meet these challenges. The National Security Strategy of the United States of America (2002), The National Strategy for Maritime Security (2004), The National Strategy for Combating Terrorism (2003), and even a National Strategy for Victory in Iraq (2005), are just a partial list of the official, public assessments issued by the Bush administration describing current threats faced by the United States and contemporary national security policy.[1]

By contrast, most observers and government officials in other countries are restrained when it comes to speaking or writing about national threat assessments. Why do most leaders and diplomats shy away from identifying threats to their own country's national security? Some might believe that by identifying states perceived as dangerous, threat assessments might become a sort of self-fulfilling prophecy. Describing other nations as potential threats might antagonize foreign statesmen, leading them to bolster their defense efforts. Candor about defense assessments could thus lead to an actual deterioration in security. Other governments might consider all threat assessments to be classified, making it difficult for officials or officers to speak publicly about national security concerns. Threat assessments also could be highly controversial in a domestic political context, resurrecting memories of militarism or the threats posed to political and economic liberties by dictatorial regimes. The "counterintelligence state," to borrow a concept from John Dziak, used foreign threats as a justification to monitor and control domestic populations, which generally resulted in human rights abuses if not a reign of terror.[2] Talk about threats to national security might simply remind everyone of the way former regimes used foreign threats to justify domestic repression. Additionally, there is a general trend toward military downsizing, especially in Europe, and drawing attention to potential threats might be viewed as something that could upset this positive development. With the end of the Cold War, many officials also might honestly believe, despite concerns about international terrorism, the proliferation of weapons of mass destruction or the supposed threat posed by a rogue hyper power (the United States), that threats to international security are minimal.

International threat assessments are not a trivial issue, especially when it comes to defense reform and restructuring. On the one hand, if threats are perceived as extremely low, little incentive exists to reform existing institutions, force structures, planning processes, or personnel policies. Because so little is at stake, virtually no political, economic, or military pressure is created to overcome the bureaucratic inertia that impedes reformers. Military establishments can safely be allowed to atrophy in terms of resources or personnel, with little danger posed to national security. On the other hand, if threats are perceived, and are cogently and calmly articulated, officials and officers could identify benefits that would flow from defense reform and restructuring, not the least of which is greater national security. Moreover, given the inherently competitive nature of military matters, institutions and nations that fail to undertake organizational, doctrinal, or operational modernization and reform will fall by the wayside. The international landscape is not a benign setting.

This chapter will posit that the four drivers of defense reform identified in this volume—globalization, economic restructuring, democratization, and the so-called Revolution in Military Affairs (RMA)—can be used to define a global-local threat matrix that to some extent affects countries everywhere. These drivers can be expected to produce global developments that shape the general international security environment. They also can be expected to have a specific impact on a given country's security situation. Although these drivers are usually discussed as grand trends that shape world politics, the chapter posits that their local effects on specific nations—shaped by unique security considerations—tend to drive threat perceptions and motives for defense reform. By exploring both the global and local effects produced by each of these drivers, the chapter will identify how the local impact of global trends can be used to estimate a nation's incentives to undertake defense reform.

The chapter begins with a brief discussion of how global trends can manifest as local threats and opportunities. It then discusses the global and local impact of globalization, democratization, economic restructuring, and the RMA. It then concludes with a brief discussion of the way these threat drivers create incentives for defense reform.

THE GLOBAL-LOCAL THREAT MATRIX

Scholars often write about threats in a general way and politicians and military officers often make brave claims about meeting threats *tous azimuts* (from all directions). But the reality of politics and defense planning forces politicians and strategists to focus on specific threats to specific interests. In the words of Thomas P. O'Neill, the former Speaker of the U.S. House of Representatives, "All politics is local." People care most about problems and opportunities that affect them directly, not about hypothetical threats, or threats that are unlikely to reach their shores. Moreover, as John Weltman once noted, "beneath the rhetoric of 'omni dimensionality'[of threats], there has been little significant doubt about the direction in which weapons were and are pointed."[3] Political conflict makes salient the possibility of military conflict; superior military capability alone does not necessarily make a neighbor a threat. Ongoing political friction, a history of conflict, or even revolutionary ideology is needed to increase the salience of a country's military capability on a potential opponent's security agenda.[4] Given this duality of threat perceptions—the idea that trends, threats, or events have to have some sort of local salience to merit the attention of officers or officials—it would be useful to highlight the potential global and local impact of globalization, economic restructuring, democratization, and the RMA. Local perceptions of global trends influence judgments about the benefits of defense reform.

Global effects might be thought of as events or developments that affect all nations more or less equally. They also include phenomena that shape the general international environment in which all states must operate. Global effects are beyond the control of any single state and require international coordination and cooperation to mitigate their impact. Even the strongest states cannot unilaterally alter global effects, despite the fact that the "weak" almost always believe that the strong can escape global constraints or capture benefits through unilateral action. In a sense, global effects shape the international commons, creating the setting for international relations.

Global phenomena, however, also produce local effects that vary from country to country depending on domestic or regional strengths, weaknesses, or problems. Some countries might have political, military, or geographic advantages that insulate them from the pernicious effects of global trends, while others might have weaknesses that exacerbate the negative effects of global developments. John Mearsheimer's recent work on great power politics, for example, highlights the impact of geography on the options available to great powers.[5] It is therefore likely that other national endowments or weaknesses could influence the impact of global trends on local politics and capabilities. Although it is impossible to predict exactly how these local effects might manifest, the possibility exists that relatively benign global trends could create difficult problems for some governments. It also is possible that states that find themselves in similar situations might find that global trends create common local problems. Because newly democratizing states tend to face similar challenges and opportunities, it is not unrealistic to expect them to share similar perspectives on the local impact of globalization, economic restructuring, democratization, and the RMA.

Globalization

The impact of globalization on national security was brought to the world's attention by the 11 September 2001 terrorist attacks on the Pentagon and the World Trade Center and has been kept in the news by the attacks on Bali, Madrid, and London that were launched by Al Qaeda and its sympathizers. The attacks highlighted three critical aspects of globalization: 1) decisions or actions by small groups of people or even individuals can have global effects; 2) global events can have an immediate and direct impact on everyday life; and 3) the pathways and networks that move goods, capital, people, and ideas can be used for nefarious purposes. Although globalization often is tied to a breakdown of sovereignty in the realm of security, the rise of global terror networks have reinforced the role of the nation-state in the matters of national and homeland defense. Governments, however, struggle in the face of globalized trade, technology, and finance to devise effective policy and institutional responses to meet these new kinds of threats. As Victor Cha has noted, "the nation-state does not end, it is just less in control."[6]

General Trends

Globalization, which is being powered by the information revolution, has produced three trends that have altered the international strategic landscape. First, a skill revolution is underway, in the sense that people are increasingly better educated, have better analytical and communication skills, and are increasingly willing to use them to evaluate critically the performance of individuals in positions of authority and to take matters into their own hands. The skill revolution was actually anticipated by some of the Internet's leading proponents. Bill Gates, founder of the Microsoft Corporation, for instance, has not hidden his hope that individuals will be empowered when they gain access to computers and the Internet. He suggested that the Internet would give individuals capabilities only possessed by bureaucracies less than a generation ago, thereby transforming the world.[7] In a series of analyses written over the last decade, James Rosenau also has identified "four flows of influence" that are transforming social and political relationships:

> (1) a technological revolution has facilitated the rapid flow of ideas, information, pictures, and money across continents; (2) a transportation revolution has hastened the boundary-spanning flow of elites, ordinary folk, and whole populations; (3) an organizational revolution has shifted the flow of authority, influence, and power beyond traditional boundaries; and (4) an economic revolution has redirected the flow of goods, services and capital, and ownership among countries.[8]

Rosenau's third item is crucial, in that he is suggesting that a change in people's attitudes toward authority is following in the wake of the information revolution.

Some readers might find the idea far fetched that people's attitudes, if not human nature, is subject to a fundamental change and that people today are far more sophisticated than their parents or grandparents. Rosenau, however, is actually on firm ground when he suggests that technology itself is not value free and that technology can alter people's attitudes toward the world around them. There is an ideology, or a logic, so to speak, embedded in every technology. This ideology affects the way individuals are likely to employ a given technology and the long-term effects a new technology is likely to have on society.[9] Sometimes the inventor of the technology recognizes and understands this ideology: Bill Gates hoped that his work would have a revolutionary impact on society by empowering individuals at the expense of traditional institutions. More often, inventors are unaware of the logic inherent in the technology they are creating. Gutenberg was a Catholic, but his printing press made the Protestant reformation possible because printing facilitated the dissemination of competing ideas (i.e., heresy).[10] The Internet and the personal computer empower people by giving them the ability to process data and communicate globally at virtually no cost, capabilities that only states or enormous bureaucracies (e.g., the Internal Revenue Service) possessed as late as the 1980s. The fact that people, not just states, have the technology needed to begin to overcome time and distance in communication will have a profound effect on international relations. Access to the Internet allows people to coordinate activities globally, to gather detailed information about local conditions and infrastructure for just about anywhere on the planet, and to move financial resources at virtually no cost. Powerful tools have been placed in the hands of individuals, and as September 11 demonstrates, they will not necessarily be put to good use.

A second trend is the relative decline of great power politics as the engine driving international security issues and the rise of so-called fourth and fifth generation warriors.[11] Fourth and fifth generation warriors come in a variety of forms, pursue a variety of objectives, and serve a range of masters, which include the warrior or warriors themselves. A host of grass-root ethnic, religious, and ideological movements are creating their own military and paramilitary organizations to use violence to further their objectives. Individuals also are attempting to use violence to become prominent actors on the world stage. Criminal syndicates, terrorist networks, and spontaneous terrorist cells have carried out paramilitary operations and asymmetric operations that have circumvented traditional police forces and military units. The rise to prominence of these new "threat agents" reflects the skill revolution in the sense that individuals and small groups find it natural and acceptable to use violence to advance their political, religious, ideological, criminal interests or even personal interests. So far, these new threat agents have largely used "off the shelf," widely available commercial technologies (e.g., the Internet, computers, global communications, commercial jet travel, high explosives) to create mayhem. But as the 2001 anthrax attacks in the United States demonstrate, it might only be a matter of time before individuals or groups begin to move beyond dabbling with chemical, biological, or radiological weapons to employ these weapons in mass casualty attacks.

A third trend is what Cha has called the homogenization of products, threats, and messages to a worldwide audience.[12] Standardized consumer goods, for example, have spread from the developed nations across the planet. But this global consumer marketplace is also mirrored in a global media and threat market place. Information about the operations of fourth and fifth generation warriors can spread quickly across the globe, creating a market niche, so to speak, in terms of their operational style and political objectives. Images of threats and local insults spread quickly via mass media that can blow incidents out of proportion as stories and images gather momentum and are used by local actors to further their own political agendas. Local political, ideological, or religious leaders and movements can disseminate their message to an international audience and, once tested in the international marketplace of ideas, become a recognized brand name. And like in commercial matters where brand recognition is an important marketing tool, terrorists can benefit from an established "brand identity" because it allows them to attract material and political support from sympathizers in the global marketplace of ideas.

Local Consequences

One immediate challenge posed by globalization in matters of a specific country's national security is the ability of political and military institutions to respond to the new threats posed by the skill revolution, the rise of fourth and fifth generation warriors, and the homogenization of threats. The September 11 terrorist attacks against the United States, for example, highlighted the structural weaknesses in the American defense establishment by literally striking along the seams of authority between domestic police forces and military and intelligence organizations that focused on foreign threats. Police were slow to respond to the threat of domestic terrorism because as members of law enforcement agencies, they were primarily concerned with prosecuting crimes, not arresting individuals who might engage in criminal activity. U.S. law greatly limited intelligence organizations or members of the armed forces from monitoring the activities of U.S. citizens. Although they remain controversial, the 2001 Patriot Act, and the creation of the U.S. Department of Homeland Defense in 2002 are a response to this structural weakness within the American defense and policy establishment. The real challenge, which the U.S. government failed to meet, is to respond to new threat agents before they overwhelm or circumvent existing police and military institutions.

A second challenge faced by governments is to assess and evaluate the new threat agents that are enabled by globalization. This is no small challenge because fourth and fifth generation warriors specialize in asymmetric attacks—operations that are intended to generate maximum political, if not military, effects with an absolute minimum of resources. Individual fanatics, terrorist networks, or criminal syndicates might have virtually no traditional military capability (e.g., mechanized units), but by utilizing asymmetric operations, they can create significant economic or political disruption. The effort to evaluate the danger posed by these new threat agents places a premium on intelligence gathered from human sources, especially information about an organization's ideology or objectives. The Aum Shynryko cult, for example, gave the nerve-agent Sarin a special place in their ideology and used it as a weapon, while Al Qaeda seems to have a preference for using high explosives to strike targets related to mass transportation systems.[13]

A third challenge confronting officials is the potential need to abandon deterrence as the primary strategy in countering new threat agents. Enraged individuals, criminal syndicates, or terrorist networks might not be deterred by threats of retaliation because they actually desire violence, accept violence as the price of doing business, or lack assets that can be held at risk. It is probably wrong to state that most government efforts to attack terrorists constitute preventive war or preemption—Al Qaeda clearly struck the opening blows in the global war against terrorism.[14] Nevertheless, governments are forced to take proactive measures in the form of preemptive strikes, police sweeps, and active intelligence operations to interdict and destroy the new threat agents before they can inflict casualties and destruction. The new threat agents are ubiquitous and relentless. Defense reform might have to be undertaken amidst ongoing, and high stakes, police, military, and intelligence operations.

DEMOCRATIZATION

Although claims that we are witnessing the end of history now appear overblown in light of the instability produced by the combination of demography, Shia-Sunni tension and fundamentalist ideology that is currently sweeping the Moslem world, it is difficult to argue with the proposition that democracy continues to be the best available method for organizing people, places, and things. The recent surge in democratization has been welcomed worldwide and scholars and policymakers alike are banking on the democratic peace to foster economic development and stability, keeping in check the reemergence of a determined competition for primacy among the great powers. The world is currently experiencing the longest period of great power peace since the Treaty of Westphalia. It might be too much to hope that the cycle of great power war has been broken by the peaceful collapse of the Soviet Union and the end of the Cold War, but democratization and market capitalism are clearly resurgent after a century marked by totalitarianism, acute racism, and extreme nationalism. Democratization is clearly a welcome development, but it can create short-term systemic problem and specific challenges to emerging democracies.

General Trends

Because one man's democracy is another's revolutionary movement, the collapse of dictatorships or kleptocracies can create regional instability or even war as countries begin what can be a slow transition to democracy.[15] Friend and foe alike can perceive moments of transition as moments of weakness, leading some states to take advantage of the temporary troubles of stronger neighbors. Saddam Hussein's decision to settle a few old scores with Iran following the fall of the Shah in 1979, for instance, probably reflected his decision to exploit Iran's disarray during a shift toward "democracy." Because democratization often involves the transfer of control over military budgets and strategy to civilians, it often produces a temporary drop in the morale and readiness of a nation's armed forces. Whether or not this fluctuation in readiness is significant is determined by the likelihood that neighboring states might take advantage of this momentary shift in the regional balance of power. To further complicate matters, Edward Mansfield and Jack Snyder have argued that in emerging democracies that lack strong civil institutions (e.g., an independent judiciary, independent opposition parties, or civil control of the military), foreign adventurism and aggression can become linked to domestic politics. Politicians can be tempted to manipulate foreign threats to bolster their electoral prospects. In other words, mature, not emerging, democracies are likely to be peaceful.[16]

Paradoxically, democratization, especially the idea of democratic peace, creates immediate pressure on governments to abandon their military establishments, or to at least cut defense spending quickly and drastically. Peace is of course a positive development, but the euphoria that accompanies the rise of democracy can lead to rash decisions that can have a long-term impact on the ability of governments to maintain an effective military. Policymakers can embrace the idea that militaries have become immediately and irreversibly obsolete and abandon capabilities that cannot easily be replaced. During the interwar years, for instance, Canadian politicians decided that their forces would never again become embroiled in major conflict, allowing them to abandon preparations to participate in operations involving more than one division. The command skills and organizations needed to maneuver on the Corps or Army level, to say nothing of conducting modern combined arms operations, were not easily reacquired once lost. That fateful decision led to weak performance and costly errors by Canadian commanders during European operations in World War II.[17] More recently, the directors of the U.S. national laboratories have noted that the decision to extend the service life of the U.S. nuclear arsenal made at the end of the Cold War might have been overly optimistic. The last generation of U.S. nuclear weapons was not built with long-term maintenance in mind, making it difficult, if not impossible to extend their service life indefinitely.[18] In the euphoria that accompanied the end of the Cold War, however, it was impossible to obtain political approval to reconstitute the U.S. nuclear arsenal with weapons deliberately designed to last for scores of years.

Another trend, fueled by the information and skill revolution, is the erosion of tradition, bureaucracy, or hierarchy as bulwarks against public and media scrutiny of officials. Moreover, this scrutiny is not just confined to local groups. Governmental and nongovernmental organizations are likely to take a keen interest in democratic transitions, especially the emergence of civilian control over the military. In the United States, for instance, the National Democratic Institute and the International Republican Institute monitor and support transitions to democracy overseas. Elected officials might be prepared for this public scrutiny, but the intensity and extensiveness of the attention focused on the military can come as a rude shock to senior military officers who have grown accustomed to the insularity created by staffs, military tradition, and in some cases, by former political patrons. The skill revolution and increased scrutiny has even caught officers within established democracies by surprise. The 1991

Tailhook convention demonstrated to senior U.S. Navy officers, for example, that private-public events are not beyond scrutiny.[19] Or, as Admiral Richard Macke, Commander in Chief, Pacific, discovered in 1995, rank offers no privilege if off-the-cuff remarks—in his case about the rape of a young Okinawan girl by U.S. servicemen—are deemed inappropriate by an attentive public.[20]

Local Consequences

Leaders of countries making the transition to democracy generally find they need to embrace new allies, which are often established democracies. These new partnerships often entail new commitments, especially when democratic states insist on democratic transition as a quid pro quo for military assistance or political support. For example, NATO has developed a program, Partnership for Peace (PfP), which offers a series of bilateral relationships to improve cooperation between NATO and individual partner countries. Although NATO officials have not described PfP participation as a sort of junior membership in NATO, the alliance does make a commitment to PfP partners to consult with them if they perceive a threat to their territorial integrity, political independence, or security. PfP focuses on military-to-military contacts dealing with issues of practical concern, but behind this cooperation is a plan to bolster forces of democratization in partner countries. To participate in the PfP, governments must make a long list of political commitments to preserve democracy, follow the principles of international law, fulfill obligations created by the United Nations Charter, the Universal Declaration of Human Rights, the Helsinki Final Act, and various international disarmament and arms control agreements. PfP is a way to increase the military and political compatibility between NATO and partner states.[21]

New alliances, especially NATO membership, create several direct challenges for militaries in emerging democracies. Although compatibility issues involving the acquisition of new hardware and weapons systems often gain the lion's share of attention, the need for the armed forces of new democracies to embrace new planning and operational standards creates daunting organizational and professional challenges. Entire systems of professional military education and development have to be transformed quickly to mirror the systems employed by new allies. Democratic norms of civil-military relations have to be created and reflected in command and control procedures and systems. Different standards of professionalism and technical competence have to be learned and then put into practice if the new democracy is going to develop productive relationships with its new allies. All of these changes are disruptive and expensive. Paradoxically, they also must occur at a time when elected officials are seeking to curtail defense spending to divert resources to social programs.

Democratic transition and new alliance relationships also can quickly make obsolete entire branches of a state's military, while simultaneously focusing defense spending on new military priorities. Defense expenditures related to PfP participation and eventual full membership in NATO, for instance, often have little to do with traditional security priorities. Large infantry forces made up of poorly trained short-term conscripts offer little benefit to NATO, while highly specialized peacekeeping, air defense, or mechanized units are extremely expensive to train and equip. A country's greatest contribution to potential allies might actually be as a base of operations, leading to the need to upgrade local facilities, air defense networks, and infrastructure to support allied military operations—all at the expense of service preferences and traditional ways of doing business. These kinds of links to new allies also introduce new political problems for officials: they might be confronted with the need to explain to concerned electorates why foreign troops are using their territory as a base of operations for wars occurring in foreign lands.

Economic Liberalization

Issues raised by economic liberalization can resemble the same types of concerns created by democratization. Rapid integration into the global political economy can cause economic dislocation as political patronage and cronyism is overtaken by increased exposure to market capitalism. Old industries and bureaucracies can suddenly lose their economic underpinnings and raison d'etre, creating an unemployment problem especially among those who recently served the old regime. Not all of the economic prospects faced by emerging democracies, however, are negative. Newly emerging democracies can benefit from the advantages of economic backwardness. Crumbling infrastructure can be replaced with the latest technology, paving the way for rapid increases in labor productivity. In some cases, an educated but previously isolated workforce can enter the global labor markets at relatively low wages, drawing global capital to bolster emerging democracies. Democratization also can be accompanied by a burst of entrepreneurial energy as individuals scramble to take advantage of economic opportunities that had been monopolized by the former regime.

Global Issues

Economists maintain that economic liberalization and restructuring are crucial if emerging democracies are going to participate in international markets based on free trade and comparative advantage. Liberalization can of course create social and economic dislocation, a process that can be made all the more painful by international scrutiny. International lending institutions, such as the World Bank or the International Monetary Fund typically place stringent fiscal requirements on governments as a condition for obtaining international loans. International bankers take a particularly dim view of defense expenditures, viewing them as a waste of precious capital. Economic liberalization also raises questions about labor fairness and environmental responsibility, issues that are increasingly championed by grass roots organizations that undertake their own surveillance programs and international campaigns. Economic liberalization opens a country to outside scrutiny and acceptance of international and institutional norms governing issues of business law, banking, finance, accounting, labor practices, and trade.

From the global view usually taken by economists, economic liberalization might produce some short-term dislocations, but these setbacks will pale in comparison to the benefits provided by free markets, free trade, and comparative advantage. In their view, consumers worldwide will benefit from the absolute gains generated by economic restructuring and reform. Although there is a minor risk that economic openness and transparency will somehow be translated into direct military advantage by a potential opponent or exacerbate some enduring rivalry, the prospect of increased transparency is a small price to pay for global economic growth and prosperity.

Local Issues

Although economists can take a global perspective of the absolute gains produced by economic liberalization, policymakers have to take a more zero-sum view of economic matters. Instead of thinking about the absolute gains that benefit the entire international community, they need to focus on the relative gains economic restructuring produces vis-à-vis potential competitors or enduring rivals. Reform and liberalization initiatives that allow competitors to pull ahead in the short run can be extremely threatening, especially if divergent economic growth rates are quickly transformed into military capability. The logic of economics dictates that absolute gains—not short-term zero-sum thinking—should guide reform and liberalization decisions, but defense officials are not always in a position to follow that logic.

The question of whether or not relative or absolute gains drive or should drive the decisions made by defense officials was a matter of great debate among political scientists in the 1980s.[22] Today, most observers generally agree that defense officials are unlikely to ignore the issue of relative gains, but the absolute gains that preoccupy economists also seem to animate public and official discussion of economic relationships. Those who champion democratization and economic liberalization are thus likely to take a dim view of concerns about relative gains enjoyed by potential competitors and/or enduring rivals, creating a tension between defense establishments and those who champion economic reform. It is unlikely, however, that the source of this tension—disagreement about the importance of relative and absolute gains—will be recognized by participants, which may lead to political charges of obstructionism and cronyism if defense officials resist disruptive economic reforms on the basis of national security issues.

The Revolution in Military Affairs

The so-called revolution in military affairs (RMA) is an idea that grew in popularity in the aftermath of the first Gulf War. A topic of infinite interest to strategists and historians, RMAs occur spontaneously as a result of three developments: 1) the incorporation of a new technology or basket of technologies into warfare; 2) the emergence of new war fighting doctrines; and 3) the emergence of new military organizations. Most observers generally agree that the twentieth century saw two RMAs. The first involved what became known as "people's war," in which peasant armies overwhelmed more technically advanced and professional militaries that utilized combined-arms operations. The Chinese communist revolution of 1949 was based upon people's war. The second occurred when nuclear weapons and long-range delivery systems, new organizations (the U.S. Air Force and the Soviet Strategic Rocket force), and the primacy of the doctrine of deterrence created a Nuclear Revolution. Especially in a situation of Mutual Assured Destruction, deterrence of war, not victory in war, became the overriding priority of military operations, creating a fundamental change in the nature, practice, and (lack of) occurrence of strategic warfare among the great powers in the second half of the twentieth century.

If one takes the theory of the RMA at face value, it becomes clear that technology, nascent organizations, and new ways of fighting have not coalesced to create a true revolution in warfare. Changes have occurred, but theorists currently argue about whether or not the information revolution, improvements in reconnaissance capabilities, precision guidance, the emergence of genetic engineering, or the growth of global networks is producing an evolutionary or revolutionary change in warfare. Reflecting this uncertainty about the likelihood of a spontaneous RMA, current U.S. defense policy incorporates the notion of transformation, the idea that new war fighting, procurement, personnel, and organizational policies and doctrines have to be deliberately cultivated to best exploit new technologies. This increasingly practical attitude toward the impact of technology on warfare is reflected in a creeping skepticism about the prospects that we are witnessing an RMA. Stephen Biddle, for example, suggests that new technologies have simply broadening traditional combined-arms operations, creating new weapons and battlefield environments to be integrated into operational and campaign plans. Technology itself is no panacea on the modern battlefield, while militaries that master combined arms operations and integrate new technologies and forms of warfare into their doctrine continue to overwhelm less accomplished opponents.[23] Colin Gray also has recently warned that regardless of technological sophistication or even mastery of combined arms operations, military professionalism and technical superiority cannot salvage strategic incompetence.[24]

Global Issues

Regardless of one's position in the RMA debate, when traditional military capabilities are coupled with the information revolution, changes occur on the international military landscape. Some analysts have described technology itself as a threat in the sense that new technologies can quickly make expensive weapons obsolete. The pace of technological change, not a specific enemy, is the greatest threat to military organizations because it holds out the possibility that organizational and material obsolescence can occur in unexpected ways. Technology also seems to be eliminating demographic and quantitative advantages as an important aspect of warfare. Numerically inferior armies that master modern combined arms operations are delivering quick defeats to their larger opponents, and new kinds of precision-strike weapons are now capable of circumventing large armies to engage in what Thomas Schelling has called the "diplomacy of violence."[25] It is increasingly possible to take out high-value economic, military, and political targets with long-range, precision-strike weapons without first defeating an opponent's military. These changes also might be coalescing to shift the offense-defense balance in war in favor of the offense, making it easier for states or even non-state actors to go on the offensive. If military technology favors the offensive over the defense in war, then international relations can be expected to become increasingly war prone.

The information revolution also is not having a uniform impact on all battle environments. Air power clearly has been transformed by new technology. Battlefield surveillance, and precision-strike capabilities allow air forces to hold all kinds of targets at risk at increasingly long ranges. Naval operations also have been effected by the information revolution; although the relative absence of naval combat makes it impossible to judge how new technology has transformed war at sea. Land warfare, however, still remains relatively unaffected by new technologies, especially when one considers the impact of technology on small unit tactics. Infantry engagements today still seem to have more in common with their World War II predecessors than warfare occurring in other strategic settings (e.g., strategic bombing).

The process of transformation—the integration of new technologies and doctrine in warfare—has created forces that can quickly overcome more traditional military units. This gross imbalance has created pressures for state and non-state actors to seek asymmetric responses to militaries that have harnessed the information revolution to their conventional military capabilities. These asymmetric strategies and capabilities seek to inflict the maximum political impact with minimal resources by avoiding direct, force-on-force, attritional engagements with an opponent's conventional military units. A surge in international terrorism, interest in information warfare, and the proliferation of chemical, biological, and nuclear weapons are influenced by the process of transformation, as various actors struggle to overcome the conventional military superiority of their opponents. Because they are often directed at countervalue targets—civilian populations, symbols of national or cultural history, and power, economic performance, and commercial infrastructure—and are capable of producing massive numbers of casualties and significant destruction quickly, asymmetric strategies and operations tend to escalate conflict quickly.

Local Issues

For newly emerging democracies, the RMA raises issues of interoperability and affordability. Because technological transformation has had the greatest impact on military surveillance and command and control, new software and hardware needs to be acquired before military units can operate alongside of more sophisticated allies. Because of the great cost of these kinds of systems, it is unlikely that entire military organizations can be equipped with new hardware, so national strategies have to be devised to prioritize among units and capabilities to be integrated into alliance structures. Even for the richest militaries, however, the cost of surveillance, communication, and weapons systems has escalated to the point that relatively small numbers of the most advanced systems are purchased. The RMA is likely to raise equipment and training costs for new democracies, while creating increasing pressure to cut the overall size of military organizations. The RMA also seems to favor long-term professional volunteer forces over short-term conscript armies, which are often inherited by new democracies.

In the United States, the process of transformation has profound budgetary implications for military organizations, and it is likely to produce similar effects in newly emerging democracies. Because new equipment is extremely expensive and the process of transformation is open ended, resources have to be obtained from existing programs to prevent defense budgets from spiraling out of control. In other words, legacy systems must be abandoned to pay for the process of transformation; it is prohibitively expensive to continue to maintain existing capabilities while adding an endless stream of new weapons and systems. Transformation advocates in the United States have only been partially successful in overcoming the services preference for traditional weapons and modes of operation. Instead of eliminating entire legacy systems, purchases of enhanced types of legacy systems are delayed or scaled back and existing inventories of weapons are slowly reduced as aging systems are not replaced. In the absence of a true RMA, other militaries are likely to encounter the same pressures as entrenched service and bureaucratic interests fight to preserve known weapons and procedures at the expense of untried doctrines and combat systems.

The tradeoffs facing newly emerging democracies might thus be different than the tradeoffs facing the U.S. military. In the United States, the tradeoff is between maintenance and modernization of relatively sophisticated legacy systems and the purchase of more exotic weaponry. A shrinking military is the result as relatively inexpensive technology is substituted for relatively expensive, volunteer military personnel. Leaders in new democracies face a choice between relatively expensive military technology and relatively inexpensive conscript armies. Transformation might thus create profound political and social upheaval in emerging democracies as the employment opportunities and social privilege offered by military service evaporate in the process of military modernization and transformation. The paradox faced by new democracies is that increased military spending might actually lead to the eruption of social and political discontent as militaries confront the personal economic consequences of "rightsizing."

Officers and officials thus face several choices when it comes to coping with the RMA and transformation. First, they might assess that a traditional approach to military affairs can keep traditional opponents at bay and that the economic, social, and political risks of transformation are not worth the military benefits. In this case, officials could be expected to maintain existing organizations and traditions (e.g., conscription), while doing their best to use limited funds to modernize equipment and to update training and operating procedures. Defense reform in this option would focus on improving the ability of existing forces to conduct modern combined-arms operations. Second, they might attempt to modernize specific units within their armed forces, bringing them up to allied standards so that they can participate albeit with a few select units, in coalition operations. For example, officials might decide to develop modern peacekeeping or air defense forces that could be fully up to NATO standard so that they can participate fully in allied operations. This sort of selective modernization would require updated command and control and training and education, but these efforts could be limited to a few units within a much larger military. The tradeoff here would be that modernization of the rest of the military would be slowed or even curtailed as resources are devoted to a few select units. Third, officials might decide to abandon their traditional military, greatly reducing the size of their armed forces and fully embrace the RMA by modernizing a small force made up of long-time professionals. This type of modernization could involve the complete abandonment of entire services. Naval forces might be replaced by air-based maritime patrol. Air forces might be replaced by allied units in the event of crisis or war: resources could instead be supported to bring air bases and air defense systems up to NATO standards, for instance.

CONCLUSION

Several conclusions emerge from this effort to explore how globalization, economic restructuring, democratization, and the RMA produce a global-local threat matrix. First, while global trends are generally positive, regime change—even toward democracy—is not completely free of risk when it comes to local security issues. Whether or not democratic peace theory withstands the tests of time and academic fashion, the shift toward democracy can create vulnerabilities that can be exploited by potential opponents. And, if Mansfield and Snyder are correct, new democracies themselves might be belligerent. Politicians and citizens in new democracies, however, are likely to be banking on the peace dividend produced by the turn toward market capitalism and entrepreneurship that usually goes hand in hand with the process of democratization. Despite the potential threats created by the process of democratization, it is quite possible that local audiences might turn a deaf ear to warnings about continued international threats. Defense officials might face some difficult challenges in maintaining readiness in this kind of political environment. Given the possibility that threats might actually be exacerbated by the transition to democracy, defense reform offers an important way to bolster national security.

Second, the broad economic, political, and social trends that interest our contributors generally produce absolute gains when viewed in a global setting (the RMA clearly is a far more zero-sum proposition). The externalities created by these positive global trends can fall disproportionately on military establishments, especially on those within emerging democracies. They must persevere to protect the state in the face of a surge in outside scrutiny, new allies and new political leaders, just as most civilians come to believe that their role or mission is obsolete. The transition to democracy does not necessarily denote the end of the armed forces, but it does mark the beginning of a difficult period for militaries inherited from the former regime as they scramble to adjust to their new circumstances. Defense reform offers important benefits by helping military establishments adjust to the new circumstances brought about by the transition to democracy.

Third, like other national political and military leaders, those who govern newly emerging democracies cannot ignore the relative gains produced by globalization, economic restructuring, democratization, and the RMA. One would hope that most states are unthreatened by potential enemies or are not engaged in enduring rivalries, but this is clearly not the case today. Policymakers and strategists thus have to be concerned about the economic and social impact of global trends on their own states and how these trends might favor long-time regional competitors. Defense reform is one way elected officials and military officers can better harness their own national resources and advantages to make sure that the balance of relative gains vis-à-vis potential rivals is in their favor.

Fourth, transitions to democracy are occurring during a moment of history in which military technology is also undergoing profound changes. The need to devise some sort of strategy to cope with the prospect of an RMA only complicates the issues faced by democratic leaders because it forces them to deal with new types of threats with forces that are irrelevant to these new threats or are facing complete obsolescence. Military reform will be fiscally expensive because it will entail replacing cheap conscripts with expensive technology. It also will be socially expensive because it might involve abandoning conscription and downsizing the armed forces, choices that can lead to social, economic, and political turmoil. These constraints suggest that new democracies will probably only transform in a limited way, adopting new technologies and procedures to the extent that they advance overall international objectives. In other words, new democracies might be interested in forming a few modern peacekeeping units that can participate fully in NATO operations; they are less likely to abandon their existing, albeit increasingly obsolete, military infrastructure to embrace fully the RMA.

Finally, the certainty of the Cold War, in terms of threats and allies, has been replaced by a more fluid military and diplomatic landscape. Broad demographic, technological, political, and even religious trends are shaping global threats in ways that are sometimes difficult to predict. Many political and military leaders in emerging democracies might believe that they are not targeted by these threats, that terrorists or weapons of mass destruction are unlikely to reach their shores. But given the uncertainty surrounding today's security situation, they cannot dismiss the possibility that their territory might be used or attacked by state or non-state actors. Defense reform is one way that militaries can improve their ability to meet international threats, but the merits of and prospects for defense reform are shaped by both global trends and the way these global trends create localized effects.

NOTES

1. All of these documents can be found at http://www.whitehouse.gov.
2. John Dziak, foreword by Robert Conquest, *Chekisty: A History of the KGB* (New York: Ballantine Books, 1988); and Thomas C. Bruneau, "Controlling Intelligence in New Democracies," *International Journal of Intelligence and Counterintelligence* 14 (Fall 2001): 323–341.
3. John Weltman, "Managing Nuclear Multipolarity," *International Security* 6 (Winter 1981): 8.
4. Stephen M. Walt, *The Origins of Alliances* (Ithaca, NY: Cornell University Press, 1990); and Stephen M. Walt, *Revolution and War* (Ithaca, NY: Cornell University Press, 1996).
5. John J. Mearsheimer, *The Tragedy of Great Power Politics* (New York: W.W. Norton, 2001).
6. Victor Cha, "Globalization and the Study of International Security," *Journal of Peace Research* 37, 3 (May 2000): 392.
7. Bill Gates, *The Road Ahead* (New York: Penguin, 1996).
8. James N. Rosenau, "Stability, Stasis, and Change: A Fragmegrating World," in Richard L. Kugler and Ellen L. Frost, eds., *The Global Century: Globalization and National Security*, vol. I. (Washington, DC: NDU Press, 2001), 137.
9. There is a rich literature on the effect of the information revolution on society. Several critics are especially provocative. See Gene I. Rochlin, *Trapped in the Net: The Unanticipated Consequences of Computerization* (Princeton, NJ: Princeton University Press, 1997); Theodore Roszak, *The Cult of Information* (Berkeley: University of California Press, 1986); and Neil Postman, *Technopoly: The Surrender of Culture to Technology* (New York: Vintage Books, 1993).
10. Printing increased literacy because it provided common people with something to read. Without printing, Martin Luther could not encourage people to read the Bible themselves.
11. T.V. Paul, James J. Wirtz, and Michael Fortman, eds. *Balance of Power: Theory and Practice in the 21st Century* (Stanford, CA: Stanford University Press, 2004); Thomas X. Hammes, "War Evolves into the Fourth Generation," *Contemporary Security Policy* 26, 2 (August 2005): 189–221.
12. Cha, "Globalization and the Study of International Security," 395.
13. Jessica Stern, "Terrorist Motivations and Unconventional Weapons," in Peter Lavoy, Scott Sagan, and James J. Wirtz, eds., *Planning the Unthinkable* (Ithaca, NY: Cornell University Press, 2000), 202–229;

Lewis Dunn, "Can al Qaeda be Deterred from Using Nuclear Weapons?" Occasional Paper #3, Center For the Study of Weapons of Mass Destruction, National Defense University, July 2005.

14. James J. Wirtz and James Russell, "Preventive War and Preemption: Reassessing the U.S. Policy toward Iraq and the War on Terrorism," *Non-Proliferation Review* 10, 1 (Spring 2003): 113–123.
15. Jack Snyder, *From Voting to Violence: Democratization and Nationalist Conflict* (New York: W.W. Norton, 2000); and Walt, *Revolution and War.*
16. Edward D. Mansfield and Jack Snyder, *Electing to Fight: Why Emerging Democracies Go to War* (Cambridge, MA: MIT Press, 2005).
17. John English, *The Canadian Army and the Normandy Campaign: A Study of Failure in High Command* (New York: Praeger, 1991).
18. Bruce T. Goodwin, Frederick A. Tarantino, and John B. Woodward, "Sustaining the Nuclear Enterprise—A New Approach," UCRL-AR-212442;LAUR-05-3830;andSAND2005-3384,20May2005,available at http://www.nukewatch.org/facts/nwd/SustainingtheEnterprise.pdf; accessed 8 May 2006.
19. Several female officers at the convention claimed that they were sexually harassed by their male colleagues and that their superiors attempted to cover up the incidents. In the firestorm that followed, officer promotions were held up and both the Secretary of the Navy (Lawrence Garrett III) and the Chief of Naval Operations (Admiral Frank Kelso) resigned. See Forney Todd, "Tailhook Convention," in Peter Karsten, ed., *Encyclopedia of War and American Society* (Thousand Oaks: Sage Publishers, 2006), 817–819.
20. Macke had made a remark about three U.S. servicemen who had been accused of raping a girl on the island Okinawa: "I think it was absolutely stupid. I have said several times: for the price they paid to rent the car (used in the crime), they could have had a girl [prostitute]"; see CNN "Fired Admiral Gives Public Apology," 20 November 1995, http://www.cnn.com/WORLD/9511/macke_speaks/; accessed 4 May 2006.
21. "NATO: U.S. Assistance to the Partnership for Peace," U.S. General Accounting Office, GAO Report GAO-01-734, Washington, DC, 2001; and "Partnership for Peace," at http://www.nato.int/issues/pfp/index.html; accessed 4 May 2006.
22. Joseph M. Grieco, "Anarchy and the Limits of Cooperation: A Realist Critique of the Newest Liberal Institutionalism," *International Organization* 42, 3 (Summer 1988): 485–507; and Robert Axelrod and Robert O. Keohane, "Achieving Cooperation under Anarchy: Strategies and Institutions," *World Politics* 38 (October 1985): 226–254.
23. Stephen Biddle, *Military Power: Explaining Victory and Defeat in Modern Battle* (Princeton, NJ: Princeton University Press, 2004).

24. Colin S. Gray, *Recognizing and Understanding Revolutionary Change in Warfare: The Sovereignty of Context* (Carlisle, Strategic Studies Institute, US Army War College, 2006).
25. Thomas Schelling, *Arms and Influence* (New Haven: Yale University Press, 1966).

Part II

Case Studies and Conclusion

5

Democratic Consolidation in Chilean Civil-Military Relations: 1990–2005

Marcos Robledo

Introduction

During the past three decades, democratization has become confirmed as a global trend, one that is having a tremendous impact on civil-military relations around the world as societies demand that the armed forces meet liberal democratic standards. Most of the ideas about how democratization really affects civil-military relations, however, were crafted early in the so-called Third Wave of democratization. Decades later, it is legitimate to question current mainstream theories about how democracies can be or are being consolidated. This chapter aims to explore these questions, especially the role of civil-military relations in a process of democratic consolidation, by analyzing the experience of Chile between 1990 and 2005.

Chile has had one of the most successful Latin American experiences of democratic consolidation during the 1990s.[1] According to much of the academic literature written at the time of its transition, however, Chile was not supposed to have such a destiny. Instead, this literature observed that, with some of the least democratic political institutions and highest level of military prerogatives in the region, Chile was primed to become one of the most unstable and most military-driven countries in Latin America. Today, there is a broad consensus among scholars that Chilean leaders have been successful in this process of consolidation, and part of the explanation for why early predictions did not materialize can be found in the evolution of civil-military relations in Chile.[2] At the core of this seeming paradox is the fact that although Chile had a limited democratic institutional framework up until constitutional reforms were passed in 2005, both civil-military relations and the country as a whole became increasingly stable and democratic. Civilians have changed the historically dismissive behavior they displayed toward the military before the 1973 coup, which is by itself an important step toward democratic civil-military relations.[3] Equally important, the Chilean military have been changing their political attitudes and ideas about democracy.

If, during the democratic regime that endured until the 1973 coup led by General Augusto Pinochet, the military was characterized by what some scholars labeled a *constitutionalismo formal* (formal constitutionalism characterized by nominal military subordination), during the second half of the 1990s the military began to play a constructive role in the Chilean political process, and to exhibit a new attitude toward democratic values.[4] Military officers have showed an increasing acceptance of elected officials' political authority; a growing enthusiasm for the civilian formulation of defense policies; full respect for the judiciary and rule of law; and a gradual, internal acceptance of democracy and human rights. Contrary to most of the predictions contained in the academic literature and despite the undemocratic institutions Pinochet imposed on the first democratic administration of President Patricio Aylwin in 1990, the military began to play an important and constructive role in the political process of consolidation even before the 2005 laws to reform civil-military relations. In Chile, political dynamics, culture, and ideas moved ahead of institutions, but little of explanatory value has been written about this phenomenon.[5]

This chapter does not pretend to offer an alternative theory about the role that democratization plays in consolidating civil-military relations, but to advance a preliminary and partial interpretative framework that examines how both institutional and cultural change are necessary parts of any democratization process. Institutions have played an important role in Chile since 1990, but interests and ideational factors have undergone much greater change than have institutions. The actors have changed their self-perception, interests, and values, consequently altering the value of institutions that were shaped within an authoritarian ideational context. The institutional framework remains a causal variable in explaining social disputes and power relationships; but it must be complemented and enriched by the inclusion of other variables such as interests, values and ideas, many of which derive from transnational processes of democratization and globalization. This chapter will focus on the evolution not only of institutions, but also of attitudes toward democratic reform, and the ideational framework of civil-military relations.

Explaining changing attitudes within the Chilean military regarding democracy and human rights demands a focus on a complex process of political learning.[6] Changes in ideation may become a causal variable in democratic consolidation if it produces changes in actors' interests and the value they attach to institutions. This would be especially true if Chilean history showed that one of the causes of the democratic breakdown in 1973 was the lack of genuine adherence to democratic institutions by civilian, and especially military, actors. Civilians who reject compliance with democratic institutions may be forced by the state to comply; when military leaders do not comply, however, democracy breaks down. To address these issues, this chapter will examine the current theoretical tools applied to democratic consolidation and civil-military relations, and the uses and shortcomings of the literature on the Chilean case since 1990. The following section will describe the dynamics that led to the changes in military discourse. Finally, the conclusion will summarize what can be learned from the Chilean experience, and suggest a basic agenda for further research.

Democratization, Civil-Military Relations, and the Institutional and Cultural Dimensions of the Chilean Transition

If we were to focus exclusively on the legacies of transition that constrained the democratic regime, we would observe that Chile was characterized by one of the highest levels of military prerogatives in the region. The three democratic governments elected between 1990 and 2005 labored under significant antidemocratic restrictions, organized in a network of authoritarian "enclaves" that included the military, which observers correctly pointed out as obstacles to Chilean democratic consolidation.[7] Until 2005, the main nondemocratic constitutional features were the restriction of political representation through a binominal majoritarian electoral system that overrepresented conservative political sectors; a Congress that required a very high quorum to reform itself; the mandate for nine designated, rather than elected, members of the Senate (20 percent of the total), four of whom were appointed by each branch of the armed forces and the police (Carabiñeros de Chile); and the existence of institutions that provided opportunities for continued military tutelage.[8] The constitution assigned a political role to the military (as so-called guarantors of the institutionality through the National Security Council; prevented the president from removing the chiefs of the armed forces during their four-year tenure except by parliamentary impeachment leaving the membership of the National Security Council outside of presidential control). There were also organic laws granting the military high levels of functional autonomy, and these could only be reformed with a large parliamentary quorum. These obstacles were compounded at the constitutional level by provisions that granted the military additional powers during states of emergency. The powers of elected leaders were also restricted by nondemocratic (albeit nonmilitary) institutions such as the Constitutional Court, the Central Bank, and the Contraloría General de la República (general accounting office). The Chilean military's prerogatives extended to the policy-making arena as well, effectively granting them what several authors have called "functional autonomy" to define institutional policies and budgets. The main legal bases for this autonomy are the Ley Orgánica Constitucional de las Fuerzas Armadas of 1989 and the laws regulating special defense resource allocation for arms acquisitions.[9] These provide the Chilean armed forces with guaranteed levels of resources.

The focus of this literature on antidemocratic obstacles, however, does not allow a wider picture of the consolidation process in its civil-military dimension, not to mention a more complex and consistent theory of consolidation.[10] The outcome has been an unintended trend toward determinism, overstressing the importance of reducing military privilege as a measure of progress toward democratic consolidation while missing the effect of alternate variables, such as the strength of the state, the importance of well-developed bureaucracies, or other types of explanations provided by alternative theoretical frameworks.[11] The influence of electoral dynamics; political learning and changes in ideology and attitude; the importance of political elite dynamics, especially the emergence of a civilian leadership with expertise on defense policy; or the influence of the international environment are also scarcely explored paths whose relationship to democratic consolidation theory has not been discussed.[12] Of critical importance in this regard are the ideas and aspirations transmitted through globalization processes.

The role of political culture as a dependent, intervening, or independent variable of Chile's consolidation process has been studied by researchers who seek to explain the origins of the political crisis of 1973, and the post-1990 democratic progression, by measuring civic culture and social capital; in this second period, however, little has been done concerning civil-military relations. Although political culture was not the only variable at the root of the 1973 crisis, studies have shown that it was one of the more important ones. In their widely accepted study on the period, Arturo Valenzuela and Juan J. Linz broke new ground by highlighting not only the role played by both the Chilean presidential and party systems, but also the centrality of elite attitudes, from political parties to the armed forces, toward democratic institutions.[13] The 1973 crisis was, in this view, a product of the erosion of democratic values among elite groups and, in the latter period, also among ordinary citizens, whereby democracy was seen not as an end in itself but more as a means to some other end. Significant numbers, or even the majority, of both civilian and military elites had this instrumental view of democracy.

Instrumental Democracy and Formal Constitutionalism

The studies of elite—civilian or military—attitudes toward democracy before 1973 are few but very indicative of their fragility. A more recent contribution by Felipe Agüero shows that the Chilean civilian elite harbor an essentially instrumental view of the military, which has been confirmed by previous and later studies about Chilean political crises.[14] They do not consider themselves responsible for formulating defense policies or supervising the military, and tend to concentrate almost exclusively on the domestic dimensions of the military, according to their ideological and political perspectives.[15] Most important, civilian attitudes toward the military over the twentieth century were characterized by a covert, ambiguous, but clearly recognizable message reiterated at different historical moments, which revealed that the democratic idea was never an absolute. According to this message, violence was an acceptable and even legitimate method to solve domestic political disputes under the right circumstances.[16]

It is not surprising, therefore, that studies also concur that the military's compromise with democratic institutions was weak. What most characterized the evolution of twentieth-century Chilean military culture was a trend toward professionalization that in fact led to increasing politicization of the officer corps.[17] Most of the scholarly research shares the conclusion expressed by Augusto Varas that, in 1973, military culture was characterized by a "formal constitutionalism," which represented the culmination of a long process of divorce from the civilian leadership; construction of a "total" national security doctrine; assignment of armed forces' roles and missions by the military leadership itself; and their emboldened assertion of prerogatives.[18]

The authoritarian period of Pinochet's rule (1973–1989) was a period in which the military made explicit its values and skepticism toward democracy and turned them into political action. This is especially true of the institutional engineering embedded in the constitution of 1980 and the complex network of organic and ordinary laws designed to sustain the authoritarian institutions even in the eventual case of democratization. This restricted notion of democracy ended the traditional Chilean constitutional doctrine of "obediencia y no deliberación de las Fuerzas Armadas" (obedience and non-deliberation of the armed forces) honored since 1833, and changed it to "esencial obediencia" (essential obedience), according to which the military obeys the elected civilian authorities as representatives of an impersonal institutionality.[19]

Political Culture and Attitudes toward Democracy in Chile, 1990–2004

Despite the comparatively high levels of regime legitimacy, efficacy, and efficiency manifested in the evolution of Chile since 1990, the available information about public opinion shows that the Chilean polity is still far from being a consolidated democracy. The data provided by Centro de Estudios de la Realidad Contemporanea, one of the few available long-term public opinion research projects related to democracy in Chile, and by *Latinobarómetro*, a region-wide poll regarding attitudes toward democracy, shows at least two important features.[20] First, despite the almost complete normalization of political life, Chilean society still shows serious divisions, further influencing the strongly political and ideological cast of public opinion.[21] Second, as in most of Latin America, Chilean public opinion does not exhibit high levels of support for democracy and has low levels of trust regarding both interpersonal relations and democratic institutions, except for a gradual increase in support for human rights values.[22]

Answers to polling questions about the military diverge over the role of military in government and the role of the military as a state institution.[23] On the one hand, opinions about the authoritarian regime clearly illustrate a political cleavage, dividing Chileans into a slight but clear majority of democrats and a strong minority of non-democrats, in percentages that are very close to those obtained by the 1988 plebiscite. On the other hand, military (and police) institutions receive some of the highest levels of public trust compared with political parties and the Congress.[24]

Changing Military Political Culture, 1990–2005

The task of measuring military attitudes toward democracy in Chile, especially at the officer level, is more difficult (but not impossible), because of a lack of public surveys within the armed forces. If the starting point for the Chilean case was the existence of a nondemocratic culture in 1990, and a culture of "formal constitutionalism" within the previous democratic regime until 1973, three questions arise: Are military leaders committed to defending the authoritarian structures and, therefore, the authoritarian political culture embodied in the institutions created by the Pinochet regime? Have they returned to the previous formal constitutionalism of the earlier democratic regime? Or, are they advancing toward a new, more democratic political culture?

The available evidence indicates that the latter alternative is clearly emerging, but the phenomenon not been adequately studied because much of the research done on Chilean civil-military relations was conducted during the first (and more conflictive) period of the post-Pinochet democratic regime. An updated study of the evolution in civil-military relations should assess levels of civilian control and the resultant attitudes among military personnel, either of contestation or compliance/subordination, through analysis of: the military's relationship with society and state power (i.e., rule of law); and, its relationship with the civilian leadership regarding defense and military policies, strategic assessment and plans, and military force structure and doctrines.

1990–1994: Contestation but Subordination

Chilean civil-military relations since 1990 can be divided into distinct periods.[25] The most difficult one was, of course, during the first years of the democratic regime led by President Patricio Aylwin (1990–1994), characterized by permanent conflict between military and civilian leaders on constitutional, human rights, and accountability issues.

During this period, the armed forces maintained an authoritarian attitude, affirming their self-perception of a tutelary role over the society and the state. It was sustained by the opportunities for political activism provided by their institutional framework, but this attitude was also grounded in an ideological orientation. Beyond defense of the constitution of 1980, one sector of the military also developed a total vision of the military as a profession whose main role should be not only the traditional one of national security, but also devotion to the protection of societal values.[26]

The military entered the democratization process in 1990 with a nondemocratic political culture, characterized by deep polarization and strong distrust of the ruling political coalition. Opposition to the executive was pronounced, including the exercise of all special privileges, and even a willingness to use illegitimate force if necessary, as the crises of the *ejercicio de enlace* in 1990, and the 1993 *boinazo* (unauthorized military mobilizations in the capital city) clearly demonstrated. Opposition also included a defiant position regarding the judiciary.[27] The armed forces openly contested President Aylwin's policy on human rights, rejecting the Informe Rettig (the Rettig Report), the first serious attempt to advance on the extremely sensitive issue of the *desaparecidos* (the "disappeared,"—more than a thousand people who were spirited away during the Pinochet period by security forces, and presumably killed).

The attitude of the military to political institutions, especially the political parties, was also clear. A still-energetic General Pinochet was commander in chief of the army during this period, and, as the former leader of the authoritarian regime, remained the informal chief of the political opposition. President Aylwin sent a package of constitutional reforms to the legislature aimed at full institutional democratization, including the dismantling of military political prerogatives, but it was blocked by the opposition in the Senate.[28] This served to reinforce the association in the public's mind between the Chilean military and the rightist parties, and to further alienate the military institutions from the rest of society and the polity.

Advances at the societal level during this period of conflict were tempered by what was initially called "democracia de los acuerdos" (the democracy of pacts).[29] Despite all the difficulties faced and criticism endured, this deliberate search for political agreements to establish basic stability created a new cultural zeitgeist of consensus-building, and set a needed departure point for important norms in civil-military relations in the new democratic Chile.[30]

In the political field, the government was also able to return the police to the operational control of the Ministry of the Interior; and weaken the role of the military in internal security through the creation of a small, civilian-led intelligence agency. Furthermore, President Aylwin confronted Pinochet on the appointment of top-ranked officers within the armed forces, blocking their nominations and thus signaling to the military that he could effectively shape the high command.[31] This practice was reinforced in 1997, when Pinochet tried to promote a colonel accused of personal involvement in human rights violations, but whose promotion was blocked by Aylwin's successor, President Eduardo Frei.

During this period, there were advances in defense and military policies, but these were very limited because of political conditions favoring a defense of the military legacy of the authoritarian period and a relative lack of proactive civilian leadership in this area.[32] Military prerogatives nevertheless were seen to be limited within the framework of the most presidential of all Latin America's democracies. After the 1973–1990 interregnum, the military resumed its long-standing culture of recognizing presidential authority and military subordination to the executive, softening the ambience and easing the formalities of the civil-military relationship. As Francisco Rojas and Augusto Varas explained, Pinochet's authoritarian regime distinguished and separated political roles from the institutional, and the professional character of the military institutions was kept and set an important difference regarding other Latin American countries.[33]

CHANGING CULTURAL PATTERNS: 1995–1999 AND 2000–2004

After the first democratic administration of Patricio Aylwin, civil-military relations began to change more rapidly. The two administrations that followed, led by Eduardo Frei Ruiz Tagle (1995–2000) and Ricardo Lagos (2000–2006) can be treated as a new period in terms of the military's relations with society, the state, and political institutions.

Relations with Chilean Society

During this second period of democratization, the relationship between civil society and the military experienced a shift, primarily because the consensus-building practices initiated in 1990–1994 were extended to civil-military relations and deepened. Some of these practices had previously been initiated by both the civilian and military, through academic-type meetings before and after the regime change, and via the opening of military academies to civilian students.[34] Following the political program of his coalition, the Frei administration, through Defense Minister Edmundo Pérez Yoma, began to formulate an explicit defense policy in 1995 through a series of civilian and military debates, to be published as the first defense white paper.[35] These discussions included officers from the ministries and armed forces, and also civilians from the Congress, think tanks, academic institutions, and other nonmilitary organizations.[36]

This process produced several simultaneous outcomes. It demonstrated that, for the first time in Chilean history, civilian elites understood they had an important role in, and assumed responsibility for, the formulation of defense and military policy. It made explicit what until then was only a surmise for officers—that civilian elites, including leftist parties, considered the professional military to be a legitimate institution in democratic society and were willing to state it publicly. As a result of this change in civilian attitude, significant trust developed between civilians and military officers, while the polarization of political culture eroded among most key members of the democratic Chilean elite.

Through their cooperation, both groups of actors changed their attitudes and experienced political learning, despite past rivalry and enmity. During negotiations, both sides realized that they were in a different (but better) position than they had expected to be, and therefore adopted a more ambitious agenda, raising the goals to be reached through cooperation. On the one hand, civilians moved away from their historical neglect of the responsibility to formulate defense and military policy, and overcame previous views about military roles. This was especially true of the leftist parties, which abandoned their reflexively Marxist and revolutionary conceptualization of the military. On the other hand, the military leadership realized that their own previous perceptions and expectations of conflict with civilians about defense and military issues were wrong. Also, and despite certain "authoritarian enclaves" in the defense field, the officers modified their initial claim of full autonomy and began to accept the right of elected officials to set defense and military policy in a modern, accountable democracy.[37] In this sense, consensus-building did not mean equalization of hierarchically related actors like elected officials and military officers, but an exercise in persuasion and cooperation.

In the end, the practice of consensus-building in both the 1990–1994 and 1995–1999 periods did not solve the problems of civil-military relations, but it did create a base upon which to build and from which to search for solutions in other areas, and it provided a political methodology that would become increasingly useful to address important civil-military issues. In 1999–2000, such methods were used to address pending human rights issues, in 2001 to initiate the first reform since 1904 of the military draft, and to produce the second defense white paper in 2003. What is relevant is that in all these exercises, the military has been formally participating as an institutional actor, while not all the eligible civilians of the ruling elite have participated. Government authorities and some members of Congress, and advocates from human rights organizations and other societal institutions have been most active.

A second significant evolution in the armed forces' relations with society, particularly since the Lagos administration (2000–2006), is what could be labeled a process of gradual "secularization," by which the military service chiefs have openly begun to speak about bringing their institutional values in line with those of the broader society. In this way, the Chilean military are gradually beginning to abandon their past authoritarian ideology, which had helped legitimize the armed forces' nondemocratic roles in current civil-military institutions.

The first milestone of this process was the 1999–2001 Mesa de Diálogo de Derechos Humanos (Roundtable on Human Rights), created by Minister of National Defense Edmundo Pérez Yoma to address pending human rights issues in Chile. The chiefs of the armed forces sent formal delegates, who participated along with human right lawyers and representatives of different churches and the Freemasons, as well as public personalities. In its final declaration, the military delegates signed a text in which they described a revised understanding of the democratic breakdown of 1973, and of the human rights violations they had previously perpetrated, then justified and neglected.[38] As an example of this new attitude of societal participation, in its initial statement at the Mesa, the army spokesman stated that,

> ...the uniform that we wear with pride nurtures itself from the esteem in which we are held by the society we want to serve and protect. We are not a static compartment, we are in and with society, we are the Army of Chile and we will share forever the destiny of this Republic.[39]

Since then, the commanders in chief have consistently encouraged a gradual consolidation of this changed relation with society through what the Chilean media has called symbolic political *gestos* (gestures). Army chief General Ricardo Izurieta named an important military base "General René Scheider" for the army leader assassinated in 1970, and invited Scheider's family to the ceremony in which he passed the command to his successor, General Juan Emilio Cheyre.[40] In his turn, General Cheyre went further. In September 2002, he ordered a mass in remembrance of General Carlos Prats, former commander in chief of the army. This was the first time the army denounced the assassination of General Prats and his wife by agents of Pinochet's secret police in 1974, and the first time since then that General Prats's family was invited to the Military Academy. In January 2003, General Cheyre released a public statement regarding the thirtieth anniversary of the 1973 coup, in which he renewed the institutional compromise of the Mesa de Diálogo, and declared that the army was neither a political actor nor the heir of any regime, because "the Army is not the counterpart of any political party or social sector. It belongs to all Chileans, whom it is called to serve equally."[41] Later, in June 2003, Cheyre made an additional statement repeating the Mesa de Diálogo "nunca más" (never again) pledge in relation to human rights violations and democratic breakdown through political violence.[42]

The navy and air force have developed similar policies, but with different intensities, circumstances, and nuances regarding their relations with society, mostly associated with human rights issues. For example, both institutions participated in the Mesa de Diálogo. In stark contrast to his highly politicized predecessor, Navy Admiral Miguel Vergara Villalobos has defined the navy's mission as essentially professional, stressing that "we wish to be a support to all Chileans . . . . We wish to be a modern navy in service to the country." The Chilean air force has been clearer regarding its willingness to increase its connection with Chilean society. After a period of political conflict with the government in 2002, the newly appointed service chief, General Osvaldo Sarabia, was explicit on this point during his remarks at the ceremony marking his assumption of command.[43]

Finally, in November 2004, the same month that constitutional reforms were agreed upon, President Lagos released the "Report of the National Commission on Torture and Political Prisons," an extensive document in which, for the first time, the Chilean state officially and in detail acknowledged that torture was practiced against political opposition leaders and citizens during the seventeen years of authoritarian rule.[44] In stark contrast to their reaction to the 1991 Rettig Report, on this occasion the armed forces reacted positively.

Since the Mesa de Diálogo in 1999 the Chilean military has been concerned with developing a more broad and open relationship to Chilean society, as will be seen with regard to human rights and other professional issues, such as the integration of women and homosexuals into the military, and the handling of conscientious objectors to the compulsory draft.[45] This does not mean that the armed forces agree on every issue with the majority opinions of civil and political society. However, the services have increasingly abandoned their historically authoritarian posture, have come to generally support governmental policies, and are tolerant of public debate on defense and military issues. In this sense, the Chilean military services today are increasingly secular institutions that must be understood in the wider context of Chilean cultural liberalization.[46] Much of this progress comes as a result of the military leadership's reassessment of their relative position in public opinion and Chilean society, which reflects high levels of autonomy from state and society, and also increasing experiences of subordination to presidential authority.

Relations with the State

During the Frei and Lagos administrations, the armed forces found themselves in public disagreement with several governmental decisions, but there were also a growing number of episodes of military subordination and acceptance of civilian decisions. The evolution of military culture, however, went beyond this formal acceptance of civilian control, and included changes in attitudes and beliefs about constitutional reforms, compliance with civilian decisions, democracy, and human rights.

In the constitutional realm, the most significant change began in July 2001, after the new Lagos administration insisted, as had Aylwin and Frei before, on sending a package of constitutional reforms to Congress regarding the roles of the military and the National Security Council, and the retirement of commanders in chief. In contrast to the previous debates in which the military openly rejected the possibility of reforms, on this occasion Defense Minister Mario Fernández demanded that the Senate not directly request an opinion from the heads of the armed forces, but follow formal channels through the

Ministry of National Defense, to avoid having the military publicly deliberate on government policy. Fernández requested a response from the commanders in chief, and then he personally explained their as well as the government's opinions in public hearings before the Senate's Constitution, Legislation, and Justice Commission (Comisión de Constitución, Legislación y Justicia). In his remarks, the defense minister stressed that for the first time since 1990, the service chiefs had explicitly noted that their opinion was not a veto, because they were going to accept the final decision of the Congress, whatever the outcome.[47]

Laying the military "veto" to rest was not a minor issue. In 1990, the army had informally vetoed the appointment of a moderate socialist as undersecretary of war (second in the Chilean Defense Ministry). By 2002, however, the elimination of the veto was demonstrated by the election of President Lagos and the composition of his administration. Not only had the Chilean people again elected a socialist as president in 2000, but Lagos also broke new ground in civil-military relations by naming Michelle Bachelet as defense minister. She was the first socialist in this position since Orlando Letelier served during Allende's government, and also the first female minister of defense in Chilean and Latin American history. She would become the first woman president of the Republic of Chile on 11 March 2006.[48]

The turning point in the military's relationship with the Chilean state came on 11 November 2004. On that day, there was an agreement on forty-eight constitutional reforms between the government and the opposition, most of them pending since they were first proposed in 1990. From an institutional perspective, the reforms ended fourteen years of authoritarian constitutional constraints imposed by the Pinochet regime. The agreements modified Article 90 of the constitution, eliminating the military and police role as guarantors of constitutional order. They also shifted control of the police from the Ministry of Defense to a new ministry in charge of public security. Article 93 was also reformed, giving the president the administrative power to remove the commanders in chief of the armed forces and the general director of Carabiñeros after informing the Senate, even before the end of their four-year term. Changes to Article 95 transformed the National Security Council from a decision-making into a purely advisory entity, balanced the number of civilians (the president of the Republic and of the Senate, the Supreme Court and the Comptroller General) and military personnel (commanders in chief and the General Director of Carabiñeros) serving on it, and reserved to the president the power to call the Council into session. As of 10 March 2006, the reforms also eliminated senate seats held by the military and former presidents appointed for life, thus ending nonelected representation. Finally, the binominal electoral system was removed from the constitution and downgraded to the rank of constitutional organic law, thus easing the way for future reforms.[49] Equally important, the 2004 agreement on constitutional reforms, which are the institutional basis of democratic civil-military relations, was received without public comment by the armed forces and the police, behavior that remained unchanged up through adoption of the new constitutional text.

Other important milestones of military reorientation from conflict to subordination were those related to the appointment or retirement of the chiefs of the military and the police.[50] In 1995, President Frei was openly challenged by the general director of the police, Rodolfo Stange, who exercised his prerogatives and refused to resign despite an open request from the government.[51] Finally, after several weeks, Stange had to acquiesce because he realized that the power of the Chilean presidential system over the police was enormous, and his institution was paying a high cost for his refusal. The second democratic administration had to face not only the General Stange crisis in 1995, but also the crisis produced by the army's resistance to the Supreme Court's conviction of retired general Manuel Contreras for the assassination in 1976 of Orlando Letelier, former minister of defense for Allende. Contreras was chief of Pinochet's secret police until 1978, responsible for most of the extrajudicial executions and disappearances that took place during that period, and one of the symbols of human rights violations committed during the authoritarian period. After several days of negotiations Contreras was imprisoned, one of the first episodes of significant military compliance with human rights law since 1990. Another important moment was Pinochet's replacement after his retirement from the army in March 1998, when the government was able to appoint General Izurieta instead of more hard-line candidates. Military subordination to the president and the defense minister was confirmed during President Lagos's tenure when General Patricio Ríos, chief of the air force, decided to resign after the media revealed that he had mismanaged the air force's contribution to the Mesa de Diálogo by appointing a general who deliberately hid information about some "disappeared" persons from the other roundtable members.

The real turning point for Chile's armed forces in relation to the rule of law came with Pinochet's 1998 arrest and trial in London.[52] It accelerated several incipient trend dynamics and set off an explosion of trials for human rights abuses by the military in Chile itself. Previously, many of these cases had been dealt with gingerly by the judiciary, even though several of them were not covered by the Amnesty Law of 1978 that excluded all prior cases of human rights abuses by the security forces from prosecution. The new conditions placed the military on the horns of a dilemma: either accept trials of military officers, or else violate the rule of law and democratic institutionality. In practice, their options to resist short of outright confrontation were limited, and in addition, the London detention strongly shook the expectations of the military and forced them to confront the evolution of international politics and law in the area of human rights.

Relations with Political Institutions and Processes

Finally, the armed forces' own calculations of their political strength forced them not only to accept the changes, but also to take the initiative to look for a different approach to problems. This in turn led to the creation of the Mesa de Diálogo. Since the Mesa, the military has initiated an era of full cooperation with the courts, although not without occasional conflict, as the General Ríos episode showed. This has included a significant effort to shed light on the fate of *desaparecidos*, despite the high risk of judicial punishment for personnel involved in human rights abuses committed during the authoritarian period, even those previously shielded by the 1978 Amnesty law.[53] It is important to stress that the military reached the Mesa de Diálogo agreements despite the fact that they did not have guarantees about the treatment of accused active or former service personnel. According to Zalaquett, as of 2003, the number of persons who had served time for human rights violations are about 40, while about 250 were undergoing trial.[54]

The Mesa de Diálogo has been a second important turning point toward full military compliance with the rule of law and subordination to the state. This was the first time in Chilean history that the military demonstrated a deep understanding of and commitment to democracy and human rights, and have accepted the immediate practical consequences of such a posture by failing to put up any resistance in subsequent trials. Since then, there has been a growing perception in Chile that, except for some parts of the left and center parties, there is not a comparable process of ideological and political cultural change among the political classes.[55]

It is worth noting that the way in which the human rights problem was faced relied on continuing the practices of consensus-building that were initiated in 1990 and strengthened in 1995 to address other areas of civil-military tension. Since there were no preconditions for meetings, nobody was forced to renounce his beliefs and opinions before meeting with the others. What followed was an exercise of mutual exchange in which each one confronted the other's opinions, and learned from them. The political parties accepted, for the first time, the assertion of military leaders that in 1973 the armed forces had acted together with the political parties rather than alone, and that all the actors had differing degrees of responsibility in the violent democratic breakdown. Furthermore, the military agreed, for the first time, that the responsibility for human rights violations had been institutional and not personal, and that there was no justification for the abuses committed during this period.[56]

The military's relationship with other political institutions, such as the national parties, has changed as well over the Frei and Lagos administrations. The Frei period began with clear signals of a consolidation of the military-political right alliance, for example in the rejection in 1995 of the second set of constitutional reforms proposed by the president, and in other signs of an even more "organic" relationship.[57] In 1994, after his forced resignation as General Director of Carabiñeros, General Rodolfo Stange joined Renovación Nacional, the center-right and more liberal Chilean political party, in which he successfully ran for the Senate from the state of Llanquihue, in the Chilean south. In 2001, even after the Mesa de Diálogo, Admiral Arancibia resigned as the commander in chief on the Navy because he decided to run (also successfully) for the Senate in Valparaíso as the candidate of the Unión Demócrata Independiente, another Chilean rightist party.

Links between the armed forces, the right, and the authoritarian regime were in evidence during Pinochet's detention in London, when many of the most prominent rightist leaders openly organized his defense. Since the mid-1990s, however, the relationship between the military and the rightist parties as institutions has begun to suffer a gradual erosion because of the changing logic of the electoral dynamic, a process also experienced in other Latin American countries.[58] At the heart of this trend is the growing possibility that rightist parties might win the presidency for the first time in four decades. In 1999, the right presented a populist candidate, Joaquín Lavín, who openly campaigned as nonpolitical and center-oriented, separating his candidacy from Pinochet, and obtaining the highest vote for the right since 1938.[59]

The outcome of the electoral dynamic has been a growing and mutual process of differentiation between the military and the rightist parties. This shift is in its early stages and not immune to setbacks. Nevertheless, it has already achieved some important milestones, the most important being General Cheyre's statement in January 2003 declaring the independence of the army from the authoritarian regime and from any political party, and situating the army in a professional role.[60] The consequences of this change for democratic consolidation are, however, still to be seen. Having ended the military's veto on constitutional reforms, this new reality may help dilute the still-present military-right alliance in the Senate, and promote further progress in the institutionalization of civilian control of the military.

Defense Policy

The attitude of military leaders toward civilians concerned with defense and military policies also changed significantly since 1995 when the Frei government formulated the first public policy agenda in the history of Chilean democracy and publicly claimed the rights of elected civilians to set defense and military policy, a practice that was further developed during President Lagos's administration.[61] Although in the beginning this practice met with resistance from the military, the policy arena covered during these two governments grew continually, and President Lagos's first defense minister summarized them as La Agenda de Defensa in 2001.[62]

These changes in policy formulation led to the first two defense white books in 1997 and 2002, and they represented the first time in Chilean history that the main features of defense policy were publicly defined, opening the road to accountability. Signed by the presidents and defense ministers of each period, since their publication the books have framed an increasingly dense number of military policies. These white books have been widely accepted by the armed forces as mandatory documents, not least because the participatory process through which they were developed incorporated military opinions and visions, but also because officers perceive them as state, rather than administration, policy, increasing their legitimacy among the services.[63]

Civilians have developed policies for both the domestic and international dimensions of defense policy. In 1997 and 1998, the Defense Ministry modernized its personnel policies by introducing incentives for increasing professionalization.[64] In 1996, the Ministry began a modernization of the draft that was continued in 2001 when the government sent to Congress the first global reform to compulsory military service since 1904. In 2003, the Ministry submitted the first reform of the military pension system since 1990. Other symbolic and sensitive changes have taken place in relation to gender policies that were developed or strongly reinforced by Defense Minister Bachelet. The air force graduated its first female officers; the army opened combat-support specialties to female participation; the navy, for the first time in its history, incorporated women into its service, admitting the need for an open study of opportunities for women in the institution.[65]

Institutional policies have aimed at strengthening joint structures and operations, while the services have begun to adjust their development policies, including force structure, acquisitions, doctrines, and educational programs, to match those formulated by the Ministry of Defense. At the joint operational level, in 2003 the minister of defense introduced an important reform creating joint theatres under a single operational command that were tested for the first time during the military exercises of that year in the north of Chile. In one of the clearest cases of civilian control, in 2002 the government authorized the purchase of ten F-16 fighters from the United States, but introduced an offset policy as a condition for the purchase, an option that had not been considered by the Chilean Air Force. In 2003, the government decided for financial reasons to suspend the navy's modernization project calling for several new frigates to be built both abroad and in Chile; it instead demanded that the navy buy used vessels, initially through international competition, but finally by a direct government-to-government agreement with Holland. At the strategic level, in 1997 President Frei and his defense minister directed and approved the first strategic assessment since 1990. President Lagos's administration advanced civilian leadership by reviewing and approving the first national strategic plan in 2002, and the first strategic defense plan in 2003, while in 2004 the Defense Ministry began to develop the first joint doctrine for the armed forces.[66] These documents established, for the first time in Chilean history, a centralized strategic planning system within which the Chilean Armed Forces can frame their land, naval, and air strategy, with important changes for force structure, doctrine, and institutional development.

The governments of Presidents Frei and Lagos also innovated in the way they have incorporated the military into their foreign security policy. Despite years of resistance, skepticism, and distrust based on a history of geopolitical rivalries since the 1990s, the Chilean government has openly integrated the armed forces into its cooperative policies of strategic stabilization at both the bilateral and regional levels, through military participation in confidence-building measures and increasing defense and military transparency. Furthermore, the Chilean military has enthusiastically embraced new policies of international cooperation on the global level, through increasing participation in peace support operations such as Lagos's 2004 commitment of more than 500 military personnel to the United Nations stabilization force in Haiti.[67] In September 2005, the Ministry of Defense sent to Congress legislation proposing the most ambitious defense reform since the post–World War II reorganization.[68]

Conclusion: Democratization and the Role of Attitudinal Changes in Defense Reform

As this chapter has shown, there is sufficient evidence to conclude that the military's culture, attitudes, and ideas about democracy and human rights have undergone a consistent, if imperfect and even contradictory, process of transformation in Chile. The Chilean Armed Forces have abandoned their defense of the institutions and political culture created by the authoritarian military regime, and are no longer committed to the continuation of those structures. But perhaps even more important, military leaders have not returned to their previous culture of formal constitutionalism exhibited during the democratic regime that collapsed in 1973. The evidence shows that the military is gradually advancing toward an increasingly democratic political culture featuring formal subordination to civilian authority and commitment to the rule of law. In short, the new democracy that began emerging in 1990 has made the long transition toward the reestablishment of its civil-military relations, according to the standards of any consolidated liberal democracy. Thus, civil-military relations in the end became a cornerstone to the process of democratic consolidation.

Global Trends and the Chilean Case

The study of Chile's transition suggests the need for further research regarding the influence of other global determinants on defense reform. The ideas that accompanied the Third Wave of democratization clearly placed an emphasis on the articulation and institutionalization of civilian control of the military, more clearly than during any previous period of democratization, either globally or within Chile. As Bruneau and Trinkunas point out in Chapter 3, these ideas and norms were part of the agenda of international foundations and agencies. In Chile, the historical links to European and International Socialist and Christian Democratic organizations have undoubtedly been historically very important. It is clear that democratization introduced a sea change in Chile in traditional patterns of civil-military relations and sparked the deepest defense reforms since World War II. In stark contrast to previous reforms led by the military during the twentieth century that were intended to increase military prerogatives, the reforms led by civilians in the post-1990 democratic governments were the first in contemporary Chile aimed at strengthening the country's democratic institutions. They served to both consolidate civilian authority and alter military attitudes toward democracy. For the first time in the history of Chile, civilians began to formulate defense policies, put strategic planning under policy guidelines, control the allocation of funds according to strategic plans, and even initiate reforms to institutionalize civilian control over the decision-making process. Within this context, defense reforms also are advancing the efficacy and efficiency of defense institutions.

The available evidence further suggests the need of a wider research agenda that describes the interaction among other global trends affecting Chile's defense reform, on at least the regional and national levels. At the regional level, cooperative work on democratization, economic liberalization, and regional integration between Brazil, Argentina, and Chile beginning in the 1990s sparked the most important strategic change in Latin America since the nineteenth century. Together with the end of the Cold War-based conflicts in Central America, this tripartite rapprochement allowed the development of an increasingly dense network of cooperative defense policies.[69] By ending mutual threat perceptions and thus transforming geopolitical rivalries into security cooperation, the consequences of this shift for defense policymaking in the participant countries, and eventually throughout the region, were enormous. As the second defense white paper put it in 2002, Chile moved from its traditional defense posture based purely on deterrence and the traditional territorial axis, to a mixed one that included both deterrence and international cooperation, and thus toward diversification and globalization of Chile's strategic interests.[70] Democratization, economic liberalization, and integration as a regional phenomenon helped to diminish the importance of traditional defense assumption and made new cooperative defense ventures possible.

At the national level, globalization and economic liberalization also pushed defense reform, because foreign and economic policies fostered both the diversification of Chile's global economic activities, and its growing profile in international politics. The continuing success of the Chilean economic model and its growing success in addressing the social dimension of this model gave great credibility to Chile both diplomatically and vis-à-vis important international financial institutions. Unlike many developing states subject to the prevailing logic of economic liberalization, Chile did not face the same pressures from international financial actors to reduce defense spending abruptly as part of structural adjustment or economic liberalization processes. This allowed civilians in government and the armed forces to engage in a long-term process of consensus-seeking on defense policy, rather than take short-term crisis-driven decisions about military spending. In essence, the success of the economic and social model of the democratic period is part of what provided the space for the civilian and military cultural change process to take place. This stability is also part of what allowed the production of long-term defense policy planning, embodied in the two white books, which has credibility with all key civilian and military actors in this process. This in turn has allowed Chile to increase the already substantial levels of efficiency and efficacy of its defense forces, and has contributed in some particular areas to support the great credibility of the international policies of the democratic administrations, particularly in the area of international peace and stability, including participation in the UN mission to Haiti.

The Need for a Comprehensive Theory of Democratic Consolidation

Chile has become an increasingly stable democracy in Latin America since 1990, and has been able to advance toward democratic civil-military relations despite the lack of an institutional framework during these years. On the contrary, until September 2005, military leaders had clung to their prerogatives, but in real terms these powers had been gradually abandoned because of attitudinal change among military leaders regarding democracy, political violence, and human rights. Therefore, political institutions were not the causal variable in Chile's democratic consolidation. This institutional transformation occurred in 2005, but by then political attitudes already had changed as the result of years of conflict, interest calculations, negotiations, consensus-building, and political learning.

Some conclusions can nevertheless be drawn. First, much of the initial impetus for and gradual acceptance of change within the military was the result of political calculus rather than conviction, as well as a response to internal bureaucratic politics. In 1999 when the Mesa de Diálogo was established, the wider context included Pinochet's arrest in London and a rocketing number of lawsuits against former regime members across the country, putting the army under unprecedented pressure to accept the rule of law. The only alternative was to use illegal force against the government, which would have entailed enormous national and international costs, and which had minimal internal support (none at all from the navy and air force). This is not to say that every decision that followed was purely cynical and calculated. The outcome reflected the growing isolation of the hardliners within the army, and the emergence of professional opportunities for military officers who supported democracy, or who were changing their perceptions toward democracy and civilian control.

Second, it is worth putting the military's institutional evolution within the wider national context, which also had several implications regarding calculation and political learning. During the years following 1990, the military gradually realized that the democratic leadership was being politically and economically responsible. After years of human right abuses following the 1973 coup, many military personnel expected vengeance, the ascendancy of leftist ideology, economic stagnation, and a return to civilian disinterest in and ignorance of military affairs. Instead, officers found moderation, responsiveness, a culture of consensus-building, and an extreme sensitivity toward military and defense policy. Because civilians had changed their culture, so could the military. The new democratic management of the country also shifted military perceptions regarding their most important institutional interests. The armed services now enjoy greater legitimacy within civil society, more input into new defense policies, and a stable budget that has allowed for the most important defense modernization in decades. Thus, democracy has served the best interests of the military by creating a spillover effect between the wider processes of democratic stabilization, consensus-making, sustained economic growth, and increasing social cohesion, including a positive dynamic in civil-military relations.

Third, there is an important caveat to raise about these observations. While the institutional behavior of Chile's military has clearly changed, there is no scientific evidence to support such an observation as there would be in the civilian realm, where opinion polls are the norm. Systematic polling within the military has not yet been possible in Chile. The question of how deep, open, and extended is the change of discourse within the military is thus a legitimate one. This is not to say that the observable change is not real or genuine, but it should be complemented with systematic research in the future.

NOTES

1. Mario Fernández, "El Sistema Político Chileno: Características y Tendencias," in Cristian Toloza and Eugenio Lahera, eds., *Chile en los Noventa* (Santiago: Presidencia de la República/Dolmen Ediciones, 1997), 27–51; Juan Samuel Valenzuela, "Reflexiones sobre el Presente y el Futuro del paisaje Chileno a la Luz del Pasado," *Estudios Politicos* 75 (Winter 1999): 273–290; Detlef Nolte, "El Congreso chileno y su aporte a la consolidación democrática en perspectiva comparada," *Revista de Ciencia Política. Chile en Democracia: 30 años después* 22, 2 (2003): 43–67.
2. On the seriousness of the process, see Valenzuela "Reflexiones sobre el Presente"; Peter Siavelis, *The President and the Congress in Postauthoritarian Chile: Institutional Constraints to Democratic Consolidation* (University Park: Pennsylvania State University Press, 2000); David Altman and Anibal Pérez-Liñán "Assessing the Quality of Democracy: Freedom, Competitiveness and Participation in Eighteen Latin American Countries," *Democratization* 9, 2 (2002): 85–100; Nolte, "El Congreso chileno y su aporte a la consolidación democrática." The contributions of civil-military relations are emphasized by Felipe Agüero, "30 años después: La ciencia política y las relaciones Fuerzas Armadas Estado y Sociedad," *Revista de Ciencia Política. Chile en Democracia: 30 años después* 23, 2 (2003): 251–272; and Paul E. Sigmund, "The Chilean Military: Legalism Undermined, Manipulated, and Restored," *Revista de Ciencia Política. Chile en Democracia: 30 años después* 23, 2 (2003): 241–250.
3. Felipe Agüero, *Soldiers, Civilians, and Democracy: Post-Franco Spain in Comparative Perspective* (Baltimore, MD: Johns Hopkins University Press, 1995); Richard H. Kohn, "How Democracies Control the Military," *Journal of Democracy* 8, 4 (October 1997): 140–153.

4. Augusto Varas, "La Intervención civil de las Fuerzas Armadas," in Hugo Fruhling, Carlos Portales, and Augusto Varas, eds., *Estado y Fuerzas Armadas* (Santiago: Stichting Rechtshulp Chili/FLACSO, 1982), 59–82.
5. For this discussion we use the concept of culture according to Gabriel Almond and Sidney Verba *The Civic Culture. Political Attitudes and Democracy in Five Nations* (Newbury Park, CA: Sage Publications, 1963), and the constructivist concept of idea, which assumes social causes, as proposed by Alexander Wendt in "Anarchy Is What States Make of It: The Social Construction of Power Politics," *International Organization* 46, 2 (Spring 1992): 391–425.
6. Jennifer L. McCoy, ed. *Political Learning and Redemocratization in Latin America: Do Politicians Learn from Political Crises?* (Miami: North-South Center Press, 2000).
7. For early neoinstitutional works focused on Chilean civil-military relations, see Brian Loveman, "Misión Cumplida? Civil Military Relations and the Chilean Polítical Transition," *Journal of Interamerican Studies and World Affairs* 33, 3 (Fall 1991): 35–74; Loveman, "Protected Democracies and Military Guardianships: Polítical Transition in Latin America, 1978–1993," *Journal of Interamerican Studies and World Affairs* 36, 2 (Summer 1994): 105–189; Loveman, "Civil-Military Relations in Spanish America: The Past as Prelude," paper delivered at the Conference on Civil-Military Relations, Riverside, California, 19 February 1999; Gonzalo García and Juan Esteban Montes, *Subordinación Democrática de los Militares. Exitos y Fracasos en Chile* (Santiago: CED, 1994); Wendy Hunter, *Eroding Military Influence in Brazil* (Chapel Hill: University of North Carolina Press 1997); and Larry Diamond, *Developing Democracy: toward Consolidation* (Baltimore, MD: The Johns Hopkins University Press, 1999). The wider constitutional debate can be traced in Oscar Godoy, ed. *Hacia una democracia moderna. La opción parlamentaria* (Santiago: Ediciones Universidad Católica de Chile, 1990); Augustin Squella and Osvaldo Sunkel, eds. *Democratizar la democracia: Reformas pendientes* (Santigo: LOM/Centro de Análisis de Políticas Públicas Universidad de Chile, 2000).
8. Oscar Godoy, "Parlamento, Presidencialismo y Democracia Protegida," *Revista de Ciencia Política. Chile en Democracia: 30 años después* 23, 2 (2003): 7–42. Fernández, "El Sistema Electoral Chileno. Dilucidando Equívocos y Adaptando Fórmulas," in Agustín Squella and Osvaldo Sunkel, eds., *Democratizar la Democracia: Reformas Pendientes* (Santiago: LOM/Centro de Análisis de Políticas Públicas Universidad de Chile, 2000), 113.Eugenio Guzmán "Apariencia y realidad: Comentarios al Sistema Electoral chileno de Mario Fernández," in Squella and Sunkel, eds., *Democratizar la Democracia: Reformas Pendientes*, 130.
9. These are Law No. 7.144 and Law No. 13.196. The former was passed during World War II, however, and the second dictated soon after the 1973 coup. Therefore, the special allocation corresponds more to historic military prerogatives; the military only made it more rigid

(distributing funds by thirds). The real innovation was introduced by the *Ley Orgánica de las Fuerzas Armadas* of 1989, which prohibited budgetary decreases lower than levels of absolute expenditure in that year. See Guillermo Patillo, Fernando Bustamante, and Miguel Navarro, *Cuál debe ser el gasto militar en el Chile de los 90?* (Santiago: Editorial Atenea/Centro de Estudios del Desarrollo, 1991); and Francisco A. Rojas, ed. *Gasto Militar en América Latina: Procesos de decisiones y Actores Claves* (Santiago: FLACSO-CINDE, 1994).

10. Guillermo O'Donnell, "Illusions about Consolidation," in Guillermo O'Donnell, ed., *Counterpoints: Selected Essays on Authoritarianism and Democratization* (Notre Dame: University of Notre Dame Press,1999), 175–194.
11. See Guillermo O'Donnell, "On the State, Democratization and Some Conceptual Problems: A Latin American View with Glances at Some Postcommunist Countries," in *Counterpoints*, 134–157; on strong military bureaucracies, see David C. Kozak, "The Bureaucratic Politics Approach: The Evolution of the Paradigm," in David C. Kozak and James M. Keagle, eds., *Bureaucratic Politics and National Security. Theory and Practice* (Boulder, CO: Lynne Rienner, 1988), 3–15; O'Donnell, *Counterpoints*, 134–137). The concept of weak and strong states comes from Joel S. Migdal, *Strong Societies and Weak States: State-Society Relations and State Capabilities in the Third World* (Princeton, NJ: Princeton University Press, 1988); and Theda Skocpol, "Bringing the State Back In: Strategies of Analysis in Current Research," in Peter B. Evans, Dietrich Rueschemeyer, and Theda Skocpol, eds., *Bringing the State Back In* (New York: Cambridge University Press, 1985), 3–37.
12. Among those who have discussed electoral dynamics, see Wendy Hunter, *Eroding Military Influence*. On political learning, see McCoy, *Political Learning and Redemocratization in Latin America*; and on the dynamics of political elites, see John Higley and Richard Gunther, eds. *Elites and Democratic Consolidation in Latin America and Southern Europe* (Cambridge: Cambridge University Press, 1992); Rut Diamint, *Democracia y Seguridad en América Latina* (Buenos Aires: Grupo Editor Latinoamericano, 2001). For the Chilean case, see Patillo, Bustamante, and Navarro, *Cuál debe ser el gasto militar en el Chile de los 90?*; Augusto Varas and Claudio Fuentes, *Defensa Nacional, Chile 1990–1994: Modernización y Desarrollo* (Santiago: FLACSO-Chile, 1994); Rojas, *Gasto Militar en América Latina*; and Miguel Navarro, "El Ministerio de Defensa y la Organización Política de la Defensa," *Fuerzas Armadas y Sociedad* 12, 4 (October–December 1997), 19–25. Several scholars have examined the influence of international environment on consolidation, including Michael C. Desch, "Threat Environments and Military Missions," in Larry Diamond and Marc F. Plattner, eds., *Civil-Military Relations and Democracy* (Baltimore, MD: Johns Hopkins University Press, 1996), 12–29.

13. Arturo Valenzuela, *The Breakdown of Democratic Regimes: Chile* (Baltimore, MD: Johns Hopkins University Press, 1978); and Juan J.Linz, *The Breakdown of Democratic Regimes. Crisis, Breakdown, and Reequilibration* (Baltimore, MD: The Johns Hopkins University Press 1978).
14. Felipe Agüero, *Brechas en la Democratizacion: las Visiones de la Elite política Sobre las Fuerzas Armadas* (Santiago: Nueva Serie FLACSO, 1998); Augusto Varas, Felipe Agüero, and Fernando Bustamante, *Chile, Democracia, Fuerzas Armadas* (Santiago: FLACSO 1980); Carlos Maldonado, *La Milicia Republicana: Historia de un Ejército civil en Chile, 1932–1936* (Santiago: Servicio Universitario Mundial, WUS-Chile, 1988); José Díaz Gallardo, "Administración de la Defensa: la Experiencia Chilena en el periodo 1932–1973," *Fuerzas Armadas y Sociedad* 11, 4 (October–December 1996), 6–14.
15. Agüero, "Brechas en la Democratizacion," 12–19. Simon Collier and William S. Sater, *A History of Chile, 1818–1994* (Cambridge: Cambridge University Press, 1996), 326. Linz, *The Breakdown of Democratic Regimes*; and Valenzuela, *The Breakdown of Democratic Regimes: Chile.*
16. Paul E. Sigmund "La democracia en el pensamiento liberal, católico y marxista," in Ana María Stuven, ed., *Democracia Contemporánea. Transición y Consolidación* (Santiago: Ediciones Universidad Católica de Chile, 1990), 57–70.
17. Frederick M. Nunn, *The Military in Chilean History: Essays on Civil-Military Relations, 1810–1973* (Albuquerque: University of New Mexico Press, 1976); and Carlos Maldonado, "Entre reacción Civilista y Constitucionalismo Formal: las Fuerzas Armadas en el periodo 1931–38," Serie FLACSO No. 55 (August 1988), Santiago.
18. Varas, Agüero, and Bustamante, *Chile, Democracia, Fuerzas Armadas*; García and Montes, *Subordinación Democrática de los Militares.*
19. Godoy, "Parlamento, Presidencialismo y Democracia Protegida," 20.
20. Carlos Huneeus, *Chile un país dividido: La actualidad del pasado* (Santiago: Catalonia, 2003); on the *Latinobarómetro* study, see Marta Lagos, "Democracias en borrador," in Agustin Squella and Osvaldo Sunkel, eds., *Democratizar la democracia: Reformas pendientes* (Santiago: LOM/Centro de Analsis de Politicas Publicas Universidad de Chile, 2000), 13–28.
21. Valenzuela, "Reflexiones sobre el Presente"; Eugenio Tironi and Felipe Agüero, "¿Sobrevivirá el Nuevo Paisaje Chileno?" *Estudios Públicos* 74 (Autumn 1999): 151–168; Alan Angel "Party Change in Chile in Comparative Perspective," *Revista de Ciencia Política. Chile en Democracia: 30 Años Después* 23, 2 (2003): 88–108; and Eugenio Ortega Frei, "Los partidos políticos chilenos: Cambio y estabilidad en el comportamiento electoral 1990.2002," *Revista de Ciencia Política. Chile en Democracia: 30 años después* 23, 2 (2003): 109–147.

22. Numbers vary according to the studies. The Centro de Estudios de la Realidad Contemporanea (CERC) shows that in 1990, democracy was supported by 63 percent of public opinion, by 53 percent in 1998, and 48 percent in 2000; see Huneeus, *Chile un país dividido*, 101. *Latinobarómetro*, by contrast, showed 54 percent in 1996, 53 percent in 1998, and 57 percent in 2000; see Lagos, "Democracias en borrador," 139. According to culturalist theories, the lack of trust is an obstacle to the creation of social capital, thus complicating Latin American democratic consolidation. See Robert Putnam, *Making Democracy Work* (Princeton, NJ: Princeton University Press, 1993); Francis Fukuyama, "Social Capital," in Lawrence E. Harrison and Samuel P. Huntington, eds., *Culture Matters: How Values Shape Human Progress* (New York: Basic Books, 2000), 98–111; Marta Lagos, "Between Stability and Crisis in Latin America," *Journal of Democracy* 12, 1 (January 2000): 137–145; and Lagos, "Democracias en borrador," 2001.
23. Valenzuela "Reflexiones sobre el Presente"; Tironi and Agüero, "¿Sobrevivirá el Nuevo Paisaje Chileno?"; and Ortega, "Los partidos políticos chilenos."
24. Huneeus, *Chile un país dividido.*
25. Claudio Fuentes, "Militares en Chile: ni completa autonomía ni total subordinación,"in *Chile 96. Analisis y Opiniones* (Santiago: FLACSO–Chile, 1997); Rodrigo Atria, "Estado, militares y democracia: La afirmación de la supremacía civil en Chile," *Fuerzas Armadas y Sociedad* 15, 2 (January–March 2000), 39–46; Gonzalo García, "La Defensa Nacional y las Fuerzas Armadas," in Cristian Toloza and Eugenio Lahera, eds., *Chile en los Noventa* (Santiago: Presidencia de la República/Dolmen Ediciones, 1997), 161–179; and García and Montes, *Subordinación Democrática de los Militares.*
26. Milan Marinovic Pino, "Fuerzas Armadas y sociedad: marco teórico para un debate político," Documentos de Estudio, Centro de Estudios Sociedad y Fuerzas Armadas, Instituto de Ciencia Política, Universidad de Chile, 1990; Alejandro Medina Lois, "El pensamiento militar," Ensayo No. 15, *Documentos*, Centro de Estudios de la Nacionalidad, Santiago, Chile, 1990; Omar Gutiérrez, "La Profesionalidad de las Fuerzas Armadas," in *Comunidad Chilena y Defensa Nacional* (Santiago: Centro de Estudios de la Nacionalidad, 1988); Gutiérrez, "La Profesionalidad de las Fuerzas Armadas," in *Seminario: Comunidad Chilena y Defensa Nacional* (Santiago: Centro de Estudios de la Nacionalidad, 1988); and Gutiérrez, "La identidad cultural y la defensa nacional: Elementos sociológicos y psicológicos intervinientes," in *Hay Patria que defender? La identidad nacional frente a la globalización* (Santiago: Centro de Estudios del Desarrollo, 2000), 198–208.
27. Augusto Pinochet, "Discurso de S.E. el Presidente de la República con ocasión de la ceremonia de conmemoración de su nombramiento como Comandante en Jefe del Ejército," original text released to the press on

23 August 1989. Augusto Pinochet, "Discurso de S.E. el Presidente de la República, Capitán General Augusto Pinochet Ugarte, en rancho de cuartel en Escuela Militar," original text released to the press on 23 August 1989.

28. Claudio Fuentes, " Resisting Change: Security-Sector Reform in Chile," *Journal of Conflict, Security, and Development* 2, 1 (April 2002): 121–131.
29. Stuven, *Democracia Contemporanea.*
30. Gustavo Cuevas Valenzuela, "La nueva democracia en Chile," in Paz V. Milet, ed., *Estabilidad, crisis y organización de la política. Lecciones de medio siglo de historia chilena* (Santiago: FLACSO-Chile, 2001), 85–110.
31. Hunter, *Eroding Military Influence in Brazil*, 151.
32. Varas and Fuentes, *Defensa Nacional, Chile 1990–1994*, 18–23.
33. Francisco A. Rojas, "Transición y Relaciones Civiles-Militares en Chile: Aportes en un Nuevo Marco Internacional," in Jorge Domínguez, ed., *Seguridad Internacional, Paz y Democracia en el Cono Sur* (Santiago: FLACSO-Chile/Diálogo Interamericano, 1998), 148; and Augusto Varas, *Los Militares en el Poder* (Santiago: Pehuén, 1986).
34. Varas and Fuentes, *Defensa Nacional, Chile 1990–1994.*
35. *Libro de la Defensa Nacional de Chile*, Ministerio de Defensa Nacional (Santiago: Antártica, 1997).
36. The list of participants is in ibid., 5–6.
37. See Pinochet, "Discurso de S.E. el Presidente de la República con ocasión de la ceremonia de conmemoración de su nombramiento como Comandante en Jefe del Ejercito." This in an official text released to the press on 23 August 1989 by the Chilean Army.
38. "Acuerdo de la Mesa de Diálogo: Hacia el reencuentro de todos los chilenos," Gobierno de Chile (Santiago: Ministerio Secretaría General de Gobierno, 2000). Available at http://www.cepchile.cl/
39. Quoted in Juan Carlos Salgado, "La Participación del Ejército de Chile en la Mesa de Diálogo sobre los derechos humanos," in *Anuario Nuevo Gobierno: Desafíos de la Reconciliación, Chile 1999–2000* (Santiago: Libros FLACSO-Chile, 2000), 201.
40. General Scheider, commander in chief of the army, was killed in 1970 as a result of attempts by the United States and Chile's extreme right to prevent Salvador Allende from assuming the presidency. Scheider refused to lead a coup against the new president.
41. Juan Emilio Cheyre Espinoza, "Exclusivo: General Cheyre habla del golpe," *La Tercera*, 5 January 2004.
42. Juan Emilio Cheyre Espinoza, "General Cheyre: Nunca Más," *La Segunda*, June 2004, 13.
43. "General Sarabia renueva compromisos adquiridos por la FACH," *El Mercurio*, November 2002, 5.
44. President Lagos eventually submitted a law to Congress recognizing the right of the victims to at least symbolic state reparation. The report

is available at http://www.cepchile.cl/dms/lang_1/doc_3480.html; accessed April 2006.

45. General Cheyre said in 2004 that the army tolerates homosexuals if they behave in a private way. *Las Ultimas Noticias*, 13 July 2004.
46. Eugenio Tironi, *La irrupción de las masas y el malestar de las elites. Chile en el cambio de siglo* (Santiago: Grijalbo, 1999).
47. Mario Fernández, "Exposición del Sr. Ministro de Defensa Nacional ante la Comisión de Constitución, Legislación y Justicia del Senado," original text. (Valparaíso, 17 July 2001, 2). Available at the official website of the Ministry of Defense of Chile. www.defensa.cl.
48. Salvador Allende was the leader of the Chilean Socialist Party.
49. See "Mensaje Number 24.342" from the president of the Senate to the president of the Chamber of Deputies, 11 November 2004. Available at the official website of the Library of the Chilean Congress, at www.bcn.cl.
50. The Chilean Constitution established a four-year term for the commanders in chief of the armed forces and the general director of Carabineros.
51. The presidential request was issued after General Stange was implicated in the killing of three Communists in 1985.
52. For an exhaustive account of this period, see Ernesto Ekaizer, *Yo, Augusto* (Buenos Aires: Aguilar, 2003).
53. See "Bachelet y FFAA renuevan espíritu de Mesa de Diálogo," *La Tercera*, 3 October 2004.
54. In a significant gesture, in May 2003 General Cheyre refused to use his right to testify in writing, and personally spoke at a trial presided over by Judge Jorge Calvo, who was investigating executions in Cheyre´s regiment at La Serena, north of Chile, after 1973. See "DDHH: Por primera vez Cheyre declaró cara a cara ante un juez," *El Mostrador*, 25 May 2003. Also, Pinochet himself had been in danger of facing trial, despite the ruling of various courts, including England's, that his physical and mental condition would not allow a fair trial.
55. Sigmund, "La democracia en el pensamiento liberal, católico y marxista."
56. For a detailed account of the Mesa de Diálogo, see Elizabeth Lira, "Mesa de Diálogo de Derechos Humanos en Chile: 21 de agosto 1999–13 de junio de 2000," in Varios Autores, ed., *Nuevo Gobierno: Desafíos de la Reconciliación, Chile 1999–2000* (Santiago: Libros FLACSO-Chile, 2000), 203–219.
57. Fuentes, " Resisting Change."
58. Hunter, *Eroding Military Influence in Brazil.*
59. Manuel Antonio Garretón, "Cambio, continuidad y proyecciones de las elecciones presidenciales de fin de siglo," in *Nuevo Gobierno: Desafíos de la Reconciliación, Chile 1999–2000*, 103.
60. Cheyre, "Exclusivo: General Cheyre habla del golpe." Several authors have stressed this new trend in the relationship between the right and the military. See Garretón, "Cambio, continuidad y proyecciones de las elecciones presidenciales de fin de siglo"; Paul W. Drake, "El nuevo

escenario político," in *Nuevo Gobierno: Desafíos de la Reconciliación, Chile 1999–2000*, 109–117.

61. See García, "La Defensa Nacional y las Fuerzas Armadas"; Atria, "Estado, militares y democracia," 39–46; Fuentes, " Resisting Change."
62. Mario Fernández, *Clase Magistral del Ministro de Defensa. Mario Fernandez Baeza, en la Inauguración del año Académico de las Fuerzas Armadas*. Santiago, Chile, 24 March 2000. Official Text released by the Ministry of National defense, available at www.defensa.cl.
63. Vergara, *Conferencia Inaugural del Mes del Mar 2004*.
64. In 1997 and 1998 Congress passed two laws, the Estatuto del Personal de las Fuerzas Armadas, DFL No.1 (G), and the Estatuto del Personal de Carabineros de Chile, DFL No. 1 (C), sent by the administration, to modernize the military and police.
65. Michelle Bachelet, "Clase magistral de la Ministra de Defensa Nacional, Michelle Bachelet Jeria, en la inauguración del año lectivo de las academias de las Fuerzas Armadas," official text, released by the Ministry of National Defense of Chile, 2004, available at http://www.defensa.cl/paginas/public/noticias/2004/1803clase_magistral.htm; accessed 9 October 2006.
66. Juan Carlos Salgado, "Exposición JEMDN con motivo del aniversario del Estado Mayor de la Defensa Nacional, año 2004," *Santiago*, 16 July 2004.
67. Alberto Van Klaveren, "Inserción Internacional de Chile," in Eugenio Lahera and Cristian Toloza, eds., *Chile en los Noventa* (Santiago: Dolmen, 1998), 117–160; Marcos Robledo and Francisco Rojas, "Construyendo un régimen cooperativo de seguridad en el Cono Sur de América Latina," *Fuerzas Armadas y Sociedad* 17, 1 and 2 (January–June 2002): 5–31.
68. The full text of the reform is available at the official site of the Chilean Congress: http://sil.congreso.cl/pags/index.html; accessed 3 October 2006.
69. Rojas and Robledo, "Construyendo un régimen cooperativo de seguridad en el Cono Sur de América Latina."
70. *Libro de la Defensa Nacional 2002*, Ministerio de Defensa Nacional (Santiago: Antártica, 2002).

6

Preserving Autonomy in Conflict: Civil-Military Relations in Colombia

Douglas Porch

> To find an intelligent soldier in Colombia is like a miracle, and miracles don't happen.
>
> —Colombian expression, provided by General Alvaro Valencia Tovar

Introduction

This chapter will argue that, although the global drivers of defense reform and civil-military relations upon which this book is based are undeniable, there nevertheless is a case to be made for Colombian exceptionalism—the persistence of internal dynamics in Colombia's case—for at least three reasons: first, unlike many of its neighbors, democracy is not an alien concept belatedly grafted onto an authoritarian political culture. On the contrary, Colombian democracy, while restricted and imperfect, formed part of that nation's birthright. Indeed, Colombia has one of the most impressive records of democratic continuity in Latin America. This has included a century of civilian control of the military and ongoing attempts to foster a spirit of professionalism among soldiers, which implies a respect for boundaries between political and military roles. Professionalism, however, has hardly translated into apolitical behavior among Colombian soldiers. Rather, the history of civil-military relations in Colombia illustrates in full measure what British historian Hew Strachan calls "the political consequences of professionalism."[1]

A second Colombian dynamic has been the historical one—the central fact of Colombian history is the precariousness of the nation state, and the weakness of state institutions.[2] The consequence has been persistent and violent challenges to the legitimacy of the state. "Contingent sovereignty" has always been a reality in a country where geographic fragmentation, an absence of communications, a weak or nonexistent school system, and sub-national loyalties to Liberal and Conservative Party networks combined with the hostility of the Church toward Liberal administrations to undermine national cohesion and state legitimacy. Massive urbanization in the latter decades of the twentieth century, encouraged in part by conflict in the countryside, has weakened these once intense local loyalties, reduced the influence of landowners, and diminished the authority of the Colombian Church. Unfortunately, this historic dynamic has persisted and even intensified over the last quarter-century as the state's ability to foster a spirit of national unity has been sabotaged by insurgency, organized crime, and right-wing, paramilitary groups.[3]

Finally, while the Colombian armed forces have proven subordinate to political authority, Bogotá has struggled to make effective use of military power. The ability of the state to synchronize policy, strategy, and operations, is arguably the most important national security function of civil-military relations. The problem in Colombia can be traced to dysfunctional institutions tasked with the making of strategy, and to the delegation of the responsibilities of making war to small professional forces drawn from narrow sectors of society.

The perseverance of insurrection in Colombia for a half-century has shaped the military's roles and missions in ways that are extremely contemporary. While "human security" is described lately as "a response to the challenges in today's world," and a "broadening" of traditional definitions of human development, many, if not most, of its principles and strategies would be familiar to counterinsurgency specialists of decades past, including Colombian officers who formulated imaginative approaches to combating *La Violencia* (1948–1958).[4] The debate in Colombia has focused on the nature of the insurgency, its center of gravity, and critical vulnerabilities. This has drawn the military into the political arena as interpreters of the causes of conflict, advocates for particular solutions, and as interlocutors between the government and its citizens on both the national and local levels.

In short, while military forces are perpetually challenged to contain their political activities within boundaries acceptable to standards of democratic civilian control, wartime, and especially counterinsurgency missions in which the frontier between war and peace is obscured, invite a high level of political engagement by the military and a heightened potential for dysfunctional civil-military interaction, for at least four reasons. First, Colombia seems no more able than some other Western democracies to evolve a coherent counterinsurgency strategy. This is in part because it lacks robust institutions through which to conduct a strategic dialogue. But also, considerable scope for disagreement exists between and among soldiers and civilians on the causes and nature of any insurgency, much less that of Colombia that is anchored in no ethnic or religious discontent, or even, some argue, in ideology. Without a clear net assessment of the problem, strategy formulation becomes a source of debate over the relative merits of political versus military counterinsurgency approaches, not just between soldiers and civilians, but within military institutions as well.

Second, strategic confusion complicates the task of evolving credible measures of success and hence demonstrate progress against an insurgency. Because counterinsurgency wars are inevitably wars of attrition fought out over years, patience and faith in ultimate victory may become early casualties unless military forces can produce tangible evidence of incremental success. This may cause the government or the military to force the pace of the war in quest of a rapid victory, which brings up a third problem—collateral damage. Because the modus operandi of the insurgent is to secret himself within the population, to represent certain economic sectors like the coca harvesters, to ally with organized crime groups, or to form legitimate organizations like NGOs, to participate in the political dialogue, insurgencies offer a multiplicity of targets, many of which may be only partially amenable to military action. For their part, soldiers may become exceedingly frustrated at the unwillingness or inability of the government to attack the insurgency on judicial, financial, or social fronts.

Finally, because insurgents are equated with dissidents, rebels, and heretics, they are usually considered to be beyond the reach of international law and the laws of war. Indeed, governments may insist that they are not at "war" at all, but in fact are facing a "law and order" problem that falls under a purely domestic legal jurisdiction. This may invite skepticism in the domestic and international community. It also allows the insurgency to employ captives and POWs as leverage to force the government to the negotiating table on "humanitarian" grounds, and hence bestow de facto recognition on the armed opposition, a situation that the military may view as a betrayal. For these reasons, all of which pertain in spades in Colombia, the formulation and application of policy and strategy as a process of civil-military dialogue becomes particularly difficult in an environment of civil strife.[5]

While democracy is part of Colombia's birthright, it has been a work in progress that included the demise of the National Front in 1974, the abandonment of bipartisan coalition governments in 1986, and the creation of a new constitution in 1991. However, if one measures the success of Colombian civil-military relations in terms of effective strategy formulation as a product of civil-military dialogue about how best to ensure national security, then Colombian civil-military relations may be said to have been less harmonious.[6] This is both because institutions that might serve as a forum for civil-military dialogue are weak or atrophied, and because the military regards war as its special province, a territory that few politicians are willing to invade. Attempts to tighten and formalize mechanisms of civilian control have not had much bite, in large part because reforms have taken place in the context of a conflict of escalating intensity.

The impetus for extending civilian controls over the Colombian military has come principally from internal reformers eager to make more efficient use of the state's resources, to reinforce the state's legitimacy at home and abroad, and to counter the increasing technological, tactical, and operational efficiency of the insurgents. International factors, however, have shaped the conflict in various ways. First, the failure of the European Union and Latin American countries to ante up for the original non-military dimensions of Plan Colombia has encouraged the militarization of strategy under President Alvaro Uribe (2002–to date). The globalizing influence of the United States, the absence of a coordinated, interagency approach to funnel U.S. aid to Bogotá, has in some cases worked to bolster the independence of the military and the police.[7] U.S. counterdrug priorities have shaped Bogotá's strategies, as well as supplied models for military reform. Pressure from Washington, Europe, and NGOs has also compelled the Colombian military to adjust to international human rights standards.

Given the history of war, the view that civilians lack the competence to pronounce on professional military matters, popular indifference to a conflict perceived as remote, it is hardly surprising that little political incentive exists to engage the military in a strategic dialogue. Congressional oversight is largely cosmetic, limited to parochial concerns, while the military leadership has established a strong, direct relationship with the president, who may on occasion punish a general insufficiently attentive to political direction, *pour encourager les autres* (to encourage the others). But this hardly constitutes strong institutional control, or an understanding of how to craft operations and strategy to achieve the ends of policy. Although the Ministry of Defense (MOD) blends civilians and soldiers in a collaborative enterprise up to a point, the high command remains by far the stronger institution. The greatest degree of civilian control is exercised over the budget. However, even this is minimized as most resources are committed to salaries and operating costs, leaving only scraps for discretionary spending and investment.

Second, the endemic conflict that Colombia has suffered at least since 1946, and that has intensified in the 1990s, has required Colombian soldiers to adapt their professional approach to an ever-changing landscape of conflict. As with democratic control, some of the impetus for technological and organizational adaptation has come from civilians eager to increase the effectiveness of the forces and hence ensure the survivability of the state. International factors shaping the response of the Colombian military include the U.S. military, which has served as an organizational and doctrinal model, as well as a resource base to support modernization. U.S. support has sharpened and accelerated the Colombian response to tactical and operational challenges, and has even helped to resolve internal debates within the forces. Reforms borrowed from the U.S. model such as force integration and the introduction of combatant commanders—regional commanders under whom all services fall—have "depoliticized" the military insofar as they have concentrated professional concerns along internal channels. Nevertheless, force augmentation and reorganization have failed to produce a spike in standards of professionalism and performance.

Finally, the "liberal" technocratic policies of Colombian governments since the late 1980s have produced a reluctance among government officials to expend scarce resources on defense despite the serious insurgent threat. When taken together with the preference of Colombian administrations to negotiate with enemies of the state rather than strive for military victory, this has inculcated fear of a political "stab-in-the-back" among soldiers. Nevertheless, while there are certainly aspects of the Colombian military's relationship with their civilian masters that soldiers find objectionable, the criticism has stopped short of open rebellion because, even as the state negotiated with its enemies, it has also taken steps to strengthen the forces. Furthermore, elements of the military acting alone or in collaboration with paramilitary groups have and can act as a spoiler when government policy toward the insurgency veers off in a direction they oppose. Therefore, Colombian soldiers see no need to step outside of the democratic framework. However, this has hardly translated into an efficient use by the Colombian state of military power, because soldiers have mastered the art of democratic maneuver, even undemocratic sabotage, to preserve their relative autonomy and to militarize policy and strategy.

THE 1991 CONSTITUTION AND CIVILIAN CONTROL OF THE MILITARY

The 1991 constitution, seen as a way to redemocratize Colombian society and end the violence that had spiraled in intensity in the 1980s, was greeted with euphoria in the country. It proved not to be the panacea for Colombia's problems for reasons that need not detain us here.[8] Nor has the 1991 constitution done much to alter the fundamental relationship between the government and its soldiers. The sub-autonomy of the military has been largely respected. Civilian control requires the effective coordination of all branches of government to participate in the oversight of budgeting, strategic and operational planning, intelligence, personnel actions (promotions, assignments, retirements), generating requirements and conducting acquisitions.[9] Andrés Dávila Ladrón de Guevara, director of the Division of Justice and Security in the National Department of Planning, believes that the Colombian system is misunderstood: "Many think that Colombia has an authoritarian system with a lack of civilian control. But that's not so. There are lots of controls over the military. But subordination is exaggerated as well. The problem is that there are very few people in Colombia who understand about defense and security issues."[10]

In truth, Colombian society's sense of connection with the military, and the war it is fighting is tenuous. The country's elites traditionally have boycotted the military and shown little interest in military affairs. "Colombia doesn't have a strong military tradition like other Latin American countries," notes Alfredo Rangel. "The military attracts lower to lower middle class. Those who join the officer corps are looking for social promotion." Nor are Colombians agreed on what their war is about. Colombia's unpleasantness historically has been interpreted as a political and social rather than a security problem. "From the 1970s to the mid-1990s, people said that we had a conflict because Colombia was a closed democracy with elites that oppressed the rural population," Vice Minister J.M. Eastman contends. "If that's the view, then the conflict is not seen as a security problem, but as a problem of democracy and political process, even one of economic development. So, there was no link with defense policies."

Narcotrafficking, however, has intensified the conflict from the 1980s and muddled the debate on what the "conflicto" is about. Neoliberals in the *Centro de Estudios Regionales* (CERE) in the *Universidad de los Andes* theorized in the 1990s that poverty could not be the origins of Colombia's problems by demonstrating that insurgency prospered in areas where there were resources, not in the poorest areas. The problem, they said, was the weakness of the state that allowed criminal violence to spread. Violence caused the social situation, not vice versa. Therefore, Colombia has a security problem, not an economic or social problem. This has informed Uribe's approach to the conflict. If you end the violence, you will fix the social problem because it will allow economic development.

Drugs have altered the dynamic of Colombian politics. "The old Liberal/Conservative conflict has been changed by drugs," according to Mauricio Wiesner. "This has broken down traditional party loyalty, as peasants have been driven off the land by drug barons. So, the country is largely apolitical. The state institutions don't work. Impunity and corruption are rife. The legal system doesn't work, so people take the law into their own hands and have no fear of being caught." "There isn't a civil society here and an armed guerrilla society on the other side," Colombian Communist chief Jaime Caycedo told Steven Dudley. "They are two integral parts of the same society."[11] "It's difficult to say why we have guerrillas," Eastman reflects. "Other countries have poverty but no guerrillas. I think that Colombia has a national identity. It's not that no one cares." For its part, polite society, urban society, confused about the nature of the conflict and aghast at its violence, has recoiled from *la guerra sucia*.

Nowhere is the social inequality of Colombia more apparent than in the military's conscription policies. While the military has taken steps to professionalize its ranks, the burden of fighting the conflicto falls heavily on the peasantry, no matter which side enlists them. Colombians might admire the military from a distance, but that does not translate into a desire to send their children to serve. Attempts by the MOD to introduce a lottery system in 2004 failed to get a final reading in Congress. "I get calls all of the time asking how to get a son out of military service," Juan Carlos Gómez said.

"For Colombians, the problem of the FARC is the problem of the government. This is reflected in conscription. We have a class system in this country. Everyone has an interest in the status quo—so long as I get along. I talk to my classmates. It's a horrible thing to say, but they ask: 'What will happen if we finish this war? We will lose our jobs.' There are people who think like that. The same for the NGOs. Everyone has an interest in the status quo." "We don't have a tradition of military service in Colombia," Eastman believes, "at least not one for the middle classes."

Congress

Congressional control over the military is weak, hardly more than "the noise of the sands."[12] This has several causes. Electoral reform has splintered the once omnipotent Liberal and Conservative blocs into a myriad of fifty political parties and movements, only eight of which hold more than two seats, led by men and women of scant experience, some of whom are beholden to drug and paramilitary interests. The parties are electoral machines divested of "any capacity for governance," without "the ability to draw up or carry out public policies." This absence of "legitimacy" weakens Congressional pretensions to oversight of the military.[13] The cliché that all politics are local has proved especially true in Colombia where historically representatives and senators have evinced terminal parochialism, far more focused on local than national issues.[14] The result is that Congress is not the venue to host a national debate on the major strategic issues confronting Colombia. "Its impact on policies is zero," according to Sergio Jaramillo, ex-aide to Defense Minister Marta Lucía Ramírez and now head of a prominent Colombian think tank. "The government is the President and his ministers. Congress is not part of the government. There is not a clear link with Congress."

But to argue that the Colombian Congress is highly dysfunctional is not to say that it is irrelevant.[15] Congressional authority is felt especially in the budget. The Second Commission of the Congress and an Interparliamentary Committee of Public Credit have budgetary oversight of defense spending. "The problem is that the civilians on these committees don't know enough about defense and security issues," Ladrón de Guevara believes. "The Congress has no technical capacity to carry out oversight," Vice Minister J.M. Eastman pointed out. "From time to time a special committee will look at things. The main prerequisite of Congress is to oversee the external debt. They get involved when we ask for money to buy weapons systems abroad. But they don't really say no. They don't have the capacity to do this. But they can play tough if they want to."[16] Jaramillo also points out that it is difficult for planners to become too intimate with Congress, "because you cannot share information with Congress. It will be leaked."

When it comes to legislation directly affecting the military, soldiers participate directly in the negotiation of laws, such as pension reform, and exercise their influence. "For example, the vice minister of finance who was negotiating pension reform had to be changed because the military refused to negotiate with him," recalls Ladrón de Guevara. "The military is very good at moving Congress toward the outcomes it wants," Jaramillo insists, "through contracts, etc." A colonel is in charge of liaison with Congress. He maintains a line of information to the Ministry.

President

In Colombia, civilian control begins with the president, who enjoys a direct relationship with the military. Unfortunately, the concentration of power in the hands of the president, and especially the direct president-military relationship, has actually become an obstacle to civilian control in Colombia, a problem accentuated under President Uribe. Presidential power increased during the National Front when, by agreement between the two parties, legislation required a two-thirds vote for passage, forcing the president to take extraordinary measures to maintain a functioning government. Presidential power also has been enhanced by the indifference and ignorance of Congress in defense matters. "The president is like a small god for the military," Vice Minister Peñate insists. But that is true only if the president follows policies approved by the high command, as President Ernesto Samper (1994–1998) discovered.[17] Military hostility, emboldened by accusations of corruption and pressure from the United States to act on narcotrafficking, left the unfortunate Samper bereft of a coherent security policy. Even his own defense minister worked to sabotage his boss' policy when he launched *Convivir* in 1994, a plan for military sponsorship of self-defense groups crafted by the national intelligence service, the Departamento Administrativo de Seguridad (DAS), to undermine Samper's negotiating strategy with the insurgents.[18]

The fall of the town of Las Delicias in August 1996 to the Fuerzas Armadas Revolucionarias de Colombia (FARC), who bagged sixty Colombian soldiers as prisoners, changed the momentum of civil-military relations. Scrutiny was increasingly placed on military use, or misuse, of resources. Pressure mounted on the military to deliver on the battlefield, to respect human rights, to look for efficiencies. This benefited Samper's successor, Conservative Andrés Pastrana. Although the new president, elected in 1998, courted military ire when he continued Samper's appeasement strategy by offering the FARC a *zona de despeje* (cleared zone) as a prelude to negotiations, Pastrana sought to achieve more balance in the civil-military relationship through better communication, cordiality, and negotiation. He appointed innovative generals to the top commands, kept them there, and allowed them to kick-start a process of military transformation that would put Colombian forces back on the offensive. Pastrana's tireless marketing of Plan Colombia in the United States supplied the resources to finance this transformation. The civilian ministers of defense were accepted by the military. Pastrana may be safely credited with laying the groundwork for the revival of Colombian fortunes in the war.[19]

In many respects, Âlvaro Uribe (2002–to date) reaped the benefits of his predecessor's preparations. Nevertheless, the new Colombian president also understood that the military sought a commander in chief willing to lead the nation in wartime. Within a week of taking office, Uribe declared a state of emergency that imposed press censorship, removed elected officials who "contribute to public turmoil," and bestowed sweeping powers on the security forces in tumultuous areas of the country.[20] Unlike Pastrana, content to provide political cover and resources so that his soldiers could get on with the job, Uribe exhibits a direct, hands-on leadership style that, in the short term, has certainly improved civil-military relations, at least as far as the presidency is concerned. The militarization of strategy, the desire to take the war to the FARC, all appeal to a military that rejects negotiations with the enemy. But the president is a trifle too "hands-on" for some tastes: "The style of this president is to call subordinate commanders directly," is how retired U.S. Air Force General and Latin America specialist Richard Goetze puts it. "This undermines the minister of defense. It undermines the military chain of command as well. This damages the concept of civil-military relations. This is a strategic vulnerability. The president is not allowing institutions to be built. And this is not just in defense. The minister of foreign relations is Âlvaro Uribe. He deals directly with the United States. There is no coordination. It's a one-man show."[21]

This absence of institution building and civil-military dialogue in security policy and strategy formulation did not originate with Uribe, although his capacity for ignoring the ministry and even the chain-of-command is legendary. The 1991 constitution assigned to the military and the police the mission of "defense of the sovereignty, independence and integrity of the national territory." The *Consejería para la Seguridad Nacional* (National Security Council) is meant to develop and oversee the process by which this is done.[22] In the United States, for instance, the National Security Council in theory offers a forum "to advise and assist the President on national security and foreign policies. The Council also serves as the President's principal arm for coordinating these policies among the various government agencies."[23] Colombia has attempted to replicate this U.S. institution, but much has been lost in translation. "The NSC was created in 1990, and for the first four years it was the center of capacity building," Eastman remembered. "It was a think tank that developed many ideas. It was a place where people began to think about long term problems. But since 1994, it has lost prestige and capacity."

Ministry of Defense

The Ministry of Defense is the hub where the interaction between civilian representatives of elected officials and soldiers who possess professional knowledge and control the means of legitimate violence are institutionalized. One goal of a ministry is to maximize the effectiveness of the military to implement national policy and provide for the security of the nation. Colombia's National Security Strategy was developed in the MOD, its supporters point out.[24] And by all accounts, nothing short of a "silent revolution" has occurred since 2001 to eliminate inefficiencies and centralize and partially privatize logistical arrangements to include the procurement of arms, ammunition, communications equipment, insurance, energy, health and food services, and aircraft maintenance.[25] Unfortunately, this has proven insufficient to reverse the broadly held view in "the military that the MOD doesn't represent military interests," according to one officer.[26] The problem begins at the top. The minister of defense has not played the strong role that the position requires.[27]

There are several reasons for this. First, there exists a genuine cultural divide between civilians and the military. Civilians are accused of being innocent of military culture and institutions, and quick to take decisions with little professional input. The dearth of civilians knowledgeable in defense matters translates into the appointment of generalists experienced in administration to head the Ministry of Defense, rather than specialists in military matters.

Second, the military is a robust institution in Colombia, far less fragile and exposed than the Ministry. "The idea that the Minister of Defense is in charge of security of the nation is an alien concept in Colombia," in the view of State Department official Paul Malstedt, "especially when you have a president who acts as his own commander-in-chief."[28] The commanding general has national presence, and does not hesitate to employ the media to project his views, even if they contradict those of the minister—especially if they contradict those of the minister. Third, the fact that the military enjoys a direct relationship with the president, one tightened under Uribe, leaves the minister sandwiched between the president and the commanding general. "Where is your constituency (if you are Minister of Defense)?" Jaramillo asks. "The Ministry may not be behind him. Not everyone in the building answers to you. If the minister doesn't have the full backing of the president, then he or she has a problem. Uribe didn't support Ramírez. He didn't want to alienate the military." The MOD is a weak institution, Malstedt believes, because "that's the way the police and the military want it."[29]

Vice ministers were created in the MOD to strengthen the civilian presence. However, confused administrative and command lines of authority give astute soldiers ample room for maneuver.[30] The lack of a policy planning unit in the MOD means that resources are allocated according to no strategic plan. The vice ministries are further weakened by the youth and inexperience of the incumbents, the lack of clearly defined tasks, and by the fact that the military do not consider them to be part of the chain of civilian control. Not surprisingly, they enjoy even lesser respect than the minister. "The civilians are sitting in the seats, but the military is running the Ministry," Goetze notes.

Rafael Pardo, defense minister in the early 1990s, began the civilianization of the MOD. It used to be said that every Colombian family of a certain standing aspired to count a general and a bishop among its offspring. Now, according to Vice Minister Eastman, many MOD civilian employees come from families with strong military ties, so that the milieu is familiar to them, and the atmosphere is that "of a big family." They are recruited by competitive examination, and usually given technical or administrative responsibilities. "In my part (of the Ministry), the civilians and the military get along well, they know each other. In any case, there is not much opportunity for conflict because there isn't much margin to improvise." Others are less convinced: "Very few civilians understand the structure and culture of the forces and the police," Rafael Nieto believes. "Those who know a little think that they understand everything." The absence of a military advisor close to the minister since the "civilianization" of the Secretary General is of special concern to soldiers.

Planning and Budgets

The idea of the reformers was that a vice minister of defense together with a section of the *Departamento Nacional de Planeación* would coordinate investment of resources. However, as civilians moved into the MOD in the 1990s, the military took over more of the planning themselves. Integrated planning is not well managed—the civilians simply take what the military sends as requirements and pass them on to the National Planning Department, although the vice ministers can veto a request.[31] Boundaries between programmatic planning and strategic planning are poorly defined and poorly laid out. Formal processes for operational planning and requirements generation that would involve mainly the military should be separated from strategic planning and acquisition that remain primarily civilian functions. This might help to rationalize planning and lessen civil-military tensions in the ministry.[32]

Most agree that civilian control is most firmly expressed in Colombia through control of the budget. The services state their needs, which are run past the civilians in the MOD, before being passed to the National Planning Department and the finance ministry. The president is also influential, and can be lobbied by the military for weapons systems. Nevertheless, in wartime it may be difficult to deny military requests. "Each branch of the service tells the civilians what they need," Eastman recounts. "U.S. civilians have much more capacity to decide on acquisitions and technology. Civilian experience is very recent in Colombia. We are also in a conflict, which puts the military in a strong position to state priorities. So, the civilian role is to make decisions on the basis of opportunity costs, rather than on the basis of what is needed."

Human Rights

The projection of human rights as a concern of the international community has become a focus of civil-military tension in Colombia.

This occurs largely because, according to the nongovernmental organization (NGO) Human Rights Watch, "Colombia leads the Western hemisphere in reported human rights and international humanitarian law violations," some of which directly implicate the military.[33] Expanded accountability for human rights runs counter to the vigilante mentality spawned by Colombia's long history of bloody internal conflicts, popular violence, and the absence of strong institutions to channel, arbitrate, and litigate social and political tensions, and even ownership disputes. Indeed, even the Church's role as a mediating and humanizing influence was compromised by its partisan engagement in the Conservative cause before 1965. There is certainly a robust rhetorical commitment to human rights in Colombia's official circles.[34] There is also a recognition that the expansion and institutionalization of concepts of human rights are at the heart of government efforts to strengthen and expand state presence.[35] It is also a central issue in the current Colombian conflict, according to ex-Vice Minister for Justice Rafael Nieto. "You need to win hearts and minds in this war, and you need human rights protection. This is a strategic problem."

The 1991 constitution expanded citizen and human rights, and created an extensive human rights bureaucracy throughout the state, including in the military.[36] Defense Minister Rafael Pardo initiated human rights training in 1991. But the acceptance of human rights concepts and the institutionalization of practices in Colombia have been slowed in part by civil-military tensions generated by the conflict. The military is reluctant to embrace an issue that has traditionally been monopolized by the Left. Human Rights Watch complains that President Uribe berates human rights advocates for "doing the work of terrorists," which echoes the view of many officers "who continue to try to link legitimate human rights work to support for guerrillas."[37]

There is also a certain degree of resentment that this issue is foisted on Bogotá by an international community that misunderstands the depths of Colombia's crisis, and is mediated through Colombia's political class. The United States in particular, whose pressure on Colombia to curb human rights abuses dates from the 1980s, is accused of "human rights imperialism," and since the scandals of Abu Ghraib, Baghram, and Guantánamo, of human rights hypocrisy by such groups as Amnesty International, Human Rights Watch, and even the U.S. Government Accountability Office, that charge the Pentagon with turning a blind eye to flagrant rights violations by units subsidized by U.S. military aid.[38] Carlos Franco credits the international community, to include the EU Parliament, Green parties in Great Britain and Germany, and the Inter-American court as well as NGOs like Human Rights Watch, Amnesty International, Americas Watch, and the Committee of Andean Jurists, with prodding Colombia toward a more responsible approach to human rights issues. "Colombia is very sensitive to criticism on this issue, especially from the United States," Rafael Nieto believes.

If human rights form the cornerstone of the Colombian state's struggle for legitimacy at home and abroad, it is also a mechanism through which Bogotá enforces civil and international values on the military. Civil-military tensions occur, however, because many soldiers and intelligence agents view human rights regulations to be a brake on operational success. There are several reasons why this is so: human rights is a vague, poorly defined concept. This has encouraged a lack of coherence and a variety of approaches that has made it difficult to target resources, or translate human rights into MOD policy and military doctrine.[39] International guidelines apply poorly to a nation at war. For instance, the United Nations "sets out really stupid requirements, like you cannot put a police headquarters close to the civilian population," Nieto pointed out. "You are not allowed to carry out operations to rescue people. This only promotes violence."

While an elaborate system of judicial investigation and control of human rights abuses exists on paper, in practice it is under-resourced, works from vague principles, and suffers from lack of cooperation from the military, police, and intelligence services. U.S. expert on Colombia William Avilés concluded of the 1990s that, "Human rights initiatives were largely in line with what the military would accept—training, public acknowledgement of a problem, and the non-enforceable acceptance of international humanitarian law."[40]

Evidence exists, however, that human rights legislation and controls are beginning to bite. Some believe that the concern for human rights has gone too far, and that the military is so petrified of judicial complications arising from a firefight with insurgents that might be considered a crime scene, that they pull their punches. This phenomenon, if it indeed exists, is called *el síndrome de la Procuraduría* (prosecutor's syndrome).[41] "Everyone is afraid of the *Procuraduría* (attorney general)," Valencia Tovar insists. "This is an issue that can destroy an officer's career. When there is an incident, the *fiscalía* investigates.[42] Support for the *fuero militar*—the right of the military to judge their own—is robust among certain elements of the judiciary.[43]

Nevertheless, although skeptics argue that the government only cracks down on human rights abuses when shamed by the international community, the trends in this sensitive area are positive. Massacres, newly displaced internal refugees and assassinations of unionists are down. The number of candidates who present themselves in local elections has doubled in recent years. “In 1994, 55 percent of human rights violations were caused by the military,” Nieto asserted. “In 2003 it was 12 percent. Now it less than one percent.” Human Rights Watch contends, however, that the improved statistics reflect a lack of energy, or worse, in the office of Uribe’s attorney general.[44] Furthermore, as human rights abuses by the military decline, those carried out by the paramilitaries, who act on tips supplied by military intelligence and DAS agents, and even have military-supplied weapons, continue to cause problems.[45]

Military Transformation

While it is certain that the roots of Colombia’s present conflict run deep, and that the patterns of violence and human rights abuses replicate those of *la Violencia,* the war intensified only from the 1990s, when the FARC, bolstered by drug revenues, went on the offensive. “For the military, having an adversary is new,” Jaramillo believes. “It was only a mid-intensity conflict until the 1990s.” Given the nature of the challenge, military modernization became important. This began in the early 1990s under Rafael Pardo, who began to shift the military’s focus to the internal conflict, rather than on rival Venezuela.[46] Between 1990 and 1995, the military budget quadrupled to pay for a multimillion-dollar expansion of the armed services. The government passed “war taxes” to create mobile brigades, increase the number of soldiers, and boost officer salaries. Unfortunately, a law that exempted anyone with a high school diploma from combat, combined with the requirement to guard over 5,000 critical infrastructure points and outposts, meant that the number of troops available for offensive operations remained steady.[47] Critics complained that economy-conscious technocrats who shaped Colombian policies were reluctant to invest in unproductive military spending.[48] But delays of significant U.S. aid in the 1990s over the *affaire* Samper also stymied modernization.[49] Real military transformation only began under Pastrana, who provided the high cover and resources for the Colombian high command to rebuild a debilitated and defensive-minded Colombian army.

"Plan Colombia made this transformation possible," notes Alfredo Rangel.

The Role of the United States

The United States Southern Command (SOUTHCOM), the Military Group (MILGP) in the U.S. Embassy in Bogota, and the Narcotics Affairs Section (NAS) undoubtedly are the major conductors of globalizing influences on Colombian civil-military relations. The goal is to build "Colombian Military capabilities in order to defeat the narcoterrorist threat,"[50] or in the words of one senior MILGP commander, "shape the military environment" by helping the Colombians to create institutional structures that they can sustain.[51] From a civil-military relations perspective, this huge plus-up of military assistance might be seen as a way for civilians, and their "globalizing" partners the United States, to whip a lethargic military organization toward modernization and efficiency, thereby strengthening the hand of the state. However, some Colombians argue that, by providing a direct conduit to the embassy and SOUTHCOM, and hence to U.S. resources, the heavy U.S. presence actually dilutes civilian control. This is in part because the U.S. effort is poorly coordinated among the various civilian and military components, so that aid sets off a free-for-all among Colombians eager to grab a share of the largesse.[52]

There are also limits on what a MILGP, even one as wealthy and ubiquitous as Bogotá can accomplish. U.S. practices like jointness are resisted because it both challenges traditional relationships within and between the Colombian services, and alters established patterns of civil-military relations. The advice of a U.S. captain or major may safely be ignored by a Colombian colonel or general, who has been fighting the insurgency his entire career, and who may fear that high casualties produced by aggressive tactics will bring a political reprimand, or judicial enquiry, down on his head. Some U.S. officers express frustration that the Colombian military does not appear to understand that insurgencies are about legitimacy. "Our role is behind the scenes, not to lead the charge," Lieutenant Colonel Valentzas points out. "Because we are not in the field, the Colombians think that they know better than us." MILGP officers note that they have witnessed significant progress in the Colombian forces. Nevertheless, the plus-up in equipment and personnel, the reorganization of battalion sectors into more versatile mobile brigades, and the introduction of jointness into command structure has failed to alter significantly

Colombian military mentalities and operational methods linked to a military culture in large part shaped by historic patterns of civil-military relations.

CONCLUSION

The feeling is pervasive among many officers that Colombia is experiencing a historic moment. Civil-military relations have stabilized under the leadership of a strong president who protects the military's core competencies from civilian encroachment. Military transformation and professionalization has resulted in efficiencies that appear to have the FARC, if not exactly on the run, at least on the defensive. The military stands high in public esteem. "Democratic security" has increased investor confidence. And yet, Colombian soldiers have been here before, in the 1960s and late 1970s when they felt that the military victory apparently within their grasp was squandered by politicians who fundamentally distrust and historically under-resource the military. The consensus is that continued success hinges on the continuity of Uribe's Democratic Security policy, which itself hinges on continued U.S. support. "If we have support and good leadership, within four years this thing will be under control," one senior officer explained.[53] Otherwise, Colombia's endemic problems are likely to resurface, among them structural problems, including economic overdependence on U.S. and Venezuelan markets, poor infrastructure, an overvalued peso, and dropping oil revenues. A return to political instability could be a real disincentive to investment and trigger an economic downturn.[54] A faltering of resolve in the war against the insurgency, combined with the endemic weakness of Colombian political parties, might, in the words of *El Tiempo* commentator Pedro Medellin, institutionalize what is already a "deep transformation of the networks of territorial power."[55]

The insurgency appears to be in retreat. The Ejercito de Liberación Nacional (ELN) leadership believed that they could create revolutionary conditions, especially if they siphoned off oil revenues in Arauca to build communities. "But the ELN can't survive for more than five years," Eastman believes. "They don't have the military power even to negotiate. They are hemorrhaging soldiers into the paramilitaries." Plan Colombia and *Plan Patriota*, the military offensive against the FARC in the south, have undoubtedly weakened the FARC, but opinion is divided on how much.[56] The movement has trouble constructing an urban agenda. Colombian city dwellers regard the FARC as a collection of violent bumpkins whose rural political agenda holds little appeal.[57] "They think that drug dollars substitutes for a popular base," in the opinion of senior military leaders.[58] "They are very rural people, very *campesinos*, their agenda is very local," Eastman, who has experience in negotiating with guerrillas, noted. "The FARC is beginning to retreat, and to fight at a distance using snipers and explosives," Nieto contends.[59] The government has enjoyed some success targeting mid-level FARC leaders, a critical link in a movement that recruits heavily among children and women, and whose op-tempo of late has left little time for political indoctrination and what might be called "professional development."[60]

Nevertheless, Alfredo Rangel believes that it is too early to declare victory. "The FARC is weakened but far from defeated. It is possible to lose what we have won. FARC's retreat may be only temporary." Rangel sees FARC in tactical retreat, not on the cusp of collapse. "The FARC still has its capabilities intact and conserves its capacity, in the South especially," he cautions. Even the government concedes that the FARC retains significant manpower and financial resources, while the reoccupation of territory controlled for years by the insurgents does not necessarily guarantee that the "hearts and minds" of the peasants grown accustomed to an illegal economy will follow.

Others suggest that the great strides in operational efficiency made by the Colombian military since the 1990s has altered the military dynamic of the conflict, and shown the FARC that they cannot win. "In the 1990s, the FARC was on the one-yard line," MILGP executive officer Lt. Colonel Carlos Berrios believes. "Now we've pushed them back to the fifty yard line."[61] But many wonder if the Colombian military packs the punch, and Washington retains the will, to finish off the FARC. The International Crisis Group cautions that *Plan Patriota* may have shot its bolt. The FARC's infrastructure has sustained the worst that the government can throw at it and survives. The offensives against the FARC in the south have passed what Clausewitz calls "the culminating point of victory," and are now actually winding down without decisive results. And while demonstrating "incremental success" in war is important to convince Colombia's people and allies of eventual victory, "excessive triumphalism" over military victories has lulled the public into a false sense of success.

To sustain offensives against the FARC, some estimate that the government would actually have to double the defense budget and expand the military and police by a third, "and even then there would be no guarantees."[62] Narcotrafficking persists, and provides both the remnants of the Autodefensas Unidas de Colombia (AUC), its criminal heirs, and the insurgency with resources to continue to resist the government. Opinion is divided over whether demobilization of the paramilitaries actually benefits the FARC. Fears that guerrillas will move to fill the power vacuums in localities where the state remains weak or absent appear exaggerated, as AUC strength is concentrated in the north, while the FARC operates mainly in the south and east. "Most of the demobilized paramilitaries stay in their areas. The problems will occur along the drug corridors," one U.S. official predicts.[63]

Even though Uribe will remain in office for a second four-year term, Colombian civil-military relations will undoubtedly face serious challenges. State institutions other than the presidency have not become noticeably stronger under Uribe—*au contraire.* Jaramillo complains, "there is a view that the various services are in a race, 'first past the post.' Uribe encourages this. There is no coordination between the army and the police, and no mechanism to do this. None of (Uribe's) advisors is telling him what the problems of the military are. They just don't understand." And even that "institutional strengthening" is totally personality driven. "This will make it difficult for Colombian institutions to react," Nieto warns, especially if the insurgency worsens. A greater challenge may occur if diminished U.S. aid combines with an economic downturn to restrict defense dollars. "This would be very grave," according to Rangel. "Uribe without Plan Colombia, (or continued support under the Andean Defense Initiative) cannot do great things." This could curtail Colombian military transformation and allow the insurgents to recover some of the ground they have lost over the past years. A loss of battlefield momentum combined with economic setbacks might encourage Uribe or his successor to negotiate with insurgents, in the manner of Samper or Pastrana. This would certainly raise the hackles of the military, encourage a renaissance of the *autodefensas*, and possibly lead to an upsurge in human rights abuses with a military, police, or intelligence connection.

While Rangel believes that negotiations with the insurgents will happen later rather than sooner, the potential for negotiations with the FARC, even if they involve only a humanitarian exchange, at the outset of Uribe's unprecedented second term is the buzz of Bogotá.[64] Where would negotiations leave civil-military relations in Colombia? The military remains Colombia's most popular institution. But this does not necessarily translate into firm support for the war. Attempts to institute a more equitable method of conscription that would share the burden across social classes and open military life to public scrutiny has failed to gain traction. Scandals help to sustain the civil-military divide and confirm the widespread perception that military service, and consequently the conflicto, is the province of the military. The war, often intense, is localized in remote areas of the country. Meanwhile, the largest cities where the majority of the population lives, struggle to maintain a sense of normalcy. Demanding minimal sacrifices from the Colombian population is probably a requirement of Uribe's—and by extension the military's—popularity. Because the military is taking care of the problem, the population can express its gratitude without actually having to send their sons in harm's way. The military might be far less popular if more people, especially the middle classes, had to serve in it.

This fundamental divide between civilians and soldiers about how this conflicto is to be resolved, lies at the heart of Colombian civil-military relations, according to Alfredo Rangel. "Civilian and military priorities are different. The civilians want peace through dialogue. The soldiers want military victory. The military is very jealous about keeping their space, and keeping the civilians out." War, apparently, is their space. Therefore, all of the combatants in Colombia—insurgents, *autodefensas*, and the military—offer mirror images of each other, none with a political strategy, all committed to a dogma of armed struggle until an elusive victory is achieved. Then what? The peace process under Pastrana, while initially welcomed among the general population, was extremely unpopular with the military. "The military was very opposed to the peace process," Eastman, who was negotiating with the ELN, remembered. "The worse thing that you can do is to dishonor the military. Some soldiers saw the peace process as dishonoring the military."

A "softer" approach to prosecuting the war would not necessarily lead to a military coup, according to Peñate: "There is no threat of intervention since Rojas Pinilla. The military can go on strike—'Operation Turtle' we call it, when the military drags their feet. Betancur ignored the advice of the military. We had the same problem with Pastrana. Negotiations destroyed morale. But they obeyed." "It's sad to say, but Colombia hasn't suffered enough," Wiesner suggests.

NOTES

1. Hew Strachan, *The Politics of the British Army* (Oxford: Oxford University Press, 1997), 112.
2. Daniel Pécaut, *Guerra Contra la Sociedad* (Bogotá: Espasa Hoy, 2002), 33.
3. While the extreme left has never commanded an extensive following in Colombia, many argue that the current insurgencies are a break with the past because the profusion of resources linked to globalized markets, especially oil and drugs, has allowed the main insurgent group, the Revolutionary Armed Forces of Colombia (known by its Spanish acronym, FARC) in particular to mount a serious challenge to the state. Others, however, see more continuity than change, among them the economist Francisco Thoumi, who argues that drugs are not the root cause of Colombia's problems, but rather that Colombia produces cocaine because it is a fractured society with dysfunctional institutions. Francisco Thoumi, "The Numbers' Game: Let's All Guess the Size of the Illegal Drug Industry," *TNI Crime & Globalisation Paper*, Amsterdam, NL, December 2003: 13, available at http://www.tni.org/crime; accessed 21 October 2005.
4. "We call it Security Assistance," a senior officer in the MILGP-COL explained. "But we are doing counter-insurgency like in the 1960s." LTC Carlos Berrios, interview 2 February 2006.
5. Counterinsurgency missions invite a high level of politicization for several reasons: first, notions of *jus ad bellum* that prevails in interstate conflicts with its emphasis on war waged by a legitimate authority, as a last resort, for a just cause, using proportionate force usually slither over into a no-holds-barred conflict, what Michael Howard calls a *bellum Romanum* or *guerre mortelle* reserved for rebels, "savages," and infidels. Michael Howard, "Constraints on Warfare," in Michael Howard, George J. Andrepoulos, and Mark R. Shulman, eds., *The Laws of War. Constraints on Warfare in the Western World* (New Haven: Yale University Press, 1994), 2–5. Second, the notion of *hors de combat* as defined by Article 3 of the 1949 Geneva Convention are often ignored in counterinsurgency operations where the enemy mingles with the population, so that inflicting collateral damage may lie at the core of a counterinsurgency strategy. This may be especially true if the counterinsurgent forces are too few and/or are under pressure to deliver quick, dramatic results that may tempt them to rely on the indiscriminate application of force—firepower, "sweeps," or "resettlement"—rather than a patient political strategy. Finally, soldiers engaged in counterinsurgency operations assume tasks that break down the boundaries of professional restraint, to include acting as policemen, warders, intelligent collectors, and executioners. As armed representatives of the state acting against an "illegitimate" and "cowardly" enemy, soldiers may feel that they are

permitted any tactic required to restore "legitimate" authority unconstrained by *jus ad bellum* or international law.

6. "The principal purpose of effective civil-military relations is national security; its output is strategy. Democracies tend to forget that. They have come to address civil-military relations not as a means to an end, not as a way of making the state more efficient in its use of military power, but as an end in itself. Instead, the principal objective, to which others become secondary, has been the subordination of the armed forces to civilian control." Strachan, "Making Strategy: Civil-Military Relations After Iraq," *Survival* 48, 3 (Summer 2006): 66.
7. Indeed, the official reference to Colombia's unpleasantness as a "conflicto" perpetrated by "narcoterrorist" grown rich on illicit gringo dollars, rather than a war carried out by an organized insurgency to challenge the legitimacy of the state, is shaped in part by a reluctance to grant to the insurgency de facto belligerent status, and hence concede to them certain prerogatives in international law and diplomacy.
8. The political system remains dominated by the same parties that lack ideological cohesion and are run by local elites. The judicial system remains clogged and ineffective; the problems with guerrillas and paramilitaries persist. Harvey F. Kline, *State Building and Conflict Resolution in Colombia* (Tuscaloosa, AL: University of Alabama Press, 1999), 175–181.
9. "MoD Restructure," CCMR Project Colombia, Bogotá, 1–4 April 2003, 10.
10. Andrés Dávila Ladrón de Guevara. All quotes come from an interview with the author on 30 June 2005, Bogotá.
11. Stephen Dudley, *Walking Ghosts: Murder and Guerilla Politics in Colombia*, (New York: Routledge, 2004), 228.
12. Ladrón de Guevara, "Dime con quien andas," 10.
13. "Colombia: NDI Analysis Finds Parties Lack Credibility, Stability." FBIS LAP20051120004003, 22 November 2005 quoting Article by Juan David Laverde Palma, "Political Parties in Intensive Care," *El Espectador*, 20 November 2005.
14. Ronald Archer and Matthew Shugart, "The Unrealized Potential of Presidential Dominance in Colombia," in Scott Mainwaring and Matthew Shugart, eds., *Presidentialism and Democracy in Latin America* (New York: Cambridge University Press, 1997), 110–159.
15. "The Congress has power," Andrés Dávila Ladrón de Guevara points out. "They can censure the minister of defense, and they vote on all bills promoted by the minister." The Senate must also approve any "state of exception" declared by the president if it runs over ninety days, a measure meant to curtail the president's pre-1991 prerogative to rule on the basis of open-ended "state of siege" decrees. Kline, *State Building and Conflict Resolution in Colombia*, 167.

16. J.M. Eastman, Vice Minister in charge of Budgets, Strategic Planning, U.S.—Colombian relations (Plan Colombia). All quotes are from an interview with the author on 28 June 2005, Bogotá.
17. Samper was continually at loggerheads with his generals over his attempt to trade a demilitarized zone in La Uribe to the FARC in return for the release of captive Colombian soldiers, a project to bring the code of military justice in line with human rights regulations, and the promotions process. Indeed, so unpopular was Samper with the military that rumors of military coups circulated on at least two occasions, while an unprecedented protest of over 200 officers occurred outside the Ministry of Defense when the president dismissed a popular general opposed to negotiations with the FARC. William Avilés, *Globalization, Democracy and Civil-Military Relations,* (Albany, NY: State University of New York Press, 2006), 169–175.
18. Ladrón de Guevara, "Dime con quien andas," 15–16.
19. Darren D. Sprunk, "Transformation in the Developing World: An Analysis of Colombia's Security Transformation," MA Thesis, Naval Postgraduate School, Monterey, California, September 2004, 39–40.
20. "Forward Operation Locations in Latin America: Transcending Drug Control," 8–9. Transnational TNIB Briefing Series no.2003/6, http://www.tni.org/reports/drugs/debate8.pdf.
21. General Richard Goetze. All quotes are from an interview with the author on 21 July 2005, in Monterey, CA.
22. Avilés, *Globalization, Democracy and Civil-Military Relations*, 54.
23. National Security Council mission statement, available at www.whitehouse.gov/nsc/; accessed 21 October 2005.
24. Jaramillo, interview 22 August 2006
25. "Gerentes de la guerra," *La Semana*, 3 June 2006.
26. Lt. Col. Juan-Carlos Gómez Ramirez, Director *Derechos Humanos y Derecho Internacional Humanitario.* [Director of Human Rights and International Humanitarian Law], Ministry of Defense. All quotes come from an interview with the author on 25 June 2005, Bogotá.
27. "MoD Restructure," 10.
28. Mahlstedt, interview 27 June 2006.
29. Ibid. Attempts by Marta Lucia Ramírez to wrest promotion away from the military were scuppered by General Mora. Interview with Admirals Edgar Cely, Vincente Eschandia, and Guillermo Barrera, 30 June 2006.
30. Ibid., 4. When a second vice minister was created, the idea was to divide their tasks between budgetary and technical issues, and international, policy-related issues. "However," says Jaramillo, "What happened was that the new vice-minister simply took over new programs like human rights, kidnapping, demobilization of the AUC (*Autodefensas Unitas de Colombia*—the umbrella organization for the paramilitaries), etc., programs that came out of the new security strategy."

31. Jaramillo, interview 28 June 2005.
32. "MoD Restructure," 5.
33. "Colombia January 2004," Human Rights Watch, Human Rights Overview, available at http://hrw.org/english/docs/2004/01/21/colomb6978.htm; accessed 23 October 2005.
34. "The first goal is legitimacy of the Colombian state. Human rights are part of that," President Uribe's Human Rights director and former guerrilla Carlos Franco asserts. All quotes are from an interview with the author on 23 June 2005 Bogotá.
35. "Human rights are part of the war against impunity," Mauricio Wiesner Acero, International Consultant. All quotes are from an interview with the author on 23 June 2005, Bogotá.
36. Avilés, *Globalization, Democracy and Civil-Military Relations*, 1.
37. "Colombia January 2004."
38. *The "Sixth Division": Military-Paramilitary Ties and U.S. Policy in Colombia* (New York, London, Brussels, Washington: Human Rights Watch, 2001), 87–92; Avilés, *Globalization, Democracy and Civil-Military Relations*, 39, 140–143, 193.
39. Nieto, interview 24 June 2005.
40. Kline, *State Building and Conflict Resolution in Colombia*, 173; Avilés, *Globalization, Democracy and Civil-Military Relations*, 151–157.
41. Ladrón de Guevara, "Dime con quien andas," 9.
42. Valencia Tovar, interview 30 June 2005; Luis Camilo Osorio, attorney general at the time of this interview, was replaced by Deputy Justice Minister Mario Iguarán on 20 July 2005. Osorio was criticized for failing to prosecute military officers accused of collaborating with the *autodefensas*. "World Briefing: Americas," *New York Times*, 21 July 2005, A9.
43. In 2006, a judge allowed a colonel and fourteen soldiers of the *Batallón de Alta Montaña* alleged to have massacred ten policemen who were investigating military involvement in drug dealing to be court martialed rather than tried in a criminal court. *La Semana*, 20 July 2006. www.semana.com. This was later reversed after widespread protests. Joshua Goldman, "Colombian Army Accused of Massacre of Drug Police," *Washington Post*, 18 June 2006. http://www.washingtonpost.com/wp-dyn/content/article/2006/06/17/AR2006061700840.html?nav=rss_print/asection; accesed 18 December 2006.
44. "Colombia January 2004."
45. Avilés, *Globalization, Democracy and Civil-Military Relations*, 214.
46. Alfredo Rangel, Director of Security and Democracy. All quotes from an interview with the author on 28 June 2005, Bogotá.
47. Andrian English, "The Colombian Armed Forces—An Update," Jane's Data Research, *Jane's Intelligence Review* (1 September 1999): 424; Thomas Marks, "Colombian Army Adaptation to FARC Insurgency," Strategic Studies Institute Monograph, U.S. Army War College, Carlisle, PA, 2002, 10.

48. The military budget was still only 2 percent GDP and lagged behind that of Chile, Peru, Honduras, and El Salvador. Avilés, *Globalization, Democracy and Civil-Military Relations*, 147–149.
49. Accusations of drug connections in the Samper administration and accusations of human rights abuses caused Colombia to be decertified in March 1996; it was recertified in 1998. U.S. aid began to flow the following year, but was earmarked for counterdrug operations only. President Clinton's Presidential Defense Directive 73 forbade the use of U.S. intelligence and military assets against insurgents. Henry L. Hinton, "Drug Control: Counternarcotics Efforts in Colombia Face Continuing Challenges," United States General Accounting Office (Testimony Before the Committee on International Relations House of Representatives, 26 February 1998, GAO/T-NSIAD-98-103), 5–6.
50. Draft, MILGP-COL REORGANIZATION PAPER.
51. LTC Carlos Berrios, MILGP Executive Officer, 2 February 2006.
52. For instance, in the 1990s, NAS, which answers to the U.S. State Department, dealt directly with the National Police on antinarcotics programs during the period when the government of President Samper was decertified (placed on Washington's list of countries considered insufficiently cooperative in the "war on drugs"). "Under Clinton, Washington gave money directly to the police," Vice Minister Peñate complained. "Sending money straight to the police weakened MOD oversight."
53. Interview with Admirals Cely, Eschandia, and Barrera, 30 June 2006.
54. Nieto, interview 24 June 2005.
55. Quoted in FBIS, 27 September 2005.
56. "Las FARC—Repliegue por 'estrategia,' o por necesidad," Centro de Analisis Socilpolitico: 3 June 2005, available at http://www.cas.org.co/articulos/articulos/VerArticulo.php?Id=77; and "Situación de los terroristas," 23 August 2005, available at http://www.cas.org.co/articulos/articulos/VerArticulo.php?Id=84; both accessed 23 October 2005.
57. I thank my former student Captain Paul Saskewitz for this observation.
58. Cely, Barrera, Eschandia interview 31 June 06.
59. One result has been an increasing number of soldier and civilian casualties caused by mines. "Objectivo: mutilar" *La Semana*, www.semana.terrra.com.co; accessed 30 November 2005.
60. These mid-tier leaders are regarded as the FARC's critical link, because of their administrative responsibilities, their role in arms smuggling, and other criminal activities, and the power they hold over the largely peasant rank and file. "Colombian Army Increasingly Effective against Middle-Tier FARC Leaders," FBIS LAP20051115347002, 22 November 2005. However, this may prove wishful thinking as the FARC structure allows for rapid promotion to fill vacancies.
61. LTC Berrios, interview 2 February 2006.

62. "Colombia: Presidential Politics and Peace Prospects," International Crisis Group, 16 June 2005, 12. Available at http://www.crisisgroup.org/home/index.cfm?id=3515&l=1; accessed 23 October 2005.
63. Liliana Gabriel, Political Section of U.S. Embassy, Bogotá. Interview conducted, 29 June 2006.
64. Negotiations would allegedly be based on the offer of a new Constituent Assembly, recognition of the FARC as a political entity, a truce, the cessation of a demilitarized zone, and a demobilization law modeled on the *paz y justicia* but tailored for the guerrillas. Alfredo Rangel, "The Thaw," *Cambio*, 3–9 July 2006. FBIS, July 14 2006; Gabriel argues that the FARC dilemma is that they need to deal with a strong president with the popular backing to make a peace agreement stick, but they are reluctant to hand a victory to their arch enemy Uribe, who they do not trust. Liliana Gabriel, Political Section of U.S. Embassy, Bogotá. Interview conducted, 29 June 2006.

7

"From National, Through Regional, to Universal . . . .": Security and Defense Reform in Romania

Liviu Muresan and Marian Zulean

Introduction

Outside observers of Romanian defense reform efforts after 1989 would be astonished by the dramatic nature and pace of transformation in Romanian institutions. Before 1989, Romania was considered a "maverick" Communist country, a member of the Warsaw Pact ruled by one of the fiercest dictatorial regimes in Eastern Europe. The regime of President Nicolae Ceausescu promulgated a well-defined defense doctrine grounded in "the struggle of the entire people"; Romania maintained a mass army of about 300,000 soldiers (with the potential to mobilize up to 900,000, out of a population of twenty-three million), and a well-developed national defense industry. Moreover, the Department of State Security (known as the Securitate) exercised a sort of subjective civilian control over the military, ensuring its ideological compatibility with ruling elites.

Today, Romania is a NATO member as well as a member of the European Union; the Romanian military consists of a flexible force of 75,000 soldiers, and makes an active contribution to international security through its peacekeeping troops, who are spread from Iraq and Afghanistan to the Balkans. The pace of reform in the country's security sector following the dissolution of the Warsaw Pact was dramatic not only in terms of downsizing the military and setting up a mechanism for democratic control of the security forces, but also in terms of strategic thinking. The global determinants of change identified in this volume influenced the countries that represented a model for democratic Romania, making the objectives sought in the defense reform process a moving target.

The main goal of this chapter is to describe the way security sector reform has been accomplished in Romania, and to explain how the process of building a democratic civil-military relations model was influenced by globalization, democratic reform, economic liberalization, and technological change. The first part of the chapter will present the stages Romania went through to set up a democratic civil-military structure. The second part will explore the factors that influenced the reform process, while the third part will describe the interplay of global factors in Romania's experience and outcomes.

From Warsaw to Brussels: Three Generations of Reforms

Romania is one of the former Warsaw Pact countries that was able to successfully transform its defense and security establishments, and within fifteen years become a NATO member. Democratization of civil-military relations was a fundamental aspect of the overall reform process, not only in Romania but in all of Eastern Europe. In the early 1990s, at a conference on civil-military relations, Joseph Nye proposed a civil-military pattern drawn from Samuel Huntington's theoretical model of "objective civilian control":

> The military must recognize that 1) armed forces are accountable to the rule of law and obliged to respect civilian authority and that 2) armed forces are nonpartisan and remain above politics. Civilians are required to 1) recognize that armed forces are legitimate tools of democratic states; 2) fund and respect properly developed military roles and missions; and 3) educate themselves about defense issues and military culture.[1]

Such recommendations were important for the policymakers who created cooperative regional institutions such as the Partnership for Peace (PfP), or special norms on democratic civil-military relations (e.g., the Organization for Security and Cooperation in Europe [OSCE] Code of Conduct). One of the main components of Huntington's theory, however, is the identification of two forces that shape every society's particular military institutions: "...a functional imperative which depends on the threats to the society's security and a societal imperative coming from dominant social forces, ideologies and institutions in society."[2] But Huntington's theory was mostly based on the assumption that the social imperatives were constant (drawn from the U.S. experience), and that the external threats alone could explain the evolution of a given state's civil-military relations.

This argument does not do an adequate job of explaining the complex transitions in Eastern Europe, where social imperatives (ideologies and institutions) were characterized by dynamic change over a brief period, with serious impacts on the structures and relationships specific to civil-military relations. Therefore, the next section will describe the dynamics of Romania's defense and security reform that took place in three stages, with the focus on the development of democratic mechanisms for civil-military relations.

First Generation Reforms: Focusing on Defense Restructuring (1990–1996)

In order to better understand the dynamics of defense reform it is necessary to introduce briefly the legacy factor. Historical legacies matter everywhere, and certainly in Eastern Europe. The ethnopolitical conflicts of the 1990s in the former Yugoslavia are clear proof of that. Despite the dictatorial Communist regime that ruled it for over four decades, Romania does not have a tradition of militarism. A regular army was established only in the third quarter of the nineteenth century. Civilian control was embedded in the Romanian constitutions of 1866 and 1923, and this pattern of civilian rule persisted until World War II.

In 1948, with help from Moscow, the Romanian Communist Party established the Romanian People's Republic under a Soviet-style constitution, and dismantled the royalist professional military. Members of the Communist Party with working-class backgrounds replaced the professional officers. After engineering his takeover of the government in 1965, First Party Secretary Nicolae Ceausescu adopted a more independent security policy within the Warsaw Pact, but tightened his own grip on the country with the help of the Securitate. During this period, military doctrine shifted to a more "national" orientation ("the struggle of the entire people") because the Communist ideology alone did not produce enough support and he feared Soviet military intervention.

Under Ceausescu's tight control, the military lost its power and influence. Although the conscript army was at the core of defense policy, many officers and soldiers also worked in agriculture and industry. In addition, officers' promotions were based on favoritism and the individual's degree of involvement in Communist politics, as much as on professional merit. These policies led to a deprofessionalization of the military.

After the end of communist rule in 1989, the major issues in reforming the defense system and setting up democratic civil-military relations were: 1) The need to reinvent the democratic tradition and establishing Western-type democratic norms; 2) a weak civil society and a lack of civilians with security expertise; 3) an oversized and mostly deprofessionalized military; and 4) a need to reform the security sector as a whole, to include police and intelligence services.

The Romanian Revolution of 1989 disrupted and dismantled the structures of the authoritarian security sector and put the military in the spotlight of the reform process. General Niculae Spiroiu, minister of defense in 1991, stated that his role was to prepare a framework for civilian control, and to hand the power to a civilian minister. Nevertheless, a systematic approach to security and defense reform captured the attention of policymakers only in the late 1990s. The undertaking was encouraged by several elements related to both democratization and globalization. First, Romania always perceived itself as different from its neighbors and Moscow, a "Latin Island within a Slavic Sea," and it sought to reestablish connections to a wider world. Second, Romania was keen to depart from the Soviet/Russian sphere of influence and establish closer relations with the West. Third, aware of the dangerous neighborhood in the Balkans and the Black Sea region, Romania was eager to enhance its security through integration into the full Euro-Atlantic set of alliances. International organizations such as NATO, the European Union, and the OSCE, each interested in its own way in promoting democratization and a shared understanding of security sector reform, played a critical part in supporting, advising, and directing Romania's reform efforts, and continue to do so today.

The first stages of reform (1990–1992) focused on the de-Communization and downsizing of the armed forces. This included the transfer of the Securitate to the control of the ministry of defense, and the withdrawal of the military from its role as free labor in state industries. An external requirement that supported the downsizing and reform effort was the Conventional Forces in Europe Treaty (CFE), signed in 1990, which mandated reductions in numbers of armaments and troops.

The Action Committee for Democratization of the Army also played a role in initiating changes. The first democratic government made a notable contribution toward setting up democratic civil control by establishing the Country's Supreme Council for Defense (CSAT), whose purpose is to coordinate planning and executive actions in situations of crisis. In addition, Romania adopted a new constitution and National Defense Law in 1991 that, alongside other legislation, paved the way toward democratic civilian control of the security and defense sectors and the armed forces. Legislators created special parliamentary committees to deal with control and oversight of the military and security institutions with the view of ensuring transparency.

During this period, the military sector opened its doors to civilians. The National College of Defense began accepting civilian students in 1992, and the first civilian (Liviu Muresan) was nominated as its deputy director. Ioan Mircea Pascu became the first civilian deputy minister of defense, followed by the appointment of Ambassador Gheorghe Tinca as the first civilian minister of defense. The state's military institutions in general increased the numbers of civilian personnel they employed.

Romania became the first Eastern European country to sign the Partnership for Peace Framework Document, in 1994. Following PfP accession, Romania's leaders adopted restructuring plans and international interoperability programs (known as the Planning and Review Process), as tools to identify and assess forces and capabilities for multinational training, exercises and operations in collaboration with NATO forces, with the ultimate goal of giving the armed forces a more international orientation. Moreover, in 1994 Romania adopted the OSCE's Code of Conduct, including a separate chapter that dealt with civilian control of the armed forces.

Second Generation Reforms: "Targeting" NATO (1997–2004)

This next generation of reforms was marked by Romania's effort to join NATO and by the 9/11 terrorist attacks. After the disappointment of the 1997 NATO Summit in Madrid, at which Romania was not invited to become a NATO member, the process of reform did not stop. Under the leadership of General Constantin Degeratu, the General Staff made substantial improvements to the defense planning process and to the system of military education. The Concept of Human Resource Management, created in 1997, established a National Defense Framework Action Plan for 2000–2003, and a

Long-Term Framework to 2010. The plans drawn up by the Romanian Ministry of National Defense, with foreign assistance, identified three force structure options for the Romanian armed forces, of which the middle option, comprising 112,000 servicemen and 28,000 civilians, emerged as the ideal size for Romania's national defense.[3]

The Romanian Ministry of National Defense reorganized in May 1997, with changes that affected both central structures and combat forces. The priorities were to improve personnel management, upgrade national C3I (command, control, communications, and intelligence) systems, enhance air defense capabilities, and upgrade general infrastructure with an eye toward facilitating the operation of NATO forces on Romanian territory.

After 1999, NATO stepped up its programs for security assistance to former Warsaw Pact states, and began a serious diplomatic effort to groom potential new members. An important moment at this stage was the so-called Washington Summit in April 1999, from which came the proposal to prepare NATO candidates on the basis of Membership Action Plans (MAPs). Up to this time the agenda of reforms focused on the armed forces, and included divesting responsibility for component structures and troops such as the Border Guards and defense industries to other agencies. At the same time, the intelligence agencies, defense industries, and Ministry of Interior had been following parallel tracks of reform, albeit at a slower pace. The new instrument, the MAP, now brought all of these issues into the spotlight.

The NATO Summit held in Prague in 2002, at which Romania was formally invited to become a member, acted as an important stimulus for continuing the reforms. The Romanian government took coherent measures toward fulfilling the MAP, including improvements in civilian democratic control. The Prague Summit was a turning point for the security and defense reformers. This invitation allowed them to pursue an accelerated path of reform with an agenda that included good governance, measurements of efficiency for institutions, adoption of the "Project Force-2007" concept with a new force structure of 90,000, and the modernization and procurement of equipment compatible with that of other NATO members.

Third Generation Reforms: Security and Defense Transformation

The new security environment shaped by 9/11 and its aftermath, as well as the new status of Romania as a full member of NATO (since 2004) and the EU (since January 2007), instigated a systematic transformation of the security sector as part of the third generation of reforms. This concept of comprehensive security sector reform, common in Europe but not in the United States, and important for both democratization and globalization in Romania, deserves further explanation.

Security sector reform as policy became prominent only recently in Europe; it first appeared in the programs of institutions such as NATO, the Organization for Economic Cooperation and Development, the UN and the EU, from think tanks such as the Geneva Center for the Democratic Control of Armed Forces (DCAF) and the Center for European Security Studies in the Netherlands. According to Ambassador Theodor Winkler at DCAF, security sector reform is composed of five elements: 1) reforms are guided by the political leadership in accordance with democratic principles; 2) the starting point is a broad view of the term "security"; 3) reform encompasses all security services; 4) security sector reform is a process; 5) reform focuses not only on structures but also on human resources.[4]

Despite the fact that 9/11 brought a new global security landscape into focus, and Romania made the decision to participate in what was being called a "global war on terror," defense reform continued to follow the established pattern until 2004, and it was geared toward the goal of NATO membership. By contrast, security sector reform as a policy became important only after membership was assured. A new National Security Strategy proposed in April 2006 not only set forth a new role for Romania as a global actor that is committed to the war on terror, but also included clear proposals for security sector transformation and good governance. The reform and transformation efforts take into account Bucharest's need to foster international cooperation to better counter the new security challenges. To facilitate these activities, Romania has been working to harmonize its legislation with that of the European Union and NATO countries. In the defense sector itself, the General Staff recently proposed a "Strategy of Transformation" that committed the Romanian army to: 1) fulfill its commitments within NATO; 2) participate in EU missions; 3) revamp the leadership, logistics, and C4I2SR systems; 4) modernize human resource management; 5) improve the quality of life for members of the armed forces; 6) redesign military education; 7) optimize the planning, programming, budgeting and evaluation system; and 8) reorganize military intelligence.[5]

Assessing Democratic Civil-Military Relations

The previous section presented the dynamics of the general process of defense and security sector reform. One priority of the reform process was to establish a democratic pattern of civil-military relations. According to Bruneau and Trinkunas in the introduction to this book, the best way to understand defense reform and the global determinants of reform is to disaggregate the dependent variable of democratic civil-military relations into a trinity—democratic civilian control, military effectiveness, and defense efficiency—and look for the influences that shaped their development. The next section will explore this question with regard to Romania's armed forces.

Civilian Control in Theory and in Practice

Democratic civilian control became a buzzword for the academics and analysts dealing with defense reform in Eastern Europe following the demise of the Warsaw Pact. The establishment of democratic civilian control over the military was demanded both by the public, during the "bloody" revolution in 1989, and by international institutions anxious to see Romania adopt democratic norms.

Democratic control of the Romanian armed forces was codified in the new constitution, and the laws on national defense and security. Romania's Constitution (ratified in 2003) stipulates that the military be subordinated exclusively to the people's will, in order to guarantee the country's sovereignty, independence, territorial integrity, and constitutional democracy. According to the Constitution, all three branches of government (executive, legislative, and judiciary) have responsibilities in the monitoring and oversight of the defense sector.

Among all the mechanisms for democratic control, Parliament's role is the most complex because legislators issue laws on national defense and security; approve public officials nominated for office; carry out interpellation, hearings, and investigations; approve and oversee the budget; grant overflight rights to foreign aircraft; and approve military deployments abroad. Parliament exerts its oversight authority by receiving reports on the military's programs and activities and, through the mediation of its commissions for defense, on public order and national security. These commissions play an important role in promoting laws on national defense and security, and in the approval of the defense budget. Parliament also has the authority to bring before it government officials, including the minister of defense, to answer specific questions regarding Romania's national security. Defense expenditures are transparent to the democratically elected public authorities, including Parliament. The activities of the intelligence services are regulated on the legislative level by the defense committees, but actual control is exercised by the special commissions for democratic oversight of the Romanian Intelligence Service and Foreign Intelligence Service. One of the strengths of the Romanian Parliament is its power of investigation, which it exercises through special committees selected to solve issues pertaining to national security and safety.

The most important mechanism of control is that of budgetary allocations, including the planning, budgeting, and acquisition system. Since 2001, a new system of planning, programming, budgeting, and evaluation has been implemented and the task of integrated defense planning was placed completely under the control of the civilian minister. The defense budget is public and subject to internal audit, as well as to the oversight of other institutions, such as the minister of finance, parliamentary commissions, or the judiciary.

Executive control is exercised through the CSAT, which organizes and coordinates all activities related to national defense and security. The nation's president represents the Romanian state, is the supreme commander of the armed forces, and serves as president of CSAT, a position that confers on him major influence over issues of national security. Decisions within this agency are consensually taken by a group of ten persons led by the president. Modifications to CSAT's structure since the end of the dictatorship reflect the dynamics of "civilian control." In 1990 CSAT included only five civilians out of the ten members; since 1997 the chief of the General Staff has been the only military officer to sit on the Council. The other members include the national security adviser and the two directors of the Romanian intelligence services (which are known by the acronyms SRI and SIE), who are directly accountable to the president; the chief of the General Staff, who is indirectly accountable to the president as supreme commander; and five ministers in the executive branch. The prime minister is the vice president of CSAT and the chief of civil protection. He leads the government's executive activity and implements defense policy, through the mediation of the minister of defense. The General Staff is part of the Ministry of Defense and is subordinate to the civilian minister.

The judiciary also plays an important part in the control of the military. The Constitutional Court guarantees the supremacy of the Constitution and treats the army as any other institution, verifying the constitutionality of the normative documents related to defense. The Accounting Court is responsible for controlling the spending of public money, while the office of the Ombudsman defends citizens' rights and liberties.

Another important aspect of democratic civilian control is transparency. Independent media, nongovernmental organizations, and independent think tanks help inform and educate civil society on issues of security. There are a quite a few foundations that are very active in the field of security policy, such as the EURISC Foundation, the Manfred Wörner Euro-Atlantic Association, the George C. Marshall-Romania Association, and "Casa NATO."[6] Throughout the years since the revolution of 1989, the mass media have acted as a genuine watchdog of democracy, considered to be the fourth power within the state. The adoption of Law no. 544/2001 on free access to information in the public interest contributed decisively to the consolidation of civil democratic oversight.

The Ombudsman exercises a certain amount of oversight and control as an advocate for the interests of the public, by investigating complaints reported by citizens. Governmental institutions impose internal controls by undertaking to investigate and assess their own activities. In addition to these domestic institutions, the European Court of Human Rights represents another external oversight mechanism, particularly in the field of intelligence. Despite these mechanisms, it remains difficult to make a reliable assessment of civilian control in practice. Two analyses described below, one based on a study of a crisis situation and the other a monitoring exercise, attempt to address this question.

Marian Zulean examined a domestic crisis that occurred in early 1999 in an effort to evaluate how well Romania's democratic institutions of civilian control actually work when put to the test.[7] The crisis arose from a coal miners' strike, whose leaders intended to force a change of government. When the government started a radical program of reforms in the mine industry that included a number of mine closures, a group of miners calling themselves the "Jiu Valley League" started a general strike, asking for pay raises and the exception of some mines from the closure programs. The government did not approve the requests and asked the Ministry of the Interior to take legal measures to defend the public order. But the well-organized coal miners started marching toward Bucharest, defeated the police and gendarmerie in skirmishes, threatened the capital, and clamored for a change of parliament and the presidency.

In response to that situation, on 21 January 1999, CSAT held an emergency meeting and urged the government immediately to adopt an ordinance that would define and regulate conditions under a state of siege and a state of emergency. Under these conditions the president of Romania was empowered to declare a state of siege; he asked General Degeratu to prepare a strategy to reestablish public order. After the resolution of the crisis, various actors drew conclusions that are relevant for civil-military relations. The former prime minister, Radu Vasile, accused the gendarmerie troops of nonprofessionalism. The media published a report by the General Staff that concluded that the mechanisms of democracy worked, but condemned the lack of swift decisions at the political level, and the tactical mistakes and confused strategy of the Ministry of the Interior.[8] It went on to propose that the government finalize the legislative framework to deal with emergency situations, prepare a crisis management system, and allocate the financial resources for response training. The main conclusion from this crisis is that, although the general norms of democratic control of the security sector were in place, the effectiveness of mechanisms of operational control varied among the branches of the security sector.

Also, certain civil society and state institutions worked cooperatively to monitor parliamentary oversight of the security sector, in order to evaluate how well the democratic mechanisms worked. In 2004, the EURISC Foundation took the initiative and, together with the Committee for Defense, Public Order and National Security of the House of Deputies, developed a monitoring exercise entitled "Instruments and Mechanisms for Parliamentary Oversight of the Security Sector in Romania." The participants in the monitoring exercise included the coordinators, Razvan Ionescu and Liviu Muresan, and a team of experts from the Romanian Parliament, as well as experts from various agencies and NGOs.

The final report of this exercise highlighted that the most frequently used instruments of control were the questions and interpellations by members of Parliament. The intelligence services, the Ministry of National Defense, and the Ministry of the Interior are the institutions in the security sector that are subjected to the most frequent questioning. The ability of the Romanian Parliament to monitor budgetary execution, the report found, was limited by the complexity of the defense planning process.[9]

The report also highlighted the reality that parliamentary oversight was confronted with a new challenge to its mandated control over the missions of the armed forces. Since peacekeeping operations became one of the most important missions of the Romanian armed forces, the decision whether to deploy had become a political one. Prior to Law no. 42/2004 on the participation of the armed forces in missions outside the country, Parliament had the final say concerning deployment of the army in international operations. According to the new law, the president of the country now has this authority. He or she approves the participation of the military in collective defense, peace support operations, humanitarian assistance, and coalition military operations, and must inform the Parliament only *after* the decisions are taken. The *prior* approval of Parliament is necessary only for operations of peace support and coalition military operations that do not occur within the framework of any international treaties signed by Romania.

Finally, the institutions subject to parliamentary oversight consider that such scrutiny had a positive effect on their activity by improving their public image and enhancing the transparency of their functions, and has thereby brought them some extra credibility. Obviously, the enforcement of Law no. 544/2001 on free access to information in the public interest has greatly contributed to this openness, not least because it led to the creation of a special department for public relations in most of the organizations visited.

In conclusion, it is apparent that the establishment of democratic mechanisms for civilian control has been the focus of defense reform after 1990. It has been a long process that occurred in at least three waves, the establishment of legal norms being the easiest part. Some problems have come to light recently, however, regarding too much focus on civilian control over the armed forces, and too little on the intelligence agencies. The errors arose from a misunderstanding by Western donors, who assumed that a sort of control had previously been exercised by the Communist Party and Securitate, and with the dissolution of these institutions, the intelligence services were not the most pressing issue facing Romania's new democracy. The extension of reform to the whole security sector was a necessary correction.

Military Effectiveness and Efficiency

Although they are important aspects of democratic civil-military relations, both military effectiveness and efficiency are issues that cannot be accurately assessed by civil society. The traditional measure of military effectiveness comes in time of war, but today, when the risk of classical war is less probable, evaluations are done either by internal audit, by the Parliament's Defense Commissions or by the expert NATO teams that determined Romania's readiness to join NATO. These evaluations suggest that the military's general mission to defend the country's sovereignty while transforming itself to deal with new threats and join NATO was a success. This section will describe in more detail the transformation of roles, missions, structures, training, and education within the defense and security sectors.

During the Communist period, Romania's military had a relatively well-structured defense policy, clear missions, specific training, and clear responsibilities for a classical total war. Thus, the main task of the political and military elite after 1989 was to replace the authoritarian model of defense with a democratic one. In accordance with the first post-Communist constitution (1991), the role of the Romanian armed forces was defined as "guaranteeing the state's sovereignty, independence, territorial integrity and its constitutional democracy."

Until 1994, when Romania applied for membership in NATO's Partnership for Peace, both the military and political establishments had been working to develop new strategic concepts and military doctrines. Clear and comprehensive definitions of security and sound mechanisms for defense planning, however, were drafted only in the late 1990s, and then with critical help from the United Kingdom, the United States, and a few other NATO countries. The first debate on a national security concept was launched in the early 1990s, but the lack of security guarantees from the West during the Balkan and Trans-Dniester crises during this period led planners to identify hundreds of threats to Romania's security and make somewhat panicky proposals for a "circular," siege-style defense. The first National Security Strategy was formulated only in June 1999, while a second one was issued in December 2001. Their general objectives were to preserve the state's independence, sovereignty, and territorial integrity, and to guarantee the constitutional order.

More recently in 2005, President Traian Basescu issued a new National Security Strategy that not only proposes a classical guideline for national security and a "pragmatic and realist" strategic vision, but also aims to systematically transform the elements of Romanian power. The main missions include participation in global security efforts; constructing a new European and Euro-Atlantic identity for Romania; a new approach to regional security that focuses on the

Black Sea area; building a homeland security system; providing good governance; strengthening the national economy; reforming the security sector; and modernizing critical infrastructure.[10]

The main goal of structural defense reform has been to create a compact, flexible NATO-compatible military that is able to provide adequately for the security of the Romanian people. The need for interoperability with NATO within the framework of the PfP has also fostered new goals and strategies for defense reform beyond the classical concept of the security sector, and comprised even such issues as human rights. Since 1999, the MAP has helped to push Romanian military reform toward power projection, and created a consistent, clear, and comprehensive approach to security and defense reform across the entire sector.

By contrast, the reorganization of the intelligence agencies started with the Revolution of 1989 and was monitored by Parliament, CSAT, and the executive branch. Although the legislative framework for the functioning and control of these agencies was put into place very early, the mechanism by which control actually functions remains poorly studied. After Romania began membership negotiations with the EU, the spotlight moved toward other security sectors such as the Ministry of Interior, where problems included border control, demilitarization of the ministry, and anticorruption measures. This asymmetrical focus is also explained in part by the lack of knowledge and divergent interest of the Western donors.

According to the law, today the main missions of the armed forces are to: 1) contribute to Romania's security; 2) defend Romania and its allies; 3) promote regional stability through defense diplomacy; and 4) assist other agencies in civil emergencies and crises. Likewise, the principal missions of the intelligence services are to: 1) defend Romania as a sovereign, unitary, and indivisible state; 2) consolidate public order; and 3) guarantee the fundamental rights and liberties of citizens.[11]

The Concept of Human Resource Management, initially created in 1997, provided the tools to streamline the top-heavy officer corps, and specifically addressed education and training for officers and troops. This was followed by a National Defense Framework Action Plan for 2000–2003 and a Long-Term Framework to 2010. The general goal of these various reforms was to restructure, streamline, and professionalize the personnel side of the defense structure, while procurement and investment were postponed until after 2005, when Romania would be a NATO member.

A key aspect of the new training and education policies was the establishment of the National Defense College and National Intelligence Academy, the former for military officers and the latter for intelligence professionals. These two educational institutions are managed under dual authorities. The National Defense College functions in the framework of the Ministry of Defense and the National Intelligence Academy is under the guidance and control of the SRI; curricula and educational standards for both institutions, however, are under the guidance of the unambiguously civilian Ministry of Education and Research.

An important aspect of the Romanian government's efforts to establish Romania's new orientation as a security provider has been the adoption of peace support operations (PSOs) as new missions. According to chief of General the Staff General Bădălan, in 2006 Romania deployed more than 2,300 soldiers abroad (out of a total strength of 75,000) in the Balkans, Afghanistan, and Iraq. Among them, 838 are deployed under the NATO flag, 122 under EU crisis management operations such as EUFOR-Althea in Bosnia-Herzegovina, and 1316 as "coalition of the willing" participants in Iraq.[12] Following the 11 September attacks, on 21 December 2001, Romania's Parliament approved the participation of military personnel and equipment in NATO's International Security Assistance Force mission to Afghanistan. On 30 April 2002, Parliament also approved the deployment of more troops to Afghanistan as part of the U.S.-led Operation Enduring Freedom.

The other important aspect of democratic civil-military relations, defense efficiency, concerns whether the military is able to accomplish its missions at a cost acceptable to society. The factor that initially most influenced military efficiency was the country's dramatic economic downturn after 1989.[13] The decreasing GDP created pressure for a more rational allocation of resources, including military spending. Following the violent fall of the Ceausescu regime in 1989, Romania faced some of the worst conditions among the transition economies of the former Soviet bloc. In addition to all the well-known market distortions and structural problems common to all transition countries, the legacy of Ceausescu's highly personalized rule was a bureaucracy that was insecure, politicized, and prone to corruption. The World Bank estimated that GDP dropped constantly from 1989, and recovered only after 2000. Not until 2004 did per capita income return to its 1989–1990 level.[14]

The legitimacy of the military as an institution is widely supported by the Romanian public. In regular polling, the armed forces have always been ranked as the second most-popular public institution, with about 70 to 80 percent support. To determine legitimacy and efficiency beyond this overall approval, it is necessary to measure the degree to which civilians and military personnel agree on the roles and missions of the military. To accomplish this, researchers conducted a study in 2005, within the framework of the European Research Group on the Military and Society (ERGOMAS) that tried to determine whether a civil-military cultural gap exists.[15] Despite some statistically significant differences of opinion on such issues as "defending the country," "sending troops abroad," and "peacekeeping operations" between the cadets and civilian students who took part in the poll, both groups gave very strong support for such new missions as "fighting terrorism" and "combating WMD."

Military effectiveness and military efficiency can be seen to be part of the broader process of building democratic civil-military relations. The ability of the Romanian armed forces to participate successfully in overseas missions and retain strong public support at the same time is indicative that they are viewed as effective and efficient, despite some disagreements over the specific nature of the missions. A strong push for these changes came from the Romanian public and policymakers, but success was determined by the guidance, norms, and assistance provided by Western institutions such as the OSCE, NATO, and the EU. The next section will explore what kinds of global factors most influenced the reform process.

Global Determinants of Defense and Security Sector Reform

From the above discussion, it is clear that defense and security sector reforms in Romania have been influenced by a complex set of global factors, such as globalization, democratization, economic liberalization, and, to a lesser extent, the RMA. Although common to defense reform in other countries as well, these factors should not be seen as separate, independent variables that act autonomously from one another, but rather as an interdependent mix of influences. Domestic factors such as historical legacy, public opinion, and demographic trends also make their contribution to defense reform, but they too are influenced by global trends.

Globalization was the "total social fact" that not only redefined the concept of security but also brought both new threats and new opportunities for cooperation. Here globalization is defined in the broader sense of growing international economic, cultural, and social activity; enhanced interdependence; and both greater vulnerabilities and opportunities for cooperation. For Romania, after the Communist experience and Ceausescu's repressive dictatorship, the influence of globalization was a real challenge. Democratization and economic liberalization were additional factors, favored by the norms of globalization, that contributed to the radical transformation of Romanian society, as well as to the particular process of building democratic civil-military relations. Gradual progress toward democratization and economic liberalization began immediately after 1990 and accelerated when Romania was invited to start negotiations to join NATO and the EU. Even though some academics question whether democratization and economic liberalization are "global" phenomena, or consider them to be a "McDonaldization" process, the reality in Central and Eastern Europe is that these factors acted as a package to promote change. The general norms for defense reform were internalized due to the open-door policies of both NATO and the EU.

Globalization was the force that opened Romanian society, favored the importation of democratic norms, and contributed to the liberalization of the economy. The consultancy firm A.T. Kearney and *Foreign Policy* magazine recently published their fifth annual "Globalization Index," which compiles and analyzes various data to measure the degree to which states' economies and political systems are integrated into the global system.[16] To understand the progress Romania has made, consider that in 1989 it was one of the world's least globalized countries, alongside Albania and Cuba; in 2005 it ranked thirty-fifth overall out of sixty-two countries, and at the top in its willingness to support international treaties.

The *Bertelsmann Transformation Index* uses a more complex set of data to assess the political management of change in developing countries on the path to democracy and a market-based economy.[17] In the 2006 BT Index category for degree of market-based democracy, Romania ranks nineteenth out of 119 countries, at the high end of the cluster of countries with "Good prospects for consolidation of a market-based democracy"; in the category for management of change by political decision makers, Romania ranks twenty-fourth, near the top of the "Successful management with weaknesses" cluster.

The most obvious factor for Romania's transition toward globalization, economic liberalization, and democratization has been the role of Western assistance in setting up a democratic civil-military model. Globalization not only brought some new security threats, but also offered means to combat them collectively within alliances such as NATO. Moreover, NATO and the EU offered a set of norms for defense reform and new military missions and practices, and assistance to implement them.

In order to realize defense and security sector reform, Romania benefited from many multilateral and bilateral assistance programs, for both military and civil society.[18] At the bilateral level, the most important donor was the United States through its military-to-military, International Military Education and Training (IMET) and Foreign Military Funding (FMF) programs. Another important project that helped Romania to prepare personnel for PSOs was the British-sponsored Regional Centre for Partnership for Peace Training.

At the multilateral level, the Partnership for Peace programs helped Romania prepare its military for PSOs and become interoperable with NATO, through the Planning and Review Process. The European Union provided resources to further facilitate security sector reform. There were also some regional cooperative security projects that helped promote the reforms. Among these, the Regional Center for Combating Trans-border Crime in Bucharest, with the cooperation of twelve former Soviet-bloc states plus fifteen observers, has gained increasing importance and recognition since 9/11 for its work targeting the nexus of transnational organized crime and terrorism, and asymmetric threats in general. This regional emphasis on working together with international institutions to address new threats also served to prevent the reemergence of old traditional views on defense that focused on the military capabilities of neighboring states.

Although the OSCE Code of Conduct (1994) set the norms for democratic control of the armed forces in Eastern Europe and Central Asia alike, only the ten former Soviet countries of Eastern Europe eventually were admitted to NATO. They were considered "graduates" because their reforms had been monitored and evaluated for effectiveness and efficiency under the MAPs. If NATO had not created the PfP and developed MAP conditionality, Romania likely would still be struggling today to adapt the Cold War concept of "war of the entire people" to a new regional reality.

Economic liberalization not only created the conditions needed for privatization and the integration of new technology, but also pressed the politicians to allocate resources in a rational way, and the Romanian public to realize that the most rational defense is to join a democratic alliance. Defense efficiency and effectiveness were promoted not only due to World Bank conditionality and budget scarcity, but also through new tools of resource allocation promoted by NATO, such as the "planning, programming, budgeting and evaluation" or PPBES system.

The revolution in military affairs is considered an answer to today's security challenges and the harbinger of future development. The introduction of new concepts and methodologies such as network-based defense and the national security network are setting new standards not only at the technological level but also for new ways of thinking. Nevertheless, the RMA was the least influential factor for defense reform in Romania. The principal reason was the way reform planning was done, as "restructuring first," investing in manpower and leaving the procurement and development side to last. Furthermore, the new missions, such as PSOs, were not terribly demanding regarding the standards of RMA, although Romania's peacekeeping troops amazed even some NATO members with the efficiency of its troop transport in operations abroad, using a "second-hand" C-130 Hercules fleet.

Globalization, democratization, and economic liberalization clearly are the main global factors that influenced defense and security sector reform in Romania after 1989. Although in the short run the economic liberalization that led to declines in defense spending appeared to be an obstacle to defense effectiveness, it is evident that these cuts promoted defense efficiency and defense effectiveness in the long run, and made an important contribution toward building democratic civil-military relations.

CONCLUSION

Romania has established both the constitutional provisions and broader legal framework for democratic control of the security and defense sectors. New missions and new defense planning mechanisms allow a yearly critical assessment of defense policy. The most important factors in democratic civilian control are those of budget allocation and transparency. Looking at the reform process, one can see that reforms were initiated by internal demands, while supported and guided by external factors (the Conventional Forces in Europe Treaty, the OSCE Code of Conduct, the PfP Framework Document, and NATO's MAP). The MAP and Western assistance brought more clarity to Romania's defense policy and reform, which led to the invitation to join NATO at the Prague Summit in November 2002.

Recent trends in security policy, such as the new National Security Strategy, set specific goals for transformation of the security sector, with intelligence reform in particular being brought into the spotlight. The creation of an intelligence community, already foreseen by the new Strategy, will increase oversight in the intelligence services. This intelligence community would help coordinate the activity of other specialized departments located in different ministries, and promote efficiency in the intelligence establishment. Furthermore, the intelligence community could compile information on all intelligence activities into reports, including recommendations and proposals for action, for the Supreme Council for National Defense.

Security sector reform in Romania is more than a summing up of reform's successes and failures in each individual component of the security sector; rather it is part of the "grand design" that includes reform of the whole society, and reflects the country's general progress toward integration into NATO and the EU. Defense and security sector reform in Romania are a success story. The saying by Nicolae Titulescu used in the title of this chapter represents the way Romanian defense and security policy has developed over time, from a nationalistic autarchy to a regional player with global aspirations, within the framework of the NATO team. The success of defense reform is due to a set of global factors, such as globalization, economic liberalization, and democratization, which were reinforced by a domestic political will.

NOTES

1. Joseph Nye, "Epilogue: The Liberal Tradition," in Larry Diamond and Marc Plattner, eds. *Civil-Military Relations and Democracy* (Baltimore, MD: The Johns Hopkins University Press, 1996), 153. The work Nye based his comment on is Samuel P. Huntington, *The Soldier and the State* (New York: Vintage Books, 1957).
2. See Huntington, *The Soldier and the State*, 2.
3. For more on Romania's defense reform and strategic plans, see Marian Zulean, "Professionalisation of the Romanian Armed Forces," in A. Forester, T. Edmunds, and A. Cottey, eds., *Transforming the Post-Communist Military* (Basingstoke: Palgrave Publishing, 2001), 115–133; and George Maior, "Personnel Management and Reconversion," in Larry Watts, ed., *Romanian Military Reform and NATO Integration* (Bucharest: Center for Romanian Studies, 2002), 57–81.
4. See Theodore Winkler, "Managing Change: Reform and Democratic Control of the Security Sector and International Order," in Alan Bryden

and Philipp H. Fluri, eds., *Security Sector Reform: Institutions, Society and Good Governance* (Baden-Baden: Nomos, 2003), 13–41.

5. C4I2SR—Command, Control, Communications, Computer, Information, Intelligence, Surveillance, and Reconnaissance. For more on the Strategy for Transformation, see "Strategia de transformare a Armatei României," Ministerul Apărării Naţionale, Bucharest 2005, available at: http://www.mapn.ro/strategie_transformare.doc; accessed 30 August 2006.
6. For more on NGOs and media activity, see Liviu Muresan, "Institutes, Media, Information Policy and Civil Society," in Jan A. Trapans and Philipp H. Fluri, eds., *Defense and Security Sector Governance and Reform in South East Europe: Insights and Perspectives*, vol. 2 (Geneva: Geneva Center for the Democratic Control of Armed Forces [DCAF], 2003), 393–402.
7. See Marian Zulean, *Armata si Societatea in Tranzitie* (Bucharest: Tritonic Publishing House, 2003), 75–81.
8. See the editorial "Raportul SMG prezentat CSAT," *Adevarul* no. 2698, 6 February 1999.
9. Razvan Ionescu and Liviu Muresan, "Monitoring Exercise of Instruments and Mechanisms for Parliamentary Oversight of the Security Sector in Romania," pilot project of the EURISC Foundation; the Commission for Defense, Public Order and National Security of the House of Deputies, Parliament of Romania; and with the support of DCAF, Bucharest, Romania, 2004, 34–40.
10. See "Strategia de Securitate Naţională," April 2006, available at www.presidency.ro; accessed 30 August 2006.
11. The National Doctrine on Intelligence, adopted in 2004, was a subject of debate within the framework of the Security Culture pilot program, which was developed by the Center for Information on Security Culture (CICS), Bucharest.
12. See report of General Bădălan about the activity of the General Staff on 2005, available at www.mapn.ro; accessed 30 August 2006.
13. Government of Romania, "White Paper on Security and National Defense, 2004," updated with information provided by MOD, Department of Defense Policy, 2006, 42–44.
14. World Bank, "Country Assistance Evaluation," Report No. 32452, 25 May 2005.
15. See Marian Zulean, "Civil-Military Cultural Gap in Romania," in G. Caforio and G. Kummel, eds., *Military Missions and Their Implications Reconsidered: The Aftermath of September 11th* (Greenwich, CT: JAI Press, 2005), 151–171.
16. The *A.T. Kearney/Foreign Policy Globalization Index* is the first comprehensive empirical measure of globalization and its impact. It measures economic, person-to-person, political, and technological integration in

sixty-two countries, accounting for 96 percent of the world's GDP and 85 percent of the world's population. Available at http://www.atkearney.com/shared_res/pdf/2005G-index.pdf; accessed 30 August 2006.

17. See the *Bertelsmann Transformation Index 2006*, Bertelsmann Stiftung. Available at http://www.bertelsmann-transformation-index.de/11.0.html?&L=1; accessed 30 August 2006.

18. For more on the role of international assistance see Marian Zulean, "International Requirements and Assistance for Defense and Security Reform," in Philipp H. Fluri and Jan A. Trapans, eds., *Defense and Security Sector Governance and Reform in South East Europe: Insights and Perspectives Volume 2; FYROM Macedonia; Moldova; Romania; A Self-Assessment Study* (Belgrade: CCMR, 2003), 405–415.

8

Global Determinants of Defense Restructuring: The Case of the United States

Jim Schweiter and Kim Wincup

Introduction

Civil-military relations within a sovereign nation are reflections of the history and culture that led to the creation of that nation. Reforms of the defense functions in a stable democracy like the United States occur within the country's federal framework of governance. When global factors influence defense reform, it is important to gauge how these factors affect the nature of the reform undertaken and achieved. Reform of the U.S. military's institutions, laws, policies, or practices may also be brought on by domestic drivers, such as alterations in the internal political situation, analytical assessments of the national security environment, or even fiscal pressures, that decision makers believe have the potential to adversely affect the ability of the United States military to respond to national security threats.[1]

Institutions invested with legal authority drive change. In the United States, the executive authorities in the persons of the president and secretary of defense can initiate change in the defense bureaucracy and its way of doing business, but the federal legislature performs a critical function in any such efforts. It is on the unique role of the United States' strong and independent legislative branch in matters of defense reform that this chapter will focus.

The chapter examines two recent situations in which significant defense restructuring was attempted and in which the U.S. Congress was a primary actor. First, legislation known as the Goldwater-Nichols Act, named after the two congressmen who wrote it, is a prime example of defense reform occurring through an exercise of civilian control (in this case the legislature) over the Department of Defense (DoD) in the name of improved military effectiveness.[2] This law, passed after various military operations demonstrated deficiencies in the military command structure, improved the ability of the military services to conduct joint operations and altered the command and control arrangements among the services, and between DoD and the president. Since enactment of Goldwater-Nichols, the American military's effectiveness in conflicts has improved as a result of the reforms adopted in this law.

The second situation is narrower in scope but worth considering because it provides insight into how the need for efficiency can impose change. Congress's reworking of the Air Force's proposal to lease new Boeing 767 mid-air refueling or "tanker" aircraft to replace the existing Air Force KC-135 fleet, and the imposition of additional requirements as a prerequisite to approval, demonstrate the important role of the legislature in defense reform, as well as the imperative to ensure greater efficiency in the acquisition process, even when the ultimate outcome of the reform effort is a negligible change from the status quo.

These two cases of U.S. defense reform are instructive for several reasons. First, they show the importance and unique influence of the legislative branch, and of the personalities it comprises, in civil-military relations and in shaping defense reform legislation. Second, these examples suggest that improved effectiveness and efficiency in governmental mechanisms is a common purpose for defense reform efforts. Third, the larger global determinants of reform posited in this book—democratization, economic liberalization, globalization, and technology improvements—are drivers only to a limited degree in these instances. They may contribute to the impetus for reform but are not central to the nature of the reforms achieved. Fourth, participation of the legislative branch in defense restructuring is no guarantee of real change. The results of the cases examined herein are mixed, and the assertion of civilian control over military reform endeavors is not, at least in these two examples, a useful gauge in determining how successful reforms will be. Finally, these cases are illustrative as a model for other political systems, particularly those with independent legislatures that have national security responsibilities.

The Historical Context for Consideration of Defense Reform and Civil-Military Relations

The U.S. system of governance emerged from events in England dating at least to the 1600s. The divine right of kings began to erode in England with the beheading of Charles I (1625–1649), and promulgation of an English bill of rights in 1689 that described the need for civilian control of the military.[3] The rudiments of a strong and independent legislative branch of government and of the notion of civilian control of the military may be seen in the U.S. Declaration of Independence. Reciting various grievances of the colonists against the King of England, that seminal document includes the following clauses that suggest the importance of both a representative legislature and the supremacy of civil power:

> He has kept among us, in times of peace, Standing Armies without the Consent of our legislatures.
> He has affected to render the Military independent of and superior to Civil power.
> He has combined with others to subject us to a jurisdiction foreign to our constitution, and unacknowledged by our laws; giving his Assent to their Acts of pretended Legislation:
> For quartering large bodies of armed troops among us....[4]

The framework provided in the Constitution establishes civilian control of the military as a key to the kind of democratic society and federal institutions that the authors hoped to achieve. The manner in which this framework is imposed and the authority respecting national security matters vested in the executive and legislative branches of government are important to understanding the role each plays in defense reform.

The first article of the Constitution speaks at length about the powers vested in the legislative branch of government. Article I provides Congress greater and more diverse authority in the arena of national security than either of the other branches. Article I, section 8 specifically provides that Congress has the authority:

1. To declare war;
2. To raise and support Armies;
3. To provide and maintain a Navy;

4. To make rules for the Government and Regulation of the land and naval forces;
5. To provide for calling forth the Militia to execute the Laws of the Union, suppress Insurrections and repel Invasions;
6. To provide for organizing, arming, and disciplining, the Militia, and for governing such Part of them as may be employed in the Service of the United States . . . ; and
7. To make all laws which shall be necessary and proper for carrying into Execution the foregoing Powers, and all other Powers vested by this Constitution in the Government of the United States.[5]

These sections make clear that the Framers intended the standing military as well as the militia to be subject to the control of civilians in the legislative branch. Moreover, the language of the next section stating that "no money shall be drawn from the Treasury but in Consequence of Appropriations made by Law," has obvious potential consequences for the executive and the DoD.[6]

The powers to appropriate money from the treasury and to provide for the military are two of the most fundamental to the survival of the nation. While the president's power as commander in chief and to make treaties is substantial, the fact remains that Congress has explicit constitutional authority over military affairs that permits it to shape national security policy and control reform.[7] Which branch ultimately has the more important role is open to debate, but it is this context of divided power that shapes any discussion of defense reform.[8]

Democratic Control of the Military

One of the oldest and most difficult challenges in democratic societies is how the body politic will secure the subordination of military forces to political authority. Civilian control of the military establishment by elected civilian government leaders is a fundamental tenet of democratic government. It permits national defense policy choices to be guided by the decisions of officials who reflect the will of the people, rather than by those of military leaders whose views tend to be more narrowly focused on national security, and who are not accountable to the public in the same way. When there is a tradition of strong civilian control and the military has focused on external defense, tension nevertheless exists when the elected civilian leadership seeks to exercise supremacy in military policy and decision making. When the military establishment benefits from high national prestige, is led by skilled bureaucrats, or feels threatened by proposed legislative changes, then the civilian leadership may face spirited challenges as it seeks to impose its will on policy decisions. Seldom, if ever, however, is the survival of the government itself at stake when reforms are initiated.[9] In a very real sense, the military's own professionalism, traditions of political neutrality, and practice of restraint in domestic political affairs guarantee de facto civilian control of military institutions. Nevertheless, within this relatively absolute maxim, the degree to which civilians exercise control over various reform policy outcomes has tended to depend on the people and the issues involved. So it is in the two cases examined here, in which civilian leaders within a relatively strong legislature have succeeded in overriding military preferences in legislating defense reform.

Global Determinants of Defense Reform

The global determinants posited in this book—democratization, globalization, economic liberalization, and technology advances—clearly can and do have a palpable effect on defense reform and restructuring in countries around the world, including the United States.[10] For example, some arms manufacturers are expanding globally, pursuing transnational mergers and alliances by establishing design, production, and market operations abroad.[11] Similarly, advances in science and technology have caused DoD to think anew about the programs and research activities it funds as a part of the national security strategy, resulting in increased investments in such disparate emerging technologies as unmanned aerial vehicles, microsensors, multiplayer gaming, and nanotechnology.[12]

To be sure, the impetus for and outcome of the episodes of defense reform described below contain elements of these global determinants. As will be seen, deployments of American military forces at various places around the world in the 1970s and 1980s showed the flaws in the military command structure and inefficiency in operations that created the imperative for reform. The Air Force would not have proposed replacing the existing fleet of KC-135 aircraft were not those airframes wearing out at an accelerated rate because of extensive operational deployments, arguably a consequence of globalization. The unique feature in the cases discussed here, however, is the primacy of the role played by the legislative branch in the reform process. Congress's intervention in defense restructuring not only yields insights about the practical aspects of reform and civil-military relations, but also demonstrates that legislative participation is more outcome determinative, at least in these instances, than any of the global factors that may otherwise influence defense reform.

The Impetus for Defense Restructuring in the United States

In the United States, wartime operational experiences from World War II, Korea, and Vietnam shaped much of its national security structure. For example, legislation to reform the way the defense establishment is organized and functions, known as the National Security Act of 1947 and the Defense Officer Personnel Management Act, resulted from operational lessons learned.[13] The structure of the American military was further shaped by its participation in events of lesser scope, such as the failed rescue of the American hostages held in Iran, the bombing of the Marine barracks in Lebanon, and the incursion into Grenada. The incremental accumulation of experience and awareness of operational inefficiencies in the military command structure likewise provided the impetus for the 1986 Goldwater-Nichols legislation that redefined and reorganized the responsibilities of the military leadership.

More recently, force deployments throughout the 1990s, to Bosnia; Iraq during Operations Desert Shield, Desert Storm, Southern Watch, and Northern Watch; Afghanistan for Operation Enduring Freedom; and Iraq again for Operation Iraqi Freedom, have resulted in accelerated use and aging of much of the U.S. military's equipment inventory. In particular, the overuse and resulting stresses on the aging fleet of more than 500 KC-135 refueling aircraft impelled the Air Force to propose replacing the entire fleet, citing high maintenance costs and aircraft vulnerability to catastrophic problems.[14] What was novel about the proposal was the Air Force's idea to lease 100 new Boeing KC-767 aircraft to perform the refueling mission, rather than purchasing the planes.[15] The secretary of defense proposed legislation to authorize a multiyear lease in 2001, and the lease was authorized in the Department of Defense Appropriations Act for Fiscal Year 2002.[16] Subsequent congressional inquiries, undertaken in the name of both reform and wringing increased efficiencies out of an acquisition system perceived not to make the best use of public resources, however, ultimately eliminated the lease authority over the course of the next several legislative cycles.

THE GOLDWATER-NICHOLS DEPARTMENT OF DEFENSE REORGANIZATION ACT OF 1986

The Goldwater-Nichols legislation is widely hailed as a landmark piece of legislative activism that has dramatically improved the functioning of the Department of Defense. The clear objectives of this legislation were to improve the ability of the armed services to conduct military operations jointly, and to improve the quality of military advice to senior political leaders. With respect to the command and control relationships among senior DoD leaders, the law explicitly stated that the services and the Joint Chiefs of Staff worked for the secretary of defense. The chairman of the Joint Chiefs was made the principal military advisor to the president.[17] Moreover, and from a war fighting reform perspective, the bill divided the world into regions and vested a regional military commander in chief with operational control over all U.S. forces within a given area, regardless of the branch of service to which those forces belong.[18]

These measures represented dramatic departures from how DoD operated, and how wars had been fought in the past. Previously, each war had a commander for each service, who reported to a designated supreme commander (such as General Dwight Eisenhower during World War II), but the supreme commander did not have any structured, statutory authority. Service chiefs developed their own strategic plans, and established operational requirements for their services without any overarching coordination with the other services. Commanders in combat theaters operated with significant autonomy and coordinated their operational activities up the chain of command through the service chiefs of staff in Washington. Inter-service cooperation was driven by necessity during wartime, but for the most part the military departments functioned as separate entities. Goldwater-Nichols changed virtually everything by changing the focus of the nation's war fighting to joint, rather than single service, planning.[19]

The legislative process that led to enactment of this law lasted more than four years. There was little prospect for success when it began. The senior uniformed leaders of DoD, particularly the chiefs of staff of the military services, who saw their bureaucratic power and autonomy to be at stake, strongly opposed the proposed changes.[20]

This legislation would subordinate the service chiefs of staff to the chairman of the Joint Chiefs, who would be designated as the principal military advisor to the president. In addition, the bill would make the service chiefs report in a chain to the secretary of defense. In normal conditions, the odds of implementing defense reform in the face of opposition from the professional leadership of DoD would be remote. That the legislation eventually became law is a testament to the supremacy of the Congress in its relations with the military.

The conditions leading to the enactment of Goldwater-Nichols covered a good part of the two terms of President Ronald Reagan (1981–1989), and were rooted in his strong emphasis on increased defense spending. At the time, the House of Representatives was firmly controlled by a Democratic majority, while in the Senate, Republican supporters of President Reagan had a thin majority. Throughout Reagan's first term, defense spending did increase, but there was concern about the manner in which this money was being spent. This concern related to the status of arms control treaties and revelations about fraud and abuse in the DoD acquisition processes. Major defense legislation relating to issues such as funding for the MX intercontinental ballistic missile, binary chemical munitions, and the Strategic Defense Initiative, as well as a number of related initiatives passed with only bare majorities. Importantly, congressional assessments of several military incidents (i.e., the failed Iranian hostage rescue attempt, the bombing of the Marine barracks in Lebanon, and aspects of command and control in the invasion of Grenada) heightened concerns that operational and decision-making procedures within DoD needed to be changed.

On a separate and somewhat related track, a subcommittee of the House Armed Services Committee began to consider reorganizing the Joint Chiefs of Staff structure to improve the quality of military advice provided to the president. Legislation passed the House in 1982 and 1983, but met with strong opposition from the military services and was killed in the Senate.[21] Finally, in 1984, a reform bill passed the House again, only to be accorded peremptory treatment by the leaders of the Senate Armed Services Committee.[22] This treatment only strengthened House members' resolve to pursue the matter.

The foregoing considerations, plus the need to improve the DoD acquisition process, led to the conduct of two studies, the first by the Center for Strategic and International Studies.[23] This study questioned "*the effectiveness and efficiency with which the United States plans, acquires, and operates its forces,*" (emphasis added) and suggested substantial changes throughout the defense establishment.[24]

The other study was conducted by the Packard Commission, a panel appointed by President Carter comprising a number of distinguished figures and chaired by a former deputy secretary of defense with strong private sector credentials, David Packard.[25] This commission addressed reform of the Defense Department's acquisition processes and other matters relating to the Goldwater-Nichols legislation. The report included recommendations for greater authority for unified commanders, stronger representation in the Joint Chiefs of Staff decision-making process for unified commanders, designation of the chairman as principal military advisor to the president, and creation of the position of vice chairman of the Joint Chiefs.[26]

All of these factors—the political imperative to improve the organization and management of DoD; failures in military operations; critical evaluations of the Department's existing procedures; and strong legislative personalities with impeccable defense credentials (Nichols was a well-known military supporter who had been severely wounded in World War II, while Goldwater was also a World War II veteran and retired major general in the Air Force Reserve)—created a set of circumstances ripe for defense reform. In particular, these congressional leaders became convinced that reform was necessary to create the kind of military that could guarantee the nation's security.

The goals of the Goldwater-Nichols legislation were several-fold. Generally, it was intended to improve military effectiveness and efficiency.[27] More specifically, Congress sought to strengthen civilian authority within DoD, improve military advice to civilian leaders, clarify the authority and responsibilities of the combatant commanders, improve strategy formulation and contingency planning, provide for more efficient use of defense resources, and enhance the professionalism and personnel management of the corps of joint officers.[28] To a remarkable degree, the law has achieved its objectives. Most observers credit this legislation with helping to ensure the success of operations conducted by the U.S. military in recent times.[29] The law also has promoted jointness, clarified the roles of the secretary of defense and chairman of the Joint Chiefs of Staff, clarified the mission of the commanders of unified commands and made the latter's authority commensurate with their responsibilities.[30] Although lingering problems remain, such as the quality of strategy, the resource allocation process, joint officer management, the administration of defense agencies, and "dual hatting" of senior officers who must make decisions that have implications for both joint operations and their parent service, Goldwater-Nichols stands out as an example where intervention by the legislature resulted in an assertion of civilian control over the military establishment, and generated real reform of its organization and processes.[31] While global events may have provided the evidence that reform was necessary, globalization per se did not materially shape the reforms undertaken in this case.

Air Force 767 Tanker Leasing

The U.S. Air Force's fleet of KC-135 air refueling tanker aircraft is critical to the effectiveness of the nation's military. A senior Air Force official stated that "our National Security Strategy is unexecutable without air refueling tankers."[32] These aircraft, built on the same airframe as Boeing 707s, refuel other aircraft in mid-air, which permits them to stay in flight longer, fly further, and carry more weapons and equipment than would be possible without this capability.[33]

It has been clear for some time that the inventory of these aircraft needs to be modernized. The bulk of the current KC-135 fleet averages forty-two years of age.[34] The Air Force had a plan to begin modernizing the fleet, but the events of 11 September brought increased U.S. military commitments around the globe and a more aggressive homeland defense posture that further drove up reliance and demands on the aging tanker fleet.[35] The military's expanding focus on Asia, and plans to decrease U.S. forces based permanently overseas, also spurred interest in acquiring a fleet of airplanes that can carry more fuel and cargo than those in the current inventory.[36] To this end, the Air Force proposed replacing the existing fleet by leasing 100 new Boeing 767 aircraft that have been converted into refueling tankers.[37] This proposal falls under the rubric of defense reform because acquiring a major military system under operating lease arrangements would mark a significant departure from the traditional federal procurement statutes.[38] Moreover, such a result would have profound budgetary and fielding implications for the entire DoD by establishing the precedent of using leases to acquire capital assets for major systems.

International military commitments were the de facto drivers of the move to modernize the Air Force's fleet of tanker aircraft. In this sense, globalization has played a role in this particular defense reform. It is also true that globalization has an impact on the industrial base that supports DoD.[39] While Boeing has sought the tanker lease as a way to keep its 767 production line going, European Aeronautic

Defense and Space, the European company that manufactures the competing Airbus 330 model, has long been trying to enter the American military aircraft market.[40] In this sense too, the decision whether to authorize a leasing arrangement with Boeing or to permit competition with other international companies has been affected by globalization.

While the Boeing 767 clearly is technologically superior to the KC-135, that superiority has less to do with the Air Force's pursuit of a leasing strategy than affordability issues.[41] Neither technology nor globalization was as important to the outcome of the reform effort as was the intervention of legislative branch officials in the leasing decision process.

With substantial urging from the Air Force and officials of the Boeing Company who manufacture the 767 aircraft, Congress provided pilot leasing authority to the Air Force for up to 100 KC-767 aircraft in the Department of Defense Appropriations Act for Fiscal Year 2002.[42] The proposal to lease capital equipment of this type was unique and was justified both by congressional supporters and Air Force officials as necessary because of the need to modernize the tanker fleet more quickly than originally planned and because budgetary constraints precluded the Air Force from purchasing these aircraft on an expedited basis.[43]

There was considerable controversy about the requirement to modernize the existing KC-135 fleet in the near term. Some doubted the accuracy of Air Force claims that increasing operations and maintenance costs and decreasing mission-capable rates for the current fleet were reaching critical dimensions.[44] Many questioned the utility and cost effectiveness of using leases as a means to acquire new aircraft and to maintain military capability.[45] Because the airplanes would have to be specially configured for the military mission—Boeing does not build commercial tanker aircraft, and there is no commercial market for these planes—it was widely anticipated that the Air Force would have to purchase the airplanes at the expiration of the lease period, thereby diminishing or eliminating any cost savings that might be achieved by the leasing arrangement.[46] Nevertheless, the situation in 2002 was such that Congress was encouraging this expedited process for modernizing the fleet of KC-135 aircraft, and the senior leadership of the Air Force was asserting a military requirement to do so.

Senator John McCain, a retired Navy captain and senior member of the Senate Armed Services Committee, was concerned about this approach, based on cost and lack of competition among companies for construction or modification of the airplanes that would be leased.[47] Several independent organizations assessed the cost of leasing versus more traditional approaches, and each indicated the cost of leasing was substantially higher.[48]

McCain actively opposed the lease plan and highlighted some of the questionable practices and unethical relationships that existed between senior Air Force procurement officials and the Boeing company.[49] Congress responded to the burgeoning controversy by modifying the lease authority, giving the Air Force permission to lease twenty new aircraft and purchase no more than eighty. Congress required the Air Force to conduct an "analysis of alternatives," examining ways to meet its air refueling requirements, and forbade the retiring of more than twelve KC-135 airplanes during fiscal year 2004.[50] As a further indication of the extent to which the credibility of the Department of Defense had been damaged by the disclosures about the urgency of the requirement to recapitalize the KC-135 fleet of aircraft, Congress required an independent assessment, by an entity outside the Department of Defense, of the material condition of the fleet of KC-135 refueling aircraft.[51] To make matters worse, the former chief Air Force negotiator on the tanker lease program was convicted of criminal conspiracy for negotiating a job with Boeing while overseeing the program. Another Boeing official was convicted of improperly recruiting the former Air Force official.[52] The secretary of the Air Force was cited by the Department of Defense Inspector General for misuse of his office when he lobbied the Office of Management and Budget in favor of the leasing arrangement.[53] The Inspector General also found that four other DoD officials had sought to evade acquisition regulations aimed at requiring best business practices and accountability.[54]

The disclosure of these deficiencies in the lease approach—the likely high long-term costs, the lack of justification for immediate action to modernize the existing fleet, an implied lack of competition among defense companies for award of the lease, and fundamentally flawed procurement practices—caused Congress to reverse its position and ultimately resulted in a restructured arrangement that forbade the Air Force from leasing any tanker aircraft and instead authorized the purchase of 100 replacement aircraft.[55] If the required analysis of alternatives did not substantiate the Air Force's contention that the existing fleet of KC 135 tanker aircraft was at a maintenance and safety crisis point, Congress may revisit even the conventional multiyear procurement authorization.[56]

What started out as a novel and potentially precedent setting idea of using an operational lease to acquire a major system has now, as a result of congressional oversight and intervention, defaulted to a traditional multiyear procurement authorization. Thus, the tanker leasing example is a case in which the involvement of the legislative branch of government in a defense reform initiative has, as a practical matter, yielded virtually no systemic reform. It remains to be seen whether the analytical and process shortcomings identified over the course of the tanker leasing debate will ultimately yield any major changes in the DoD acquisition process to ensure that problems like those uncovered can be avoided in the future.

Operational demands on the existing air refueling fleet led to the leasing proposal, and flowed from the global commitments of the U.S. military. The Air Force's desire for a more modern, technologically advanced refueling platform contributed to its decision to proceed with a tanker modernization program, if not the leasing arrangement itself. Air Force officials reached out to Boeing because they saw the 767 as the airframe best suited to the service's requirements. Boeing's allies in Congress became advocates of a leasing arrangement they saw as beneficial to the company whose employees were, in many cases, political constituents. The lack of competition between Boeing and EADS or any other airplane manufacturing company, however, was a key argument against leasing voiced by Senator McCain.

The unethical relationships and illegal conduct between Air Force and Boeing officials in the case of attempted tanker leasing has been called "the largest defense procurement scandal in decades."[57] The scandal contributed substantially to the Air Force's loss of credibility associated with the tanker leasing proposals, and the program languished for over two years while enduring the analyses required by Congress.

In the spring of 2006, the "Analysis of Alternatives" required by the Congress was issued.[58] This analysis concluded that a medium to large commercial derivative aircraft is the most cost-effective alternative for replacing the existing KC-135 fleet. In other words, this kind of aircraft would meet the military requirement at the lowest cost. However, the report also said that the decision about when to recapitalize the existing tanker fleet should be based on considerations other than present value life cycle costs.[59] Thus, the report repudiated the Air Force's argument that the high cost of maintaining the existing KC-135 fleet was key in the imperative to modernize it. The report cited arguments for and against early recapitalization of the existing fleet, but a central argument against was "the existence of critical near-term constraints on spending that would make a major near-term acquisition program very unattractive."[60]

In April 2006, the DoD undertook a new effort to replace the aging KC-135 fleet, and a request for information was issued to industry.[61] The Air Force sought $239 million in funding for Fiscal Year 2007 to start development,[62] which included $36.1 million for advance procurement.[63] At the same time, a formidable new competitor for the tanker replacement program entered the picture—the team of Northrup Grumman and EADS,[64] injecting the element of competition that had been lacking under the original lease proposal.

Congress took to heart the argument against expensive new acquisition programs. For the fiscal year 2007 legislative cycle, the House and Senate Armed Services Committees and Defense Appropriations Subcommittees refused to approve the requested $36.1 million for advance procurement[65] and permitted the Air Force to retire only twenty-nine of seventy-eight requested KC-135 aircraft.[66] Moreover, the Senate committees disapproved $199 million of the remaining $203.9 million request for research and development expenses.[67] Air Force officials contend at least $70 million is needed in fiscal year 2007 in order to proceed to contract award during this fiscal year.[68] The Senate's action would delay contract award until at least fiscal year 2008, further hamstringing a program in which debate about its myriad difficulties has seemingly eclipsed concern for the real need for improved and sustainable refueling capability.

Irrespective of the influence of global determinants of defense reform, the bottom line is that fiscal constraints were the primary impetus for the tanker leasing effort. Leasing was a bureaucratically shrewd attempt to field new airplanes sooner than the Air Force could have afforded in the course of the normal acquisition process. It is now uncertain when the Air Force will gain better refueling capability. Whenever a new contract is awarded, it will be on terms far different than those originally proposed by the executive branch. Any new contract will almost certainly be a conventional multiyear procurement. In this sense, the reform effort that the policy on tanker leasing represented has failed. This example clearly demonstrates that a principal reason for the failure of the leasing effort is the unique American component of a strong legislative branch and the personal influence of those within it, such as Senator McCain.

Conclusion

The two episodes of defense reform described in this chapter are cases in which institutional or operational shortcomings within the DoD created an impetus for reform. The global determinants posited in this book played a role in demonstrating the need for reform. Military operations in the post-Vietnam era, for the most part global operations, and the deficiencies they showed in organizational strategy, planning, and war fighting capability, led to the seemingly obvious conclusion that the individual military services cannot operate without regard to the others, and provided the analytical basis for the Goldwater-Nichols reforms.[69] Similarly, the increased demands for equipment and pace of operations around the world, combined with the desire for improved technology (i.e., better, more modern aircraft) and a constrained budget, precipitated the move to acquire new tanker aircraft through leasing. Nevertheless, it is difficult if not impossible to quantify the extent to which these global drivers actually influenced the outcome of the reform efforts. Our analysis suggests that the involvement of the legislative branch of government and the influence of the individual members of Congress in the reform debate was far more important in shaping the reforms achieved than were global determinants.

It is also important to note that the cases examined here have yielded real reform. The Goldwater-Nichols Act has been widely praised for improving the command and control structures at the senior levels of DoD and the quality of military advice provided to senior political leaders. The reform proposal to lease tanker aircraft has come a full circle. Although Congress initially granted the authority to lease new Boeing 767 tankers, suspect analytical data, inappropriate relationships, and a flawed acquisition process caused Congress to return to a conventional multiyear procurement acquisition strategy. In this sense, the reform effort failed, but in as much as no new tankers have yet been acquired, it seems likely that the final chapter on this subject has yet to be written.

These two cases are also instructive for assessing civil-military relationships and military effectiveness and efficiency. The Goldwater-Nichols instituted structural reforms aimed at improved efficiency and effectiveness, led by a strong, independent legislative branch, which resulted in meaningful change without risking the political instability that sometimes affects other countries with a less well-established tradition of professional, apolitical military services. The

Goldwater-Nichols experience proves that well-crafted reform can result in greater military effectiveness. Although reform of the procurement process has yet to be achieved in the case of tanker leasing, these examples are useful studies because of the involvement of the legislative branch. Congress, and more particularly, congressional leaders with substantial national security expertise and credibility, played critical roles in shaping the outcome of the reforms. Moreover, in the cases of Goldwater-Nichols, there was substantial opposition to proposed changes from influential elements within DoD. That such opposition failed is a demonstrable testament to civilian supremacy over the military leadership in the United States. The tanker leasing episode is notable because officials within DoD supported the proposed reforms while congressional sentiment was mixed, but Congress' scrutiny of the leasing proposal facilitated the discovery of serious improprieties, and Congress determined that the terms of the proposed lease were unsustainable.

Ultimately, what is required for military forces to be effective is context dependent. The reforms of Goldwater-Nichols have been vindicated by battlefield experience since its enactment. It is perhaps premature to judge the outcome of the tanker leasing proposal. What may be said with certainty in this case, as well as the other case, is that Congress played a central role in dictating the specific outcome of the reform effort. In this respect, the legislative element of civilian control illustrates a deliberative approach to defense restructuring in the United States that may provide a useful template for reform in other countries.

NOTES

1. B. Balogh, J. Grisinger, and P. Zelikow, *Making Democracy Work: A Brief History of Twentieth Century Federal Executive Reorganization* (Charlottesville: University of Virginia Press, 2002), 59–60. The authors suggest that the most prominent catalysts for executive branch reorganization are national crises such as World War II or the Great Depression, the quest for economy through eliminating waste, and the desire to see public policy carried out effectively.
2. Goldwater-Nichols Department of Defense Reorganization Act of 1986, Public Law 99–433, 100 Stat. 992, 1986 (hereinafter Goldwater-Nichols). The law was named after its authors, Representative William Nichols (D-AL) and Senator Barry Goldwater (R-AZ). The bill passed the House by a vote of 383-27, the Senate by a vote of 95-0, and was signed into law by President Ronald Reagan on 1 October 1986. For

a general discussion of the law, see Gordon Lederman, *Reorganizing the Joint Chiefs of Staff: The Goldwater-Nichols Act of 1986* (Westport: Greenwood, 1999).

3. English Bill of Rights of 1689, An Act Declaring the Rights and Liberties of the Subject and Settling the Succession of the Crown, clause 5 (1996), in the Avalon Project at Yale Law School, available at http://www.yale.edu/lawweb/avalon/england.htm; accessed on 26 September 2007.
4. Declaration of Independence, clause 13–15, available at http://www.law.indiana.edu/uslawdocs/declaration/html; accessed on 26 September 2007.
5. United States Constitution, Art. I, sec. 8, cls. 11–16, 18, in *The Constitution of the United States of America, Analysis and Interpretation*, Congressional Research Service, Library of Congress (Washington, DC: U.S. Government Printing Office, 1996).
6. Ibid., Art. I, sec. 9, cls. 7 and 358. See also, *Cincinnati Soap Co. v. United States*, 301 U.S. 308, 321 (1937). The statement that, "No Money shall be drawn from the Treasury but in Consequence of Appropriations made by Law," was intended to restrict the disbursing authority of the executive.
7. United States Constitution, Art. II, sec. 2, cls. 1, 2.
8. Robert Turner, "The Power of the Purse," in H. Shuman and W. Thomas, eds., *The Constitution and National Security* (Washington, DC: National Defense University Press, 1990), 76–77; see also, *Youngtown Sheet & Tube Co. v. Sawyer*, 343 U.S. 579 (1952). This decision found that the president's seizure of the steel industry was not justified by his commander in chief authority where Congress had rejected his power to seize.
9. Ibid., 146. See also, Suzanne Nielsen, "Civil-Military Relations Theory and Military Effectiveness," *Public Administration and Management* 10, 2 (2005): 12–15. See generally, Samuel Huntington, *The Soldier and the State: The Theory and Politics of Civil-Military Relations* (Cambridge, MA: Belknap Press of Harvard University Press, 1957).
10. See the introduction of this book for explanations of the terms democratization and globalization as they apply to this discussion.
11. Ann Markusen, "The Rise of World Weapons," *Foreign Affairs* 114 (Spring 1999): 40. For a comparison, see also, Peter Dombrowski, "The Globalization of the Defense Sector? Naval Industrial Cases and Issues," in Sam Tangredi, ed., *Globalization and Maritime Power* (Washington, DC: National Defense University Press 2002), 210–220. For a range of perspectives on the challenges to American national security posed by globalization, see R. Kugler and E. Frost, eds. *The Global Century: Globalization and National Security* (Washington, DC: National Defense University Press 2001).
12. See, for example, Defense Science Board, "2001 Summer Study of Science and Technology," Office of the Undersecretary of Defense

for Acquisition, Technology and Logistics, Department of Defense, May 2002, 15.

13. Act of 26 July 1947, codified in 50 U.S.C. sec. 410 et. seq.; Pub. L. 96–513 (1980).
14. Amy Butler, "Air Force Mulling Replacement for Aging, Maintenance-Needy KC-135," *Inside the Air Force*, 4 May 2001.
15. Vago Muradian, "Roche Seeks Speedy 767 Deal with Boeing to Renew Support Fleet at Low Cost," *Defense Daily International*, 12 October 2001.
16. Section 8159 of Pub. L. 107–117 (2002).
17. Goldwater-Nichols, Pub. L. 99–433, sec. 201, in H. R. Rep. 824, 99th Cong., 2nd Sess., 15, 12 September 1986.
18. Goldwater-Nichols, note ii, sec. 211, in H.R. Rep. 824, 99th Cong., 2nd Sess., 22–25, 12 September 1986; See generally, James Locher, *Victory on the Potomac: The Goldwater-Nichols Act Unifies the Pentagon* (College Station: Texas A&M University Press, 2002); on the importance of unity of effort and a unified, clear chain of command see also, U.S. Joint Chiefs of Staff, *Joint Doctrine Capstone and Keystone Primer*, Washington DC, 10 September 2001, 4–5.
19. "Joint" refers to activities, operations, or organizations in which elements of two or more services (Army, Navy, Air Force, Marines) participate. *Joint Doctrine Encyclopedia*, Joint Publication 1-02 (16 July 1997): 357.
20. Deborah Kyle and Benjamin Schemmer, "Navy, Marines Adamantly Oppose JCS Reforms Most Others Tell Congress Are Long Overdue," *Armed Forces Journal International* (June 1982): 61. For the other side, see, Gen. David Jones, "Why the Joint Chiefs of Staff Must Change," *Armed Forces Journal International* (March 1982): 68–72. He warns that "[t]he corporate advice provided by the JCS is not crisp, timely, very useful or very influential. And that advice is often watered down and issues are papered over in the interest of achieving unanimity.... Individual service interests too often dominate JCS recommendations and actions at the expense of broader defense interests."); see also, Locher, *Victory on the Potomac*, 35–36.
21. H.R. 6954, 97th Cong., 2nd Sess., (1982); H.R. 3719, 98th Cong., 1st Sess., (1983).
22. H.R. 5167, 98th Cong., 2nd Sess., (1984). This bill, the National Defense Authorization Act for Fiscal Year 1985, ultimately became a law (Public Law 98–525). Title XIII of the law dealt with Department of Defense organizational issues and made minor changes to the authority of the Chairman of the Joint Chiefs of Staff, but did not include the more far-reaching reforms that later became the Goldwater-Nichols Act.
23. W. Lynn and B. Blechman, eds., *Toward a More Effective Defense: The Final Report of the CSIS Defense Organization Project* (Washington, DC: Center for Strategic and International Studies, 1985).

24. Locher, *Victory on the Potomac,* 169.
25. "A Quest for Excellence," Final Report to the President of the President's Blue Ribbon Commission on Defense Management, June 1986. This commission was created by Executive Order 12526, 15 July 1985.
26. Ibid., 37–38.
27. H.R. Rep. 49, 97th Cong., 2nd Sess., 1–2 (1982); see also H.R. Rep. 744, 97th Cong., 2nd Sess., 1–2 (1982), stating that the purpose of the bill (H.R. 6954) was to "improve the efficiency and effectiveness of the Joint Chiefs of Staff by establishing a Deputy Chairman and implementing several changes in the functioning of the organization."
28. Douglas C. Lovelace, Jr., *Unification of the United States Armed Forces: Implementing the 1986 Department of Defense Reorganization Act* (Carlisle, Penn.: Strategic Studies Institute, 1996), 5.
29. "Beyond Goldwater-Nichols: Defense Reform for a New Strategic Era," Center for Strategic and International Studies, Phase 1 report, 14 (2004), notes that "[t]oday, many consider Goldwater-Nichols and its subsequent implementation as instrumental in the overwhelming successes of US forces in Panama, the Persian Gulf, Bosnia, Kosovo, and most recently, in Afghanistan and Iraq. The prestige the U.S. military establishment currently enjoys stands in sharp contrast with its reputation prior to the act's passage in October 1986."
30. James Locher, "Has it Worked? The Goldwater-Nichols Reorganization Act," *Naval War College Review* 54, 4 (Autumn 2001): 108–111.
31. Ibid.: 111–112; see also Peter Chiarelli, "Beyond Goldwater-Nichols," *Joint Forces Quarterly* no. 2 (Autumn 1993): 71, 75, 78–79.
32. Marvin Sambur, Assistant Secretary of the Air Force for Acquisition, "The Air Force Tanker Lease Proposal," statement to the House Committee on Armed Services, 108th Cong., 1st Sess. 57 (H.A.S.C. Doc. 108-14, 23 July 2003).
33. "Air Force Aerial Refueling," Congressional Research Service (CRS) Report for Congress No. RS20941, Library of Congress, 4 May 2004: 1; see also, Butler, "Air Force Mulling Replacement."
34. Neal P. Curtin, Director, Defense Capabilities and Management "Military Aircraft: Information on Air Force Aerial Refueling Tankers," statement to United States General Accounting Office (GAO), GAO-03-938T, 24 June 2003, 1; CRS Report for Congress #RS20941, *Air Force Aerial Refueling* (Library of Congress, 4 May 2004), 1.
35. Christopher Bolkcom, "The Air Force Tanker Lease Proposal"; CRS Report for Congress #RL32056, *The Air Force KC-767 Tanker Lease Proposal: Key Issues for Congress*, Library of Congress, 2 September 2003, 19.
36. Butler, "Air Force Mulling Replacement."
37. CRS Report, *The Air Force KC-767 Tanker Lease Proposal*, 2.

38. The legislative provisions passed by Congress provided leasing authority that departed from ordinary DoD procurement procedures by: 1) specifying a particular acquisition: (an operating lease of a commercial asset) rather than a capital lease or a conventional procurement; 2) specifying the number and type of aircraft to be leased (100 Boeing 767s and 4 Boeing 737s); 3) exempting the lease from the normal legal restrictions that govern DoD lease of assets like ships and aircraft (see 10 USC 2401, 2401a); 4) exempting the lease from the limits established in 31 USC 1553(b)(2) (commonly known as the Anti-Deficiency Act) on the amount of appropriations that, under certain circumstances, may be charged to closed appropriations accounts; 5) exempting the Air Force from the "Buy American" requirements of the Berry Amendment (10 USC 2533a); 6) establishing a special process under which approval of the lease would be through language included in either an authorization or appropriations act, or through a "new start" reprogramming action requested by DoD and approved by the House and Senate Armed Services and Appropriations Committees. Ibid., 8.
39. Defense Science Board, "Final Report of the Task Force on Globalization and Security," Office of the Undersecretary of Defense for Acquisition and Technology (December 1999), 1–2. The report notes that the defense industrial sector comprises firms that will increasingly rely on commercially developed technologies to produce military capabilities. The Boeing lease deal for a modified 767 illustrates this point perfectly.
40. Leslie Wayne, "Boeing Must Compete for Tanker Contract," *New York Times*, 23 November 2004, C2; see also CRS Report, "The Air Force KC-767 Tanker Lease Proposal," 30–32.
41. CRS Report, "The Air Force KC-767 Tanker Lease Proposal," 22–23. The 767 has more flexible refueling capability, can carry more patients when configured for medical evacuation, has a cargo carrying capacity twice as large as the KC-135, can operate on much shorter runways than the KC-135, and would be more available for operational missions because of better projected maintenance. Neal P. Curtin, Director, Defense Capabilities and Management, "Military Aircraft: Observations on the Proposed Lease of Aerial Refueling Aircraft by the Air Force," statement to GAO, GAO-03-923T, 4 September 2003, 10, 20. The GAO concludes that neither the Air Force nor DoD has been willing to make the difficult decision to reallocate procurement funds from other programs to support funding the KC-135 by conventional acquisition funding.
42. Department of Defense Appropriations Act, Fiscal Year 2002, Section 8159 of Pub. L. 107–117 (2002). This section said that the Air Force could not enter into the lease until at least thirty days after it submitted a report to the House and Senate Armed Services and Appropriations Committees on its plans for implementing the lease. This point was

modified in subsequent legislation. See National Defense Authorization Act for Fiscal Year 2003, section 314 of Pub. L. 107–314 (2002); Department of Defense Appropriations Act, Fiscal Year 2003, section 8117 of Pub. L. 107–248 (2002); Act for the Further Recovery from and Response to Terrorist Attacks on the United States, section 308 of Pub. L. 107–206 (2002) (commonly referred to as the Fiscal Year 2002 Supplemental Appropriations Act); National Defense Authorization Act for Fiscal Year 2004, sections 134–135, 345 of Pub. L. 108–136 (2003); National Defense Authorization Act for Fiscal Year 2005, section 133 of Pub. L. 108–375 (2004).

43. "Rep. Norm Dicks Says KC-767 Tanker Lease Recognizes Urgency of Replacing Older Defense Dept. Equipment," press release, 23 May 2003, available at http://www.house.gov/dicks/news/finaltankers.htm; accessed 23 September 2007.

44. The GAO noted that "[T]he problems and costs associated with operating and sustaining old aircraft is not a sudden manifestation, but rather a fact of life that the KC-135 support infrastructure has had to deal with for years. Many of the problems currently being reported as reasons to begin tanker recapitalization immediately—including corrosion, increasing operating and support costs, and reduced aircraft availability—are not new and were issues that the Air Force was addressing in the mid-1990s, when we last examined aerial-refueling matters and when the Air Force concluded that recapitalization was not urgent." Curtin, "Military Aircraft," 16.

45. Leslie Wayne, "Air Force Lease with Boeing Seen Adding Billions to Cost," *New York Times*, 27 August 2003, C1.

46. Curtin, "Military Aircraft," 17–18.

47. Amy Svitak, "Pentagon Panned for Response to Tanker Lease Alternative," *Congress Daily*, 26 September 2003, available at www.govexec.com/dailyfed/0903/092603/cdam2.htm; accessed 23 September 2007.

48. See, for example, Robert A. Sunshine, Assistant Director for Budget Analysis, "Assessment of the Air Force's Plan to Acquire 100 Boeing Tanker Aircraft," testimony before the Senate Armed Services Committee, Congressional Budget Office (CBO), 4 September 2003, 1–2. The Air Force projected that leasing would cost about $150 million more than purchasing the planes outright, but according to CBO's analysis, the Air Force's proposal would cost $1.3 to $2 billion more in present value terms than purchase. See also, Steve Ellis, Vice President for Programs, "Testimony before the Senate Committee on Commerce, Science, and Transportation, Taxpayers for Common Sense," 3 September 2003, available at http://commerce.senate.gov/pdf/ellis090303.doc; accessed 23 September 2007. "Fill 'Er Up: Back Door Deal for Boeing Will Leave the Taxpayer on Empty," report by the Project on Government Oversight, available at http://pogo.org/p/contracts/co-020507-boeing.html; accessed 23 September 2007.

49. John McCain, statement to Congress, 150 Cong. Rec. S. 11536-11542, 19 November 2004.
50. Ibid., sec. 134.
51. See the National Defense Authorization Act for Fiscal Year 2004, sections 134, 135, and 345 of Pub. L. 108–136 (2003). The deputy secretary of defense chose the Defense Science Board to perform this study. See, "Defense Science Board Task Force Report on Aerial Refueling Requirements," Office of the Under Secretary of Defense for Acquisition, Technology and Logistics, May 2004, 11.
52. Renae Merle, "Ex-Pentagon Official Admits Job Deal," *Washington Post*, 21 April 2004, A1; Leslie Wayne, "Former Executive at Boeing Given 4-Month Prison Term," *New York Times*, 19 February 2005, C2.
53. R. Jeffrey Smith, "Roche Cited for 2 Ethics Violations," *Washington Post*, 10 February 2005, A21.
54. "Management Accountability Review of the Boeing KC-767A Tanker Program," Report No. OIG -2004-171, Office of the Inspector General of the Department of Defense, 13 May 2005, 32–35; John T. Bennett, "Pentagon IG Report Pins Tanker Lease Blame on Five Former Officials," *Inside the Air Force*, 10 June 2005.
55. National Defense Authorization Act for Fiscal Year 2005, section 133 of Pub. L. 108–375 (2004).
56. National Defense Authorization Act for Fiscal Year 2004, section 134 of Pub. L. 108–136 (2003).
57. R. Jeffrey Smith, "Tanker Inquiry Finds Rumsfeld's Attention Was Elsewhere," *Washington Post*, 20 June 2006, A15.
58. Michael Kennedy et al., "Analysis of Alternatives for Recapitalizing the Air Force's KC-135 Aerial Refueling Tanker," *Rand Corp.*, 2006, executive summary at 12.
59. Ibid., at 14.
60. Ibid., at 15.
61. Undersecretary of Defense for Acquisition, Technology and Logistics Kenneth J. Kreig signed the Acquisition Decision Memorandum. David A. Fulghum, "Pentagon Officials Give Green Light to New KC-X Tanker Program," *Aviation Week and Space Technology*, 23 April 2006, available at http://www.aviationweek.com/aw/generic/story_channel.jsp?channel=defense&id=news/aw042406p2.xml; accessed 23 September 2007.
62. Ibid.
63. H.R. Rep. 109–452, 109th Cong., 2nd Sess., 106–107 (2006).
64. James Wallace, "Tanker Wars: Boeing Challenged," *Seattle Post Intelligencer*, 1 June 2006, available at www.seattlepi.nwsource.com/business/272243_tankers01.html, accessed 25 September 2007; Keith J. Costa, "'Fair' and 'Open' Competition Debate Stirs Tanker Replacement Effort," *Inside the Air Force*, 4 August 2006, available

at www.defense.iwpnewsstand.com/cs-protected/cs_display_doc_01.asp?f=defense_2001.ask; accessed 25 September 2007.

65. H.R. Rep. 109–452, 109th Cong., 2nd Sess., 106–107 (2006); H.R. Rep. 109–504, 109th Cong., 2nd Sess., 74 (2006); S. Rep. 109–254, 109th Cong., 2nd Sess., 93–94 (2006); S. Rep. 109–292, 109th Cong., 2nd Sess., 214 (2006).
66. H.R. Rep. 109–452, 109th Cong., 2nd Sess., 107 (2006).
67. S. Rep. 109–254, 109th Cong., 2nd Sess., 93 (2006).
68. John T. Bennett, "USAF Will Place Tanker Program 'On Pause' Without New R&D Dollars," *Inside the Air Force*, 18 August 2006, available at www.defense.iwsnewsstand.com/cs-protected/cs_display_doc_01.asp?f=defense_2002.ask; accessed 25 September 2007.
69. Locher, *Victory on the Potomac*, 35, quoting General David C. Jones, then Chairman of the Joint Chiefs of Staff.

9

India: Imbalance under Civilian Control

Rajesh Basrur

Introduction

The issue of civil-military relations in developing countries tends to be viewed largely in terms of the politics of power and control. Given the history of military takeovers in the postcolonial era, this is not surprising. India is something of an exception. Since Independence in 1947, its democracy has never been threatened by the armed forces. The sole threat to the liberal-democratic republic established by the Constitution of 1950—in the form of the emergency imposed by Prime Minister Indira Gandhi in 1975–1977—came from a civilian leadership that mainly used the police to control the country. However, even when civilians enjoy unchallenged authority, they may nevertheless by default, or indeed actively, allow military values and approaches to security to predominate. When this happens, as has occurred in India, the meaning of "civilian control" as a politically responsible and accountable approach to national security is eroded. Further, both military effectiveness and defense efficiency are adversely affected.

Globalization has affected India's security at least as much as it has in other countries, both developing and developed. The diffusion of technology, ideas, and power that are discussed in Anne Clunan's chapter in this volume, has impacted threats as well as responses, necessitating changes in the organization and planning of defense. These are discussed in the next section. While a range of global influences on Indian defense reform is observable, the effects have not been uniform. This chapter focuses on two critical aspects of India's security concerns: counterterrorism and nuclear security. In both cases, the external effects have been profound. The inadequacies of strategy have been recognized, reforms have been recommended, and yet, limitations remain. The thrust of my argument is that the Indian response has been hampered by a militarized, albeit civilian-led, approach to security. I conclude that while global determinants do play a major role in shaping defense reform, the key to understanding the particular pace, timing, and shape of reform lies in the domestic sphere.

Not only has there never been the threat of a military coup in India, civilian control of the armed forces has throughout been tight and unquestioned, while the professionalism of the military has been of a high order.[1] As one senior retired military officer puts it, "In a sense India has had a First World military, even as the nation has remained part of the Third World."[2] At the outset, there was certainly a subliminal fear of military takeover among political leaders, which explains the expansion of paramilitaries for the maintenance of domestic order so as to avoid too much reliance on the armed forces. But there was never an inkling of political ambition among members of the armed forces themselves.

There are four main reasons for the absence of military threats to civilian rule. First, British rule had firmly established the principle of civilian control since the days of the East India Company. Thus, a long history and culture of civilian control underscored post-Independence security politics. Second, India fought a series of wars during the first decades after Independence, in 1947–1948, 1965, and 1971 against Pakistan, and in 1962 against China. These kept the armed forces' gaze firmly outward, and even the humiliation of defeat in 1962 was not strong enough to undermine the standing of the political leadership. Third, the first two decades after Independence were marked by a relatively high degree of political stability. The Indian National Congress, which had led the country's freedom movement, was entrenched in power for three decades until 1977, when an opposition coalition ousted it, only to be replaced by the Congress in 1980. By this time, the principle of civilian control had been fully established. Finally, the heterogeneous nature of Indian society—splintered by innumerable caste, language, and religious/sectarian groups—was (and is) such as to prevent any specific social group from harboring the ambition to use the military to assume power.

Nevertheless, the character of civil-military relations in India can make national security strategy problematic because the civilian leadership has not been able to give clear direction to the armed forces.

At the domestic level, the state has been overly dependent on the army to counter political challenges to its integrity, while in dealing with external challenges, particularly since the advent of nuclear weapons, it has pursued a militarized approach to managing relations with adversaries.[3] There is proclivity toward "militarization" of policy in the state's approach to both internal and external threats,[4] and in addition, as Stephen P. Cohen argues, there is an evident propensity toward "civilian militarism" in the attitudes of the Indian leadership.[5] The content of defense reform in response to global influences has thus been shaped by civilian militarism, adversely affecting military effectiveness and defense efficiency.

Civil-Military Relations and Defense Reform in an Era of Change

The four variables that are the focus of this book have profoundly affected Indian society. Democracy has been consolidated over time in spite of considerable political conflict, sometimes violent, rooted in differences of ethnicity, caste, and class. As groups formerly occupying the lower rungs of the social hierarchy have risen through the electoral process, the composition of the armed forces has undergone change. Under British rule, the officer corps was dominated by the upper classes, while the ranks were recruited on the basis of caste and religious affiliation. In independent India, though tradition has to a considerable degree been retained in the social composition of the military, the officer corps has come increasingly to be a middle class one, while social boundaries have been broken by the formation of new composite regiments and by changing the recruitment practices of old ones.[6] Thus, the Indian armed forces have gradually changed in accordance with the democratization of the social structure, reflecting the rising power of status groups that were traditionally lower in the social hierarchy. Also reflective of society has been the growth of careerism and corruption in the armed forces. On the whole, though, the professionalism of the military has endured, and the wall between the armed forces and the civilian side of government has not been breached.

With respect to the globalization of democratic norms, restraint in responses to terrorist threats has been strengthened by global norms and by pressure from domestic and international human rights organizations. This has led to the internalization of human rights norms in the Indian Army, for instance, by the establishment of a Human

Rights Cell. Global norms against the use of nuclear weapons have also found a powerful echo in independent India. Successive Indian leaders expressed abhorrence toward the indiscriminate effects of nuclear weapons and became reluctant nuclearizers in response to their perception of nuclear threats.[7] While there has been much criticism of India's nuclear "coming out," what is remarkable about the process is that India opted for nuclear deterrence more than two decades after its first test took place in 1974. Despite the perception of nuclear threats on two fronts (China and Pakistan), and despite a series of crises with Pakistan, its nuclear weapons remain in a nondeployed state today.

Globalization and economic liberalization are closely linked in the Indian context. Until the late 1980s, the Indian economy was largely shielded from global competitive forces by a protectionist moat of tariffs and licensing, and by the dominance of a large public sector. A major debt crisis at the time forced a reluctant political leadership to open up the economy in the early 1990s, following which successive governments under diverse political parties accelerated the tempo of economic liberalization. The financial crisis did place military budgets under pressure initially, but the doubling of the rate of economic growth from about 3.5 percent in the 1980s has permitted a significant increase in defense spending without much strain. Military-to-military relations with the United States and other technologically advanced countries have undergone a quantum jump, and the search for new weapons and weapons technologies has become keener. At the same time, economic growth has facilitated the expansion of India's security horizons from the immediate region of South Asia to the "extended neighborhood" that covers the arc from West Asia and East Africa to Southeast Asia.[8] The overall effect has been the surfacing of an "emerging power" syndrome that has honed the armed forces' zest for more and better accoutrements of military capability. Globalization has had another, deeper influence on defense reform. The restructuring of the world economy and the penetration of capitalism everywhere have generated social tensions and given rise to terrorism as a global phenomenon. Domestic terrorist groups are linked to international groups in complex networks of religious fundamentalism, organized crime, and, in the Indian case, the policies of adversarial states. The boundaries between domestic counterterrorism and external defense are thus blurred, which creates enormous complications for policymakers.

Technological change in the realm of security reflects the meeting of global supply and local demand. With respect to military technology, India has simultaneously sought greater security through two kinds of revolutions in military affairs (RMAs): The nuclear revolution, and the high-technology products of the "third industrial revolution," which combines electronics, miniaturization, digitalization, and software development.[9] At the same time, the acquisition of power flowing from global factors applies not only to the Indian state but also to its adversaries, both state (Pakistan, China) and non-state (terrorist groups).

The two problem areas identified above—terrorism and nuclear weapons—are interrelated. Nuclearization has brought about a profound change in the Indian strategic milieu. With respect to India's relationship with Pakistan, the nuclear "revolution" in South Asia has ruled out conventional war because of the threat of escalation. The use of force is now restricted to the application of pressure through sub-conventional strategies. Pakistan has successfully used insurgent groups to pin down security forces in India and impose political pressure on the Indian government to negotiate on the Kashmir dispute. Indeed, the awareness that India is no longer in a position to strike back with conventional forces has allowed that country to intensify its sub-conventional strategy. Faced with a situation in which its conventional hands are tied, India has found itself caught between the nuclear devil and the sub-conventional deep blue sea. The resultant high tension has created a crisis-prone environment in which terrorists, sometimes acting as self-propelled loose cannons, have the capacity—and incentive—to bring the two countries to the brink of war. Globalization in this setting has a powerful political face: that of a loosely linked transcontinental movement by Islamic fundamentalists bent on the destruction of the "establishment," which in their view encompasses Hindus as well as Christians, Jews, capitalists, and their collaborators. The common thread running through this twin problem is that in Indian policymaking, a civilian-led strategy has not as yet been unambiguously established in such a way as to ensure a proper civil-military balance in tackling the challenge. Attempts at reform have yielded unsatisfactory results.

Insurgency and Terrorism

Despite the steady growth of democratic institutions and values since Independence, militancy and violence have been constant features of the Indian political landscape. The process of uneven economic development has been accompanied by relentless struggles among a plethora of social groups divided by caste, language, tribe, and religion competing for an adequate share of a relatively small economic pie. The volatile political environment has bred recurrent outbreaks of violence, often of an ephemeral and localized character, but periodically in the form of movements espousing the use of force against the state as well as against civilian targets. Over the decades, there has been a distinct trend toward ever-higher levels of violence.[10] While much attention has been given to the Islamic threat in recent years, the Indian experience has encompassed a wide variety of terrorist and other violent threats. During the 1980s, the chief center of terrorist activity was the state of Punjab, where Sikh extremists engaged in a very violent and long-drawn-out secessionist movement that took a heavy toll of lives, including that of Prime Minister Indira Gandhi. Since then, the number and location of active terrorist groups has expanded significantly.[11] These include not only Muslim terrorist groups active in the Indian state of Jammu and Kashmir (J&K), such as the Hizbul Mujahideen (HM), the Jaish-e-Mohammed (JeM), and the Lashkar-e-Taiba (LeT), but also non-Muslim groups such as the National Socialist Council of Nagaland (Isak-Muivah) or NSCN (I-M) in the northeast. Some violent political movements have sought revolutionary domestic change rather than secession or autonomy, for instance, the Maoist Communist Centre (MCC) and the People's War (PW), both of which are increasingly active in central, northern, and eastern India.[12]

The genesis of current terrorist movements has been internal in most cases, as with those in Kashmir in the north, and Assam and Tripura in the northeast.[13] However, spillovers from neighboring countries—Bangladesh, Myanmar, Nepal, Pakistan, and Sri Lanka—have been common. Notably, the secessionist movement in Kashmir has drawn extensive support from the Pakistan government, and attracted a large number of non-Kashmiris, who have given it an increasingly Islamic-fundamentalist character.[14] The global surge in terrorism over the past decade has provided a powerful impetus to terrorist activity in India. Islamic terrorist groups are driven by a pan-Islamist agenda that seeks to transform the world order through a "war of a thousand cuts."[15] Their cadres are drawn from far and wide and include Pakistanis, Arabs, Chechens, and Afghans.[16] All of them have a commitment to jihad and many are ideologically and operationally intertwined with Al Qaeda.[17] The latter has explicitly targeted

India. In December 1999, a fax message to the Voice of America in Washington on behalf of Nazeer Ahmed Mujjaid, military adviser to Al Qaeda, called for a war against "Americans, Russians and Indians" to ensure that "Islam will spread over the entire world."[18] Militant leaders have proclaimed Kashmir as a "gateway to India" and established links with fundamentalist and terrorist organizations in different parts of the country.[19] Terrorist activity in and around India is closely linked to another global (and globalizing) network, organized crime (drugs, weapons, human trafficking, money laundering), which has regional and global linkages.[20] For instance, Dawood Ibrahim, who controls the largest criminal syndicate in South Asia and was behind the serial Mumbai blasts of 1993 that killed 257 people, is known to have links with Al Qaeda.[21]

The government of India has followed a customary carrot-and-stick strategy in response, alternating between the use of force, especially military force, to suppress militants and negotiation to accommodate them.[22] Essentially, the approach has been not to try to defeat them, but to pressure them into negotiations.[23] But success has been limited, bringing a growing recognition that the army is not cut out for use in counterterrorist operations.[24] The success rate of the Indian Army has not been high. In the northeast, the one major success was the ending in 1986 of a twenty-year-long insurgency in the state of Mizoram.[25] In Nagaland, an older insurgency remains dormant as a result of a ceasefire and continuing negotiations, while in Assam there has been little progress against the United Liberation Front of Asom (ULFA), which has been prone to employing indiscriminate terror tactics.[26] In the northwest, the Punjab insurgency, which took a heavy toll of lives, could not be controlled by the army, and indeed was exacerbated by it. It was left ultimately to the state police to destroy the terrorist networks running rampant in the state.[27] In Kashmir, the activities of assorted terrorist groups remain at a high level in spite of a massive infusion of army troops into the region.[28]

Why has the army been largely unable to suppress insurgency and terrorism? First, armies as a rule have difficulty in identifying the enemy, which is able to blend with the local population. The Indian Army is no exception. Second, the army's sources of intelligence are limited by its lack of a local base. Third, its presence tends to alienate the people, who deeply resent the use against them of a force designed to fight external enemies. This is particularly true when cordon and search operations and village resettlement are carried out. The result is that militant groups, whose members are themselves often from the area, gain legitimacy among the local people.[29] Simultaneously, local police forces and governments are demoralized, and the mission thereby jeopardized. Fourth, there have been serious problems of coordination. Though the army has in most cases been designated the lead agency, there have been difficulties in command and control because of the plethora of agencies involved: the army itself, the civil authority, the state police, the state armed police, and central paramilitary forces. The simultaneous presence of so many organizations has tended to generate competition among them and to create problems with regard to the sharing of intelligence. Practical difficulties have also arisen with respect to the incompatibility of equipment used by the various forces.[30] As K.P.S. Gill, a leading counterterrorism expert, puts it:

> In J&K, the command and control system has been the weakest element of strategy, pitting force against force in an abrasive and antagonistic context that emphasises the paramountcy of one force over others, and dissipates energies in an unhealthy competition at the operational level. Narrow fiefdoms have been created, and individual commanders feel threatened by the operations and presence of other forces, and consequently adopt an attitude of hostility and contempt towards these.[31]

These problems have been acknowledged by the government, which in April 2000, mandated a Group of Ministers (GoM) with the task of reviewing the state of national security and recommending appropriate policy changes.[32] The GoM Report recognized the difficulties associated with the employment of the army in combating insurgency and terrorism. It called for improved intelligence sharing and for the removal of the army from counterinsurgency duties. The intensity of terrorist activity in J&K intensified in subsequent years, however, and so despite the recommendation of the GoM, the army has remained the main agency to combat terrorism. This may partly be explained by the international dimension of the problem, since much of the logistical support for the JeM, the LeT, and numerous other groups comes from Pakistan.[33] But, as the GoM Report points out, there is a need to separate the mixed roles of the army, the paramilitary border management forces, and the police. The government has sought to divest the army of its counterterrorism/counterinsurgency function by giving an enlarged role to two paramilitary forces: The Assam Rifles and the Rashtriya Rifles. At the broader level of policy planning, an integrated structure of internal and external national security planning has been established under the National Security Council (NSC) that was created in 1999. But little headway seems to have been made in tackling the surge of terrorist activity both in the northeast and the northwest, mostly because of the government's conspicuous lack of success in implementing its own recommendations.

In a perceptive paper on the role of the army, Sunil Dasgupta observes that the Indian Army has suffered from an ambiguous identity since colonial times; it has long been and remains at once an "expeditionary" force oriented toward external adversaries and a "constabulary" force charged with the maintenance of domestic order.[34] In part, this is the outcome of a grand post-Independence civil-military bargain, "an implicit agreement between the military and political leaderships that allowed the Army freedom of action within the institution in return for submitting to the new nationalist leadership on political-strategic matters."[35] But given the reality that Indian democracy has long ceased to be politically vulnerable to undue military influence, let alone a military takeover, the ultimate responsibility for the misdirection of the army's confused identity and for the state's persistence with a military approach to counterinsurgency and counterterrorism lies with the civilian leadership. Given the existence of a policymaking apparatus in which government ministers have no specialized knowledge of their subject areas and the bureaucracy is "notoriously generalist," the knowledge vacuum tends to be filled by the adoption of a militarist approach to persistent armed challenges to the state.[36]

Nuclear Weapons

Though the term revolution in military affairs or RMA is generally understood to mean the emergence of new information technologies and their application to the use of armed force, the nuclear revolution is just as much an RMA. While the former refers to a "'Meta-System' revolution, composed of computers, information, telecommunications, and high-technology conventional weapons," the latter constitutes a "single-system revolution" produced by developments in atomic physics.[37] In the present context, the information RMA does matter a great deal to India. In their external role, the armed forces have been profoundly influenced by the emergence of new military technologies. All three services—the army, the navy, and the air force—have begun reorganizing for network-centric warfare, and have begun to incorporate the new technologies.

The nuclear RMA represents an earlier phase of globalization: the gradual proliferation of nuclear military power beginning in the middle of the twentieth century. Because of the controls exercised by those able to develop it, the process of diffusion has been relatively slow. In the Indian case, self-restraint was a major determinant. Once adopted, the nuclear RMA has also brought profound changes. The Indian Army, for instance, has begun raising missile regiments for its nuclear forces. It has also recently reformulated its strategic doctrine.[38] The chief objective of the new doctrine is the reorientation of the army in accordance with the needs of the new strategic environment. The old strategy of amassing land forces for deep strikes in a war of potentially long duration has been dropped. The new one relies on integrated battle groups for quick action ("cold start") in a limited war. Yet, adjustment to the new nuclear-weapons environment has been uneven.

How does the Indian political leadership view the nuclear RMA and its strategic effects? Following the nuclear tests of May 1998, India officially adopted a doctrine of "minimum deterrence."[39] The chief components of officially declared doctrine include no first use, massive retaliation in response to an enemy strike by nuclear, chemical, or biological weapons, a moratorium on tests, and commitment to arms control.[40] More broadly, Indian strategic culture with respect to nuclear weapons reflects an ambivalence that is uncomfortable with the potential effects of nuclear possession even as it is accepted to a degree as necessary for deterrence.[41] If we treat nuclear weapons as having two divergent components—the political (they are unusable weapons meant only to deter) and the operational (they are like other weapons in the sense that they are usable military instruments)—the clear choice of the civilian leadership is for the former.[42] Thus, notwithstanding the recurrent crises that India has faced with Pakistan, notably the armed clashes of 1999 and the border confrontation of 2001–2002, Indian nuclear forces have never been deployed.

Civilian control of the nuclear infrastructure is very tight. Warheads are kept in unassembled condition under the control of scientists at the Bhabha Atomic Research Centre (BARC), and only delivery vehicles are under the control of the armed forces. The mating of warheads, should the need arise, is the responsibility of a separate group of scientists attached to the Defense Research and Development Organization (DRDO). The command and control system consists of a Nuclear Command Authority (NCA), which is divided into a Political Council and an Executive Council. The former, which is the sole body that may authorize nuclear use, is chaired by the prime minister and does not include members of the armed forces. The latter, which is the implementing body, does include the three service chiefs, but is also headed by a civilian, the National Security Advisor (NSA).

Civilian control has nevertheless been afflicted by the flaw observed above with respect to insurgency and terrorism. Under pressure, political leaders have tended toward a militaristic approach to strategy that has created the same type of imbalance we have seen in the case of counterinsurgency and terrorism. After the 1998 nuclear tests, their political understanding of the effects of nuclearization on India's conflict-prone relationship with Pakistan was erroneous. Initially, the leadership believed that nuclear weapons had brought to an end *all* forms of physical conflict between India and Pakistan. Pakistan could no longer attempt to pursue its long-standing objective of obtaining full control over the disputed state of J&K through military means. Since a military conflict was no longer feasible because of the risk of a nuclear conflagration, the strategic status quo would be permanently frozen, and India would be able to deal with its Kashmir insurgency as an internal problem.[43] This crucial error in Indian strategic thinking was exposed by the Kargil conflict of 1999. Accompanied by insurgents, Pakistani forces in civilian garb occupied territory on the Indian side of the mutually agreed Line of Control (LoC) in Kashmir. The aim was to create a crisis without officially crossing the LoC, that is, to obtain a military advantage while retaining official deniability. This would evoke a general fear of escalation from sub-conventional to conventional to nuclear conflict and thereby induce international intervention, compelling India to negotiate.

Indian leaders were completely surprised by the manifestation of the "stability-instability paradox."[44] The discovery that sub-conventional conflict was the haut relief of a nuclearized strategic canvas led to a desperate search for an apposite response. As terrorist attacks by Pakistan-backed "jihadis" increased in scale and intensity, the discourse soon shifted away from a search for political solutions to a quest for an appropriate mode of force projection against Pakistan. The options mulled over included hot pursuit of terrorists into Pakistani territory, limited strikes or special operations missions against terrorist camps in Pakistan, and a vague and undefined conception of "limited war." In January 2000, Indian Defense Minister George Fernandes asserted that nuclear weapons "can deter only the use of nuclear weapons, but not all and any war," and that Kargil had demonstrated that Indian forces "can fight and win a limited war, at a time and place chosen by the aggressor."[45] While admitting that under the nuclear shadow, there were "definite limitations if escalation across the nuclear threshold was to be avoided," Fernandes claimed that conventional war "has not been made obsolete by nuclear weapons."[46] His views on the feasibility of limited war closely matched those of several senior serving and retired military officers.[47]

The pressure from Pakistan-based terrorists intensified steadily and culminated in attacks on the J&K legislature in October 2001 and on the Indian Parliament in December. Indian leaders sought to break out of their straitjacket of inaction and turn the stability-instability paradox around against Pakistan through the exercise of coercive diplomacy. They initiated a massive conventional buildup, Operation Parakram (valor), along the Pakistan border and threatened to launch an unspecified form of limited war unless Pakistan stopped abetting terrorism in India.[48] Though nuclear weapons did not enter the picture, the mobilization did have a strong nuclear-strategic component. By threatening to initiate conventional conflict in opposition to terrorism, India raised the possibility of nuclear war, thus inviting U.S. intervention on its behalf. Thus, a linkage was established between sub-conventional and nuclear conflict through conventional mobilization. Further, India warned that if Pakistan chose to bring nuclear weapons into the fray, it (Pakistan) would suffer far more than India. On 29 December 2001, Fernandes asserted:

> Pakistan can't think of using nuclear weapons despite the fact that they are not committed to the doctrine of no first use like we are. We could take a strike, survive, and then hit back. Pakistan would be finished. I do not really fear that the nuclear issue would figure in a conflict.[49]

In the end, the exercise in compellence that stretched out over a period of ten months from December 2001 to October 2002 went unrewarded. Despite considerable U.S. pressure, Pakistan's promises to end support for terrorists operating in Kashmir were tactical and temporary, and, in the face of Pakistani countermobilization and threats of nuclear retaliation, India eventually had to withdraw its forces. It could not take the risk of treating a smaller quantum of nuclear damage as acceptable in practice, as opposed to the logic of rhetoric.

The resort to a militarized approach in a context eminently unsuitable for it was doomed, and should have been seen to be so. Fernandes' logic in downplaying the risk of a nuclear conflict was based on the untenable assumption that all military action is rational and controllable. India's eventual demobilization was an implicit admission of the inadequate intellectual foundations of its nuclear-strategic thinking. It reflected the hard reality that, when push came to shove, the risk of a Pakistani nuclear response was unacceptable. In effect, deterrence overrode compellence. Ironically, a predominantly political understanding of nuclear weapons—a strong point reflected in the Indian leadership's preference for nondeployment and arms control—proved to be a liability in a situation of intense pressure. Given their weak grasp of the operational facet of nuclear weapons, Indian policy-makers tended to conceive of these weapons as politically manipulable instruments for the attainment of their security objectives. In doing so, they brought their country close to the precipice.

Despite the existence of structured civilian control, there are signs of drift toward an operationally conceived doctrine and posture driven by the military's way of thinking. The Ministry of Defense, which is civilian-dominated, envisages a force of over 200 warheads in a triadic framework, which is considered a low figure necessary to avoid resistance from a government concerned about costs.[50] Since the 1980s, military war games have been fought in the nuclear context, and the idea of limited war has found strong support in both the civilian and military leaderships.[51] Thus, according to Michael Kraig, there are signs that "political leaders and analysts are buying into the reasoning of a new 'flexible response' doctrine that has been popular in some Indian military circles for some time now."[52] This militarization of Indian thinking and practice is attributable not simply to the armed forces' growing role in strategic politics, for the civilian government remains very much in command, but to the susceptibility of political leaders to conventional military solutions in a strategic environment (Pakistani support for terrorists in Kashmir) that they have been unable to tackle effectively. Taken together with the inevitable operational pressures arising from the creation of a nuclear infrastructure (beginning with the inclusion of the three service chiefs in the Executive Council of the Nuclear Command Authority), this opens up additional space for India's nuclear minimalism to drift away from its political moorings.

What are the reasons for this tendency toward militarization of strategy? First, though the armed forces have been kept at some distance from the formulation of basic strategy, notably in the adoption of minimum deterrence, there is evidently insufficient in-house expertise within the civilian side of the government. My personal conversations with members of the bureaucracy, though not systematic, tend to confirm this. The weakness of the civilian-led policy formulation structure, referred to above, means there is a serious deficiency at the intellectual level. During the incumbency (1998–2004) of the National Democratic Alliance (NDA) government that established the NSC, the NSA, Brajesh Mishra, was never a full-time official as he was also simultaneously principal secretary to the prime minister. The United Progressive Alliance (UPA) government that came to power in 2004 has had two NSAs: The late J.N. Dixit, a former foreign secretary, and M.K. Narayanan, a former head of the Intelligence Bureau. All three have come from the "notoriously generalist" bureaucracy, as have several members of the NSC Secretariat and the National Security Advisory Board (NSAB). The last has had on board several former military officers.

Second, civilian expertise on nuclear weapons issues is limited. Of the seven major writers who have elaborated on nuclear strategy, five have a background as career military officers.[53] Despite the broad accordance of most with the concept of minimum deterrence, their positions are frequently inconsistent with it in ways identified above, that is, in their frequent resort to American strategic discourse to strengthen their arguments about particular aspects of nuclear strategy they advocate. Of the two civilians, only one, K. Subrahmanyam, is a votary of minimum deterrence, but he has been inconsistent, raising his recommendation for the size of India's arsenal from sixty (pre-1998) to 150 (post-1998) warheads without a clear argument.[54] As a result, the bureaucracy, already lacking in expertise, lacks a resource base that is both civilian/political and conceptually sound.

Conclusion

While the entire range of variables that are the themes of this book are relevant, the main ones affecting India have been globalization and the revolution in military affairs. The first is closely related to both insurgency/terrorism and nuclear strategy, while the latter—the nuclear RMA—has been at the forefront of India's short but troubled nuclear-strategic history. In both the cases discussed here, counterterrorism and nuclear strategy, direct civilian control of the military has been strong. But civilian control has been problematic in the sense that the *policy content* has been distorted. The lack of an integrated structure of policy formulation and civilian expertise on security matters has led to an excessively militarized approach to national security in areas where this has been either counterproductive or unnecessary.

In the first case, there has been overdependence on the army to tackle a problem that it is not intrinsically cut out to do. The flawed use of the army for a role that carries inherent difficulties has meant that its military effectiveness has been relatively weak. This has in turn contributed to an unstable security environment and poor defense efficiency in the broad sense of the term. In the second, the army has been used as an instrument of policy (compellence) to try—unsuccessfully, as it inevitably turned out—to extricate the government from an intolerable situation that it had failed to anticipate in the first place. Military effectiveness has clearly been below par, and the long, difficult, and expensive process of mobilization and demobilization has reduced defense efficiency considerably. In addition, the civilian leadership's inadequate understanding of the basic nuclear-strategic posture that India has adopted—minimum deterrence—means that if the state comes under pressure, the military's operational-technical approach to force design, grounded in an alien doctrinal approach that already enjoys considerable influence because of the absence of adequate doctrinal thinking, may take the country down a path that is expansive, wasteful, and risk-prone. The effectiveness of the armed forces is bound to be reduced if resources are directed into areas of little utility such as planning for war in a nuclear environment, as the army has been doing under its revised doctrine. Defense efficiency will accordingly be reduced as well.

What is to be done? Clearly, it is vital that an effective policy planning and decision-making institutional structure be developed. The NDA government had given this some thought and attempted to establish a more effective policy structure.[55] The NSC, assisted by the NSA, is the apex body for the formulation of national security strategy, and is drawn mainly from the national-level Cabinet. The secretaries of the major ministries, including Defense, External Affairs, and Finance, plus the governor of the Reserve Bank of India (India's central bank), constitute the Strategic Policy Group (SPG). With perhaps individual exceptions, neither body has a high level of defense and strategic expertise. The NSC secretariat, which has a staff function for both the NSC and the SPG, is also responsible for joint intelligence assessment. Its capacity to serve as an effective staff for the NSC is questionable. Finally, the NSAB, a conceptually laudable innovation because it coopts outside experts, is in practice dominated by former bureaucrats, and is in any case not taken very seriously for inputs into policy formulation. The problem seems to lie not so much in the conceptualization of the structure as in its implementation. Reform has taken place, but in shadow rather than in substance.[56]

The first step toward a more effective, all-round and integrated policy would be to activate a careful selection of the NSAB, and to institutionalize its inputs into the NSC and the NSA. As a staff body, it should have the capacity to incorporate nongovernmental expertise through specialized task forces set up for specific issues. In another quarter, the relatively low-profile system of Parliamentary committees related to national security (defense, external affairs et al.) also needs to be supported by similar staff bodies drawing on public expertise. The role of Parliament in shaping national security policy, hitherto weak, needs to be strengthened.[57] Only then can we expect to see the development of more balanced civil-military relations, and more importantly, balanced civil-military content in national security policy.

The central argument of this chapter is that while global factors play a significant role in altering the strategic environment, and thus necessitating defense reform, it is in the domestic realm that the final determinants that give shape to the character of reform are located. The crux lies in the nature of civil-military relations. In the Indian case, the key determinant is not so much who holds formal power, but how it is exercised. It is generally held that in a democracy, civilian control of the military is essential. This study shows that civilian control of the military in a democratic polity can still be problematic. It warns against assuming that the positive trend of democratization in other states will necessarily bring an end to military-oriented approaches to security issues. Policies that fail to recognize the severe limitations of such an approach are liable to prove costly (politically as well as financially) in terms of both military effectiveness and defense efficiency. In the Indian case, the inadequacies of the civilian leadership—a shallow epistemic base and inadequate institutions—have led to the persistence of civilian militarism with respect to the key areas of counterterrorism and nuclear strategy. As a result, military effectiveness has been undermined as the armed forces have been tasked with missions, such as crushing terrorist networks and exercising compellence against a hostile nuclear state, unsuitable for them. In turn, the wastage of resources acts as a drag on defense efficiency. The chief lesson of the Indian experience is that globalization/liberalization and accompanying technological change create conditions that require a thoughtful and carefully institutionalized response in which mere surface civilian control is not enough. A civilian-political response that avoids the hazards of civilian militarism is essential.

NOTES

I thank Sunil Dasgupta as well as Thomas Bruneau, David Pion-Berlin, Harold Trinkunas, and the other participants in the project for their valuable suggestions and comments on the initial draft of this paper.

1. Apurba Kundu, *Militarism in India: The Army and Civil Society in Consensus* (London: Tauris, and New York: St. Martin's Press, 1998).
2. Dipankar Banerjee, "Military Professionalism of a First-World Army," in Muthiah Alagappa, ed., *Military Professionalism in Asia* (Honolulu: East-West Center, 2001), 19.
3. The domestic/external divide is not distinct. As will be seen in the section on terrorism, much of the terrorist threat to India comes from beyond its borders.
4. Sumona Dasgupta, "Militarization of the India State since the 1980s," *International Studies* 35, 4 (October 1998): 4390–4456.
5. Stephen P. Cohen, *The Indian Army: Its Contribution to the Development of a Nation*, revised edition (New Delhi: Oxford University Press, 2001).
6. Ibid., 180–200.
7. Rajesh M. Basrur, *Minimum Deterrence and India's Nuclear Security* (Palo Alto: Stanford University Press, 2006), ch. 3.
8. For a discussion on the concept of India's extended neighborhood, see S.D. Muni and Girijesh Pant, *India's Energy Security: Prospects for Cooperation with Extended Neighbourhood* (New Delhi: Rupa, 2005), 3–12.
9. The nuclear RMA is discussed below. On the "third industrial revolution," see Daniel Bell, "The Third Technological Revolution and Its Possible Consequences," *Dissent*, 36, 2 (Spring 1989): 164–176. In both cases, the basic impetus for enhancement of technology has come from outside. Though much of the credit for the nuclear RMA goes to indigenous efforts, basic Indian capabilities in terms of knowledge and materials came from outside, especially from the United States.
10. Rakesh Gupta, "India: Towards a Political Economy of Intra-State Conflicts," *Faultlines* 5 (nd), available at http://www.satp.org/satporgtp/publication/faultlines/volume5/Fault5-9rgupta.htm; accessed 19 August 2002.
11. For a comprehensive listing, see "India—Terrorist, Insurgent and Extremist Groups," *South Asia Terrorism Portal*, available at http://www.satp.org/satporgtp/countries/india/terroristoutfits/index.html; accessed 11 January 2006.
12. K. Balchand, "Spreading Tentacles," *Hindu*, 11 August 2002.
13. D. Suba Chandran, "Militant Groups in Kashmir: An Analysis," Institute for Peace and Conflict Studies, New Delhi, Article no. 258, 6 September 1999, available at http://www.ipcs.org/Kashmir_articles2.jsp?action=showView&kValue=548&issue=1012&status=article&mod=a; accessed 29 September 2007; "Major Incidents of Terrorist Violence in

Tripura, 1999–2006," *South Asia Terrorism Portal*, available at http://www.satp.org/satporgtp/countries/india/states/tripura/data_sheets/majorincidents.htm; accessed 29 September 2007; Monirul Hussain, "State, Identity Movements and Internal Displacement in the North-East," *Economic and Political Weekly*, 16 (December 2000): 4519–4523.

14. Yoginder Sikand, "Changing Course of Kashmiri Liberation Struggle: From National Liberation to Islamist Jihad?" *Economic and Political Weekly*, 20 January 2001, available at http://www.epw.org.in/showArticles.php?root=2001&leaf=01&filename=2099&filetype=html; accessed 8 August 2002.
15. Ajai Sahni, "Extremist Islamist Terror and Subversion," in K.P.S. Gill and Ajai Sahni, eds., *The Global Threat of Terror: Ideological, Material and Political Linkages* (New Delhi: Bulwark Books, 2002), 185–196.
16. Mandavi Mehta and Teresita Schaffer, "Islam in Pakistan: Unity and Contradictions," Center for Strategic and International Studies, Washington, DC, 7 October 2002, 15.
17. Rohan Gunaratna, *Inside Al Qaeda: Global Network of Terror* (New York: Columbia University Press, 2002), 208–209. There are reports that al Qaeda may be on the decline, but that the threat from other Islamic terrorist groups remains high, particularly in South Asia, the Middle East, and Southeast Asia. Beth Gardiner, "Report Evaluates al-Qaida Risks Worldwide," *Washington Post*, 10 November 2003, available at http://www.washingtonpost.com/wp-dyn/articles/A24571-2003Nov10.html; accessed 11 November 2003. Bruce Hoffman, however, argues that al Qaeda remains a major threat. Bruce Hoffman, *Al Qaeda, Trends in Terrorism and Future Potentialities* (Santa Monica, California: RAND, 2003).
18. Gunaratna, *Inside Al Qaeda*, 218.
19. Sahni, "Extremist Islamist Terror and Subversion," 212–233; Praveen Swamy, "Behind Bangalore: the Origins of the Long Jihad," *Hindu*, 9 January 2006; and "Behind Bangalore: the Long Jihad Today," *Hindu*, 10 January 2006.
20. Rollie Lal, "South Asian Organized Crime and Terrorist Networks," *Orbis* 49, 2 (Spring 2005): 293–304.
21. Ibid.: 296.
22. Kanti Bajpai, "Diversity, Democracy, and Devolution in India," in Michael E. Brown, and Sumit Ganguly, eds., *Government Policies and Ethnic Relations in Asia and the Pacific* (Cambridge, Mass. and London: MIT Press, 1997), 33–83.
23. Sankaran Kalyanaraman, "The Indian Way in Counterinsurgency," in Efraim Inbar, ed., *Democracies and Small Wars* (London and Portland: Frank Cass, 2003), 89–90, 85–100.
24. Vijendra Singh Jafa, "Counterinsurgency Warfare: the Use and Abuse of Military Force," *Faultlines* 3, available at http://www.satp.org/satporgtp/publication/faultlines/volume3/Fault3-JafaF.htm; accessed 18 August 2005. This applies equally to a domestic-type operation abroad: The

Indian Army's failed counterinsurgency operation against the Liberation Tigers of Tamil Eelam (LTTE) in Sri Lanka during the late 1980s.

25. Jafa, "Counterinsurgency Warfare."
26. For an overview of the numerous insurgencies in the northeast, see Ajai Sahni, "Survey of Conflicts & Resolution in India's Northeast," *Faultlines* 12, available at http://www.satp.org/satporgtp/publication/faultlines/volume12/Article3.htm; accessed 18 August 2005.
27. K.P.S. Gill, "Endgame in Punjab: 1988–1993," *Faultlines* 1, available at http://www.satp.org/satporgtp/publication/faultlines/volume1/Fault1-kpstext.htm; accessed 18 August 2005.
28. Navnita Chadha Behera, *State, Identity and Violence: Jammu, Kashmir and Ladakh* (New Delhi: Manohar, 2000); Sahni, "Extremist Islamist Terror and Subversion."
29. L.N. Subramanian, "CI Operations in Jammu and Kashmir," *Bharat Rakshak Monitor* 3, 2 (September–October 2000), available at http://www.bharat-rakshak.com/MONITOR/ISSUE3-2/lns.html; accessed 3 September 2005.
30. *From Surprise to Reckoning: The Kargil Review Committee Report* (New Delhi: Sage, 2000), 245–246. Though published—with deletions—through a private publisher, the report was produced by the National Security Council Secretariat of the Government of India.
31. K.P.S. Gill, "Tackling Terrorism in Kashmir: Some Lessons from Recent History," cited in Wasbir Hussain, "Multi-force Operations in Counter Terrorism: A View from the Assam Theatre," *Faultlines* 9, available at http://www.satp.org/satporgtp/publication/faultlines/volume9/Article2.htm; accessed 18 August 2005.
32. Government of India, Ministry of Defence, *Reforming the National Security System: Recommendations of the Group of Ministers*, available at http://mod.nic.in/newadditions/rcontents.htm; accessed 18 August 2005.
33. See Peter Chalk, "Pakistan's Role in the Kashmir Insurgency," *Jane's Intelligence Review*, 1 September 2001, reproduced on the Web site of the RAND Corporation, available at http://www.rand.org/hot/op-eds/090101JIR.html; accessed 14 February 2003; and Tim Judah, "The Taliban Papers," *Survival* 44, 1 (Spring 2002): 69–80.
34. Sunil Dasgupta, "The Indian Army and the Problem of Military Change," in Swarna Rajagopalan, ed., *Security and South Asia: Ideas, Institutions, and Initiatives* (New Delhi: Routledge, 2006), 80–111.
35. Ibid.: 88.
36. K. Subrahmanyam with Arthur Monteiro, *Shedding Shibboleths: India's Evolving Strategic Outlook* (Delhi: Wordsmiths, 2005), 21. See also Cohen, *Indian Army*, 173.
37. Lukasz Kamienski, "Comparing the Nuclear and Information RMAs," *Strategic Insights* 2, 4 (April 2003), available at http://www.ccc.nps.navy.mil/si/apr03/strategy2.asp; accessed 3 September 2005.

38. "'Cold Start' to New War Doctrine," *Times of India*, 14 April 2004; "Army Drafts New War Doctrine," *Hindu*, 5 March 2004; Shishir Gupta, "No Eyeball to Eyeball Any More in New War Doctrine," *Indian Express*, 6 March 2004.
39. For a detailed study, see Basrur, *Minimum Deterrence and India's Nuclear Security.*
40. "The Cabinet Committee on Security Reviews Operationalization of India's Nuclear Doctrine," Press Release, Ministry of External Affairs, Government of India, 4 January 2003, available at http://meadev.nic.in/news/official/20030104/official.htm; accessed 19 February 2003.
41. Rajesh M. Basrur, "Nuclear Weapons and Indian Strategic Culture," *Journal of Peace Research* 38, 2 (March 2001): 181–198.
42. This is not to say that the Indian armed forces favor nuclear use, but only that by the very nature of their role, they must necessarily treat nuclear weapons as usable and thus be concerned about their physical characteristics and the ways in which they might be deployed and used if necessary.
43. This view is clear from Home Minister L.K. Advani's post-test exhortation to Pakistan to reassess its policy on Kashmir. See Sabina Inderjit, "Advani Tells Pakistan to Roll Back Its Anti-India Policy," *Times of India*, 19 May 1998.
44. On the "stability-instability paradox," see Michael Krepon and Chris Gagné, eds. *The Stability-Instability Paradox: Nuclear Weapons and Brinkmanship in South Asia* (Washington, DC: Henry L. Stimson Center, 2001). For the original formulation of the concept, see Glen Snyder, "The Balance of Power and the Balance of Terror," in Paul Seabury, ed., *The Balance of Power* (San Francisco: Chandler, 1965), 194–201.
45. Cited in C. Raja Mohan, "Fernandes Unveils 'Limited War' Doctrine," *The Hindu*, 25 January 2000.
46. Ibid.
47. These include General V.P. Malik, chief of the Army Staff during the Kargil conflict, and Air Commodore (retd.) Jasjit Singh, then-director of the Institute for Defence Studies and Analysis, India's largest strategic think tank. See Sonika Gupta and Arpit Rajain, "Interview with General V. P. Malik," in P.R. Chari, Sonika Gupta, and Arpit Rajain, eds., *Nuclear Stability in Southern Asia* (New Delhi: Manohar, 2003), 153–163; and Jasjit Singh, "Beyond Kargil," in Jasjit Singh, ed., *Kargil 1999: Pakistan's Fourth War for Kashmir* (New Delhi: Knowledge World, in association with Institute for Defence Studies and Analyses, 1999), 212–240. Shortly before the India-Pakistan crisis of 2001–2002, Lieutenant-General R.K. Nanavatty, commander of the army's Northern Command, claimed that limited war was possible in a nuclear environment. See "Indian Army General Warns Pak," *Times of India*,

31 October 2001. After the onset of the crisis, chief of the Army Staff General S. Padmanabhan echoed his view. See Rajiv Chandrasekaran, "For India, Deterrence May Not Prevent War," *Washington Post*, 17 January 2002.

48. For a detailed analysis of the crisis, see Rajesh M. Basrur, "Coercive Diplomacy in a Nuclear Environment: The December 13 Crisis," in Rafiq Dossani and Henry S. Rowen, eds., *Prospects for Peace in South Asia* (Palo Alto: Stanford University Press, 2005), 301–325.
49. "We Could Take A Strike and Survive. Pakistan Won't: Fernandes," *Hindustan Times*, 30 December 2001.
50. Bharat Karnad, *Nuclear Weapons and Indian Security: the Realist Foundations of Strategy* (New Delhi: Macmillan, 2002), 616.
51. Michael Ryan Kraig, "The Political and Strategic Imperatives of Nuclear Deterrence in South Asia," *India Review* 2, 1 (January 2003): 24–30.
52. Ibid.: 30.
53. The seven are Gurmeet Kanwal, Bharat Karnad, Raja Menon, Vijai K. Nair, Jasjit Singh, K. Subrahmanyam, and K. Sundarji. Only Karnad and Subrahmanyam are civilians, the rest retired military officers. Their views are discussed in Basrur, *Minimum Deterrence*, ch. 3. Three works by civilian specialists have appeared recently: Basrur, *Minimum Deterrence and India's Nuclear Security*; Rajesh Rajagopalan, *Second Strike: Arguments about Nuclear War in South Asia* (New Delhi: Viking, 2005); and Arpit Rajain, *Nuclear Deterrence in Southern Asia: China, India and Pakistan* (New Delhi, Thousand Oaks, California, and London: Thousand Oaks, 2005). It is too early to say whether any of them will have a significant impact on the policymaking establishment.
54. The first recommendation is in K. Subrahmanyam, "Nuclear Force Design and Minimum Deterrence Strategy for India," in Bharat Karnad, ed., *Future Imperiled* (New Delhi: Viking, 1994), 176–195; the second in K. Subrahmanyam, "A Credible Deterrent: Logic of the Nuclear Doctrine," *Times of India*, 4 October 1999.
55. D. Shyam Babu, "India's National Security Council: Stuck in the Cradle?" *Security Dialogue* 34, 2 (June 2003): 215–230.
56. Ibid.: 227.
57. Shrikant Paranjpe, *Parliament and the Making of Indian Foreign Policy* (New Delhi: Radiant, 1997).

10

Defense Reforms, Civil-Military Relations, and the Defense of Taiwan

Toshi Yoshihara

Introduction

Taiwan's remarkable political transformation in the past decade, in the face of a growing (and arguably existential) military threat from China, raises some compelling theoretical and policy-relevant questions.[1] How and to what extent has democratization enhanced or undermined Taiwan's defense? In particular, how have defense reforms and associated changes in civil-military relations secured Taipei's strategic position vis-à-vis Beijing? Given that the Taiwan Strait remains a volatile and potentially catastrophic flashpoint that could pit China directly against the United States, these questions are pertinent to the stability of the Western Pacific and America's long-term position in the region. Furthermore, these questions gain urgency as China's rise has added to the fragility of the cross-strait military balance.

This chapter suggests that the consolidation of democracy and the resulting defense reforms related to civil-military relations have severely complicated the politics surrounding Taiwan's defense.[2] On the one hand, the democratic transition brought about impressive strides toward civilian control of the military and established the basis for all the benefits (at least in theory) that such a shift entails.[3] On the other hand, how civilian control has translated into tangible gains for national defense in light of the island's deteriorating military position remains far from clear. Historical legacies, the rise of ethnic politics, the inherent combativeness and peculiarities of Taiwanese politics, and other unintended consequences of democratization have either served to stall follow-on defense reforms or strained civil-military relations that could in turn undermine the long-term security of Taiwan.[4]

To explore the impact of Taiwan's democratic transition on its security, the first section of this chapter places the island within the global context of defense reforms. Second, it reviews the historical context of the island's civil-military relations and how democratization permitted significant changes that paved the way for greater civilian control. Third, it examines the civil-military problems that the democratic transition has produced, left unresolved, or exacerbated at the presidential and legislative levels. Fourth, the chapter relates the incomplete nature of the political evolution to the acrimonious civil-military debates that have impeded efforts at shoring up Taiwan's defense, including the island's threat perceptions, evolving military strategy, and the revolution in military affairs agenda.[5] Finally, this analysis ends with an assessment of the extent to which Taipei has advanced its defense reforms in the past decade.

The Global Context for Taiwan's Defense Reforms

This volume identifies globalization, economic liberalization, the revolution in military affairs (RMA), and democratization as four of the main global influences on defense reform efforts. In this broader context, Taiwan occupies a rather peculiar and often conflicted position. On the one hand, due to Beijing's vigorous efforts to enforce the "one China" principle, the island is one of the most diplomatically isolated nations in the world (especially when taking into account its political and economic standing among other nations). China has effectively locked Taiwan out of many major international forums and multilateral organizations, at least in an official capacity, while stymieing military technology transfers to the island from most of the industrialized, democratic world. Taipei has thus been denied direct exposure to the normative dimensions of civil-military relations promoted in the West and deprived of more diverse sources of critical technologies. As a result, Taiwan depends almost entirely on the United States, the only major power that has extended explicit security commitments to the island, for absorbing both normative and technological benefits in defense-related areas for the past few decades. At first glance, one might conclude that the island tends to be immune to the globalization of norms and the rapid diffusion of technologies in military affairs.

On the other hand, Taiwan stands as one of the major economic successes in Asia. The island's GNP, rapid economic growth (at least prior to the downturn in the early 2000s), industrial and technological capacities, volume of trade and financial interactions, presence in the international markets, and impressive foreign currency reserves are the envy of its neighbors and the world. Taiwan thus is truly enmeshed in the regional and global economy. Taiwan's peaceful transition to a genuine democracy that permits meaningful political competition represents a model ripe for emulation for China and other states. While Taipei's dependence on Washington certainly undermines the island's flexibility, it also accrues significant benefits because the United States often has the most and the best to offer. American foreign policy, particularly in the post–Cold War period, has been predicated in part on the promotion of democracy and civilian rule. Taiwan's semi-official political relations with the United States, strong socioeconomic ties, and continuing (albeit low profile) military-to-military exchanges certainly promoted U.S. values to politicians and security managers on the island. Washington has (and continues to) offer the ROC government cutting-edge military technologies that would otherwise be unavailable on the global arms market.

How can one make sense of the apparently dichotomous nature of Taiwan's position vis-à-vis these four global forces? One way is to appreciate the sequential and interconnected nature of the four determinants for the island's defense reforms. Taiwan's various achievements derive in large part from its economic successes. Hewing somewhat closely to the "modernization model" in the democratization literature, the island's burgeoning economy in the 1970s and 1980s created a nascent middle class that pushed for expanded political space with its newfound wealth and influence.[6] This in turn led to a gradual process of democratic consolidation and institutionalization that weaned the military from its internal preoccupations with state and society (detailed below). Taiwan's democratic experiment also coincided with the Third Wave of democratization sweeping through Asia, alongside South Korea and the Philippines in the late 1980s. Taiwan's economic rise as an "Asian tiger," and increased connectivity to the outside world during this same period, accelerated the transfer of off-the-shelf and dual-use technologies that greatly benefited the indigenous technological base, including RMA-related developments in the defense sector.

Economic success brought with it a set of vulnerabilities as well. While Taiwan escaped the 1997–1998 Asian financial crisis relatively unscathed, the devastation visited upon Southeast Asian, and subsequently, South Korean economies highlighted the ugly side of capital mobility in a globalized economy. More recently, the potential economic liabilities associated with tremendous and highly profitable Taiwanese business investments in China have raised concerns in Taipei. In particular, Beijing's efforts to promote the economic dimension of cross-strait relations have heightened fears that China is using the growing interdependence as an indirect, long-term "attraction" strategy to make future political reunion more palatable to the Taiwanese. At worst, it is feared that the Mainland could use its growing economic leverage to influence powerful business groups on the island to deter political movements from pursuing independence. Such a wedge between business and political interests could clearly sow social disharmony and divergences in threat perceptions among the Taiwanese public. This phenomenon could in turn impact the sense of urgency related to defense reforms (detailed below).

The consolidation of democracy in Taiwan has also become a source of instability in cross-strait relations. In particular, the politicization of Taiwanese identity has deeply divided the society between those who believe that the native populace is distinct (both culturally and historically) from the mainland Chinese, and those who advocate an eventual reunion with China under certain circumstances acceptable to the people on the island. The rise of nativism in Taiwan has led to increased hostilities with China, which fears that identity politics could accelerate the independence movement. The absence of consensus on what it means to be Taiwanese or Chinese therefore contributes to deep social cleavages over the extent to which Beijing poses an existential threat. This clearly has implications both for threat perceptions and for how Taiwan should respond to China's increasingly capable military.

As this chapter demonstrates below, the RMA debate in Taiwan, which was made possible in the first place by the expanding technological base of the economy, contains ingredients for cross-strait escalation in a crisis. The RMA-based promise of real-time intelligence and long-range, precision strikes emboldened many Taiwanese politicians and defense planners to advocate an offensive orientation against China, including counterstrikes against military and civilian targets on the Mainland during a conflict. The subsequent political fallout that resulted from disagreement over the prudence of such a potentially escalatory posture have had a palpable impact on Taiwan's military modernization, carrying serious consequences for the island's broader defense reforms.

In general, the four global determinants have tended to complicate Taiwan's path to defense reforms. Economic interdependence, a widely accepted beneficial phenomenon of globalization, has increased susceptibility to Chinese pressure in the political sphere while confusing domestic threat perceptions and priorities. Democratization, an outcome made possible by economic success, has spawned identity politics that also obscures assessments about China as a threat and associated policies to shore up Taiwan's defenses. The RMA, which encouraged a retaliatory outlook against China, has divided security managers over the question of escalation control and stability. Such disagreements clearly create obstacles to defense reforms.

DEMOCRATIZATION AND CIVIL-MILITARY CHANGES

Highly militarized and deeply authoritarian, the Republic of China remained under martial law, initially imposed by Chiang Kai-shek in 1949, until 1987, when the ruling Kuomintang party began gradually to loose its grip on power and allow civil society to assert primacy over government and, at least nominally, the military. Since then, democratization has been a slow and careful process, over which the specter of the Mainland and the need to meet U.S. interests—including democratic norms—have been powerfully formative influences. Successful elections, however, have not proved a sufficient guarantee of good civil-military relations.

Historical Context: The Party-Army Complex

Following the Chinese communist victory on the mainland and the Nationalist retreat to Taiwan in 1949, the Kuomintang (KMT) established its authoritarian rule modeled after the Leninist party-state system. This centralization of political authority was an interrelated response to the perceived Chinese communist threat and fears of domestic opposition to KMT's hold on power. In order to mobilize a potentially uncooperative populace on the island to defend Taiwan and to prepare for another military contest on the mainland, the KMT sought to exercise unchallenged authority.[7] Under this party-state system, the military functioned as an instrument of the party to ensure regime survival. Far from being a politically neutral institution, the military made its presence felt throughout state and society to enforce the KMT's unrivaled dominance.

During the period of martial law from 1949–1987, officers (both active duty and retired) occupied key positions within the civilian government. For decades the military enjoyed a substantial presence in the Central Standing Committee, the top decision-making body of the KMT. The military was closely involved in mobilizing votes for the KMT through the influence of local commanders and the Veterans Affairs Commission. In addition, military education imbued with KMT ideology was mandatory across all secondary schools and universities to reinforce social indoctrination.

To enforce the KMT's rule, the military implemented martial law and maintained domestic order through the fearsome Taiwan Garrison Command (TGC). The KMT empowered the TGC to supervise the civilian police force, suppress dissident activities through a variety of intrusive means, and censor the media. At the same time, the military owned a network of media outlets to propagate the KMT's message to the general public. The military also involved itself in a variety of economic activities on the island.

To guarantee the military's loyalty to the party, officers were required to be members of the KMT. A political commissar system, which paralleled the military command structure, oversaw the ideological alignment of the armed forces to the ruling party. In particular, the defense ministry's General Political Warfare Department became a powerful arm of the KMT to sustain military loyalty and to foster support for the party. Further cementing this relationship, the officer corps was almost exclusively a domain of residents who fled the mainland with the Nationalists after the Chinese civil war. Known collectively as Mainlanders (*waishenren*)—as opposed to descendants of Chinese immigrants to the island from a far earlier era—this politically powerful minority on the island enjoyed privileges and opportunities within the military.

On defense matters, civilian oversight (with the exception of the president himself) was virtually nonexistent. The defense minister, although technically a civilian as required by law, was invariably a retired general officer. Military personnel dominated the Ministry of National Defense (MND) and other key national security bureaucracies, while civilians were largely excluded from decisions related to security issues and defense policy.[8]

Furthermore, institutional arrangements ensured that the ROC president (particularly during the martial law period under Chiang

Kai-shek and, his son, Chiang Ching-kuo) had the final say on military matters. Technically, the chief of General Staff (CGS), the head of the General Staff Headquarters (GSH), was subordinate to the defense minister and thus responsible to the premier of the state organ. In reality, the CGS, who dealt with operational issues and commanded the three military services, reported directly to the president. The president's dual role as the secretary-general of the KMT further guaranteed the dominance of the ruling party over military affairs.

This dual chain of command placed the CGS outside of the parliamentary system, circumventing legislative oversight. Personal ties between the president and the CGS rather than institutional mechanisms shaped decisions on defense policy.[9] The GSH thus enjoyed a high degree of autonomy in crafting strategy, doctrine, procurement, budgeting, and force structure. Furthermore, direct access by the CGS to the president severely weakened the defense ministry as a player in formulating national security policy. Indeed, the ministry was largely left out of the deliberations between the military command and the president on important matters, such as the defense budget.

Given this set of interlocking party-military arrangements, Taiwan's civil-military relations proved problematic for several reasons. First, to the extent that key national security decision-making processes were dominated by the military, there existed the political phenomenon of partial civilian control. Second, the military's substantial presence within state and party organs rendered political neutrality of the officer corps moot. Third, the military's direct access to the president as the supreme party-state leader shielded the armed forces from executive and legislative oversight. Fourth, the military's monopoly over the internal security apparatus as an instrument of oppression alienated the populace, while the dominance of Mainlanders within the officer corps deepened suspicions among the native Taiwanese. Finally, the military's involvement in internal affairs of state, including an extensive network of economic interests, detracted from its main external mission to defend the state against the Chinese threat.

Advances toward Civilian Control

The lifting of martial law in 1987, a major milestone in Taiwan's democratization, initiated a gradual process of military withdrawal from domestic politics. During the early 1990s, important reforms began to shift the civil-military balance. In 1991, President Lee Tung-hui ended the

"Period of Mobilization to Suppress the Communist Rebellion," which maintained the fiction that the ROC intended to retake the mainland. By 1992, temporary provisions that had suspended the ROC's constitution since 1948 were abolished. This move reestablished the president's constitutional authority over the armed forces. In the same year, the government dissolved the much-feared TGC and turned over internal security duties to the civilian police. In 1992 and 1993, the Legislative Yuan passed laws that banned party activities in the military and universities. At the same time, the KMT began systematically to remove military personnel from all of the party's major policymaking bodies. The military for its part began to divest its interests in the media, the school system, and the private sector.

The democratic transition, however, remained a delicate affair. The military occasionally exhibited "conditional loyalty" to the state when civilian leaders sought to assert greater control or pursued policies perceived to challenge the military's interests.[10] The most prominent examples of such conditionality occurred in 1990. In the face of Taiwan's rapid democratization, conservative factions of the KMT began to apply brakes to the process. Then-premier Hau Pei-tsun (a Mainlander and former chief of the general staff and defense minister) explicitly warned that Taiwan's armed forces would not support the independence of the island even if a national referendum reached such a decision.[11] In other words, the military distinguished its loyalty to the ROC constitution from its commitment to defend the citizens of the island. Later, the appointment of a civilian to the defense minister's post in 1990 and 1993 respectively apparently produced frictions over civilian policy coordination with the CGS and the MND. The disagreements proved so contentious that President Lee was subsequently forced to appoint a retired general once again.

Nevertheless, civilian control over the military continued to gain ground. In 1998, Taiwan's premier stripped the GSH of its two main bureaus on procurement and research and development and placed them under MND, after a series of arms sales scandals rocked the government. The late 1990s also witnessed the first civilian-led investigations to uncover illicit activities by the MND and the armed forces.

After the 1992 legislative elections, which for the first time permitted the participation of opposition parties, the Legislative Yuan increasingly asserted its authority and expanded its oversight of the military. In September 1998, the CGS made a historically unprecedented appearance before the Legislative Yuan to explain the nation's defense policy. At this hearing, CGS Tang Fei publicly pledged the military's commitment to defend the state and constitution regardless of the sovereign status of the island. The legislature also played a critical role in demoting the General Political Warfare Department to a minor bureau and in circumscribing its activities to military morale within the MND. Finally, the Legislative Yuan began to pursue high-profile investigations of procurement scandals and conscription problems.

The Legislative Yuan's National Defense Committee now regularly holds meetings and hearings with the defense minister to discuss the defense budget and the threat emanating from China. Even the head of the secretive National Security Bureau (NSB) has appeared before legislators to explain budgetary issues. The defense committee also examines the entire defense budget through a very structured and time-consuming formal process. The high-profile acquisition pieces of the budget undergo the most scrutiny and often produce protracted debates (detailed below) among the legislators.

One of the major contributions of the legislature to Taiwan's civil-military relations is the passage of two laws, the National Defense Law (NDL) and the Ministry of National Defense Organization Law, in January 2000. The two pieces of legislation set the stage for further consolidation of civilian control by stipulating a major reorganization of the defense establishment.

Among the most important, the laws placed both the MND and the GSH under the defense minister.[12] The defense minister became responsible for overseeing both the administration and command of the military, thus ending the previous dual chain of command. This arrangement ensured that all military directives from the president would have to pass through the defense minister before reaching the CGS. The subordination of the CGS meant that the GSH could no longer monopolize decisions related to defense strategy, the budget, operational planning, acquisition, and force structure. Moreover, this single line of authority linked the CGS's accountability directly to the premier, which for the first time exposed the position to legislative oversight.

Second, to consolidate civilian control, the NDL sought to civilianize the MND. The law required civilians to staff one-third of the ministry by the end of 2003. Third, the laws established new bodies within the MND designed to strengthen the ability of the ministry to formulate the nation's overall defense policy. In other words, an increasingly civilianized ministry would gradually replace the skills and expertise that previously resided primarily within the GSH. As a part of this process, authority over key decisions on issues such as operational requirements was elevated from the three services and the GSH to the defense minister.

Fourth, the legislation centralized the authority of the GSH over the three individual services to enhance jointness. This move solidified the CGS's ability to command joint operations and narrowed the services' duties to training and doctrine. Policy issues were thus elevated to higher levels of command. Finally, the NDL explicitly forbade the participation of active-duty military personnel in political activities.[13] The implementation of these measures have helped depoliticize the military's role in state and society and to place critical decisions firmly in the hands of civilians.

The ultimate test of civilian supremacy was whether the transfer of presidential power from the KMT to the pro-independence opposition party, the Democratic Progressive Party (DPP), could proceed peacefully and without military intervention. During the 1990s, it remained largely unclear how the military would respond to such a major shift in the political landscape. The test came in March 2000 when DPP candidate, Chen Shui-bian, won a three-way presidential race to become the first non-KMT president of Taiwan. Even before Chen's surprise victory, then CGS Tang Yao-ming declared the allegiance of his forces to any successor to President Lee. Then-Defense Minister Tang Fei also publicly pledged the military's loyalty to Taiwan immediately after the election.

At a critical juncture, the military demonstrated restraint, political neutrality, and respect for democratic control. Several interrelated reasons explain this successful transfer of power. First, the voluntary nature of the transition avoided military backlash. The party-state system dissolved from within as the KMT severed its formal ties to the military. Second, a gradual approach avoided convulsive changes that might have unleashed instability. It took over a decade of bargaining to place the military unequivocally under a single civilian chain of command and to subject it to unprecedented legislative, media, and public scrutiny. Third, the skills of Taiwan's political leaders within the KMT, particularly President Lee, marginalized the influence of conservative factions that were resistant to change.[14]

Democratization and Its Discontents

Chen's rise to power ushered in a new phase in civil-military relations that has revealed the challenges of Taiwan's democratic experiment. At the presidential level, the DPP-led administration has demonstrated both a lack of confidence in its ability to lead military reforms and an abiding distrust of the armed forces. The Mainlander-dominated military, which tends to sympathize with the Nationalist outlook, remains suspicious of Chen's intentions. At the legislative level, the increasing assertiveness of a fractious legislature has stalled critical arms procurement plans that have frustrated efforts to modernize the military and deepened resentment of the officer corps toward civilians.

Constraints to Exerting Civilian Control

President Chen's relationship with the military has been rather tenuous since his first electoral victory. While he has consolidated his credibility and power vis-à-vis the armed forces by promoting native Taiwanese officers and those who have supported his national security agenda, he has had to proceed cautiously in deference to the military. The public assurances of allegiance by the CGS and the defense minister during and after the 2000 presidential elections in part reflected the delicate nature of civil-military ties. As the Chen administration entered office, many senior Mainlander officers were reportedly reluctant to serve under a DPP president. Media rumors of dissatisfaction and opposition within the officer corps circulated throughout Taipei. Indeed, there is some evidence that the charged atmosphere at the time forced Chen to postpone his first major reshuffling of the military leadership for over a year.[15]

Recent controversies in presidential politics have also spilled over into the civil-military realm. During the hotly contested March 2004 presidential elections, a bizarre assassination attempt on the president and his running mate compelled Chen to declare a state of emergency that called up tens of thousands of additional military and police personnel. Following a tumultuous vote recount that affirmed Chen's slim victory over the KMT-led coalition, the opposition accused him of depriving the military (presumably a voting bloc that would have favored the Nationalist challenger) a chance at the polls.[16] President Chen later charged that the military, at the KMT's bidding, attempted to foment a "soft coup" during the recount. He contended that retired officers conspired to convince serving generals to resign or feign illness en masse to add to the turmoil and thereby destabilize Chen's government.[17] The opposition cried foul while the MND vehemently denied Chen's allegations and repeatedly pledged its loyalty to the state. The furor over these incidents may have subsided, but they underscore the vulnerability of civil-military relations to politicization.

Several reasons account for the apparent distrust between the civilian leaders of the DPP and the military. Historical memories play an undeniable role. Many prominent members of the DPP, including President Chen, had been dissidents during the martial law years when excesses of the KMT and the military were virtually indistinguishable. Thus, to many advocates of democracy in the 1970s and 1980s who later became leading members of the DPP, the military symbolized KMT oppression of the island. Having served as the ideological mouthpiece of the KMT in the education system that espoused pro-unification policies, the military carries an additional historical baggage.

More recently, the emergence of ethnic politics designed to sharpen the divide between native Taiwanese and Mainlanders has kept wide the gulf between DPP leaders and the military. The DPP's nativist movement, which has sought to promote a unique Taiwanese identity distinct from the island's Chinese heritage, is now a major and regular feature of Taiwan's politics.[18] Indeed, President Chen has consistently exploited the identity card to galvanize support during electoral campaigns. In contrast, the officer corps, which is still heavily populated by Mainlanders, tends to identify with the Nationalist position that Taiwan is still a part of China. Not surprisingly, the military harbors genuine fears and suspicions of a DPP-led government. Many officers are deeply ambivalent of a civilian leadership that has actively promoted what they perceive as a provocative and dangerous agenda for independence.[19] Given the generational and ethnic nature of this rift, civil-military tensions are likely to persist.

Closely related efforts to civilianize the MND have been primarily cosmetic, depriving the civilian executive body of direct levers to influence defense policy. On paper, civilian presence within the defense ministry has substantially increased as required by the NDL. In reality, the vast majority of the civilians are retired military officers. This is in large part a result of the military's longstanding monopoly over security and defense issues prior to the democratic transition. Given that available civilians remain ill-equipped to handle complex military affairs, the necessity of continuity remains a powerful driving force. Appointments to senior military positions following the 2000 presidential elections reveal a pattern that continues today. After his electoral victory, Chen (to the disappointment of his supporters) appointed a retired navy admiral to the defense minister's post and chose Defense Minister Tang Fei to assume the premiership to ensure postelection stability. Bowing to such realities of military clout, the president has had to live with the KMT's legacy: retired general officers have successively occupied the position of defense minister.[20]

Legislative Politics: Vicious Partisanship and Gridlock

While the statutory power of civilian oversight is an essential quality for healthy civil-military relations, such authority can be manipulated or taken to extremes. In the case of Taiwan, a government deeply divided between a DPP executive and a KMT legislature has prevented any modicum of agreement on the nation's defense. The opposition pan-blue coalition (consisting of the KMT, the People's First Party, and the New Party) has held on to a slight majority within the Legislative Yuan and has used its position to stall the president's initiatives. The resulting political deadlock in the legislature has had a paralyzing effect on defense reforms. Despite expectations that the pan-green group (the DPP-Taiwan Solidarity Union alliance) might dislodge the Nationalists, the pan-blue coalition gained a firmer hold after the December 2004 legislative elections.[21] As such, the stalemate is expected to continue.

The most prominent victim of this legislative logjam has been Taiwan's defense procurement plans. Since U.S. President George W. Bush approved a massive arms sales package to the island in April 2001, the Legislative Yuan has made only modest progress to acquire the promised (and some would argue much needed) equipment. With the exception of a hard fought agreement to purchase four *Kidd*-class destroyers in 2003, the other major items have remained stuck within the legislature. In June 2004, the Executive Yuan submitted to the legislature an extra-budgetary fifteen-year supplemental procurement bill worth $18 billion that covered the rest of the major weapons approved by Bush three years before. The bill includes the purchase of six *Patriot* PAC-III antiballistic missile batteries, twelve antisubmarine P3-C aircraft, and eight diesel submarines. According to supporters of this deal, the weaponry is deemed critical to bolster Taiwan's defensive capabilities against China's increasingly capable military.

The debate, which quickly degenerated into a partisan struggle, reveals the range of voices (however outlandish) opposed to the bill. Many simply balked at the staggering price tag. They contended that Taiwan's sagging economy could not afford such a luxury.[22] Others expressed doubt on the military utility of these big-ticket items, including the ability of the *Patriot* systems to counter China's ongoing missile buildup. Beyond pragmatic considerations, some legislators devoted a great deal of their energies to the United States. One lawmaker argued that Taiwan could simply count on American intervention to meet the island's defensive needs.[23] Some critics accused Washington and its business interests of imposing the terms of the deal on Taipei and have described the proposed sale as an "insurance policy" to secure future U.S. assistance to the island.[24] Another, responding to American pleas to approve the arms package, likened the United States to a "mafia leader" demanding "protection money."[25]

While many of these latter reactions should be discounted as political posturing intended narrowly for local politics, they collectively demonstrate the far-reaching changes that democratization has brought to Taiwan's national security debate and process. Protracted opposition by the pan-blue coalition produced over sixty failed attempts to pass the procurement bill through the Procedure Committee of the LY, a body that determines the inclusion of an item on the legislative agenda. It was not until December 2006 that the bill secured a spot on the agenda.[26] Six years after the Bush administration decided to sell the arms, the Legislative Yuan agreed to 1) purchase the antisubmarine aircraft; 2) upgrade existing missile defense systems; and 3) study options to buy submarines. Worth nearly $300 million, the approved plan was a far cry from the $18 billion package offered by President Bush.[27] While such acquisitions represent a small bipartisan step in the right direction, Taiwan's political parties will still need to forge a much stronger consensus to shore up the island's defense.

The debate is also notable for the role reversal between the pan-blue and pan-green coalitions. During the KMT's reign as the ruling party, the Nationalists were the major proponents of arms purchases from the United States. Indeed, many of the disputed items have been on KMT wish lists throughout the late 1990s. Prior to Chen's ascendance, the DPP for its part has long questioned expenditures on defense while championing spending on social services. The swap in positions has further politicized the debate, exposing each side to accusations of hypocrisy and inconsistency. This phenomenon has certainly left the professional military questioning the seriousness with which civilian politicians are pursuing Taiwan's defense.

This political stalemate in Taipei has in turn threatened to harm relations with the United States, the island's only security guarantor and prime supplier of equipment crucial to Taiwan's military modernization.[28] Since at least early 2003, U.S. policymakers have watched with alarm as the bill languished in the Legislative Yuan. Senior American officials, including former Deputy Secretary of Defense Paul Wolfowitz and Deputy Under Secretary of Defense for East Asia Richard Lawless, have repeatedly warned that Taiwan's apparent indecision about its own defense could undermine the island's security. Wolfowitz was particularly blunt: If Taipei is not serious about defending itself, then Washington should not be either.[29] The irony is that Taiwan's democratic achievements underwrote America's rationale for supplying arms to the island. Yet, the very instruments of democracy that Washington promoted have now obstructed U.S. efforts to help Taiwan defend itself.[30]

The DPP's apparent about-face on defense procurement has reinforced perceptions within the military that the civilian leadership merely succumbed to U.S. pressure. It has also reconfirmed lingering suspicions that the Chen administration treats arms purchases as a political and economic tool to secure American support rather than as a strictly strategic and military component of Taiwan's defense. Chen's exhortations that the defense items are crucial to Taiwan's security thus ring hollow to many in the military.

While partisan politics account for much of the deadlock over Taiwan's defensive needs, other factors have contributed to this standstill. In many respects, the legislature is still unfit to fulfill its statutory responsibilities. In general, the body lacks the expertise to oversee the procurement process. Notably, the Legislative Yuan suffers from a weak professional staff dedicated to defense issues. Legislators well versed in military affairs remain a rare commodity. Many use unreliable media accounts and personal biases to distort national security issues as a way to score political points with their constituents. This has had a corrosive effect on civil-military relations. As Michael Swaine argues, the Legislative Yuan "is ill-informed or, worst yet, deliberately obstructionist, thus contributing to a sense of resentment and suspicion with the professional military."[31] Clearly, the island's civil-military relations face systemic and generational challenges that will not be resolved in the short- to medium-term.

DEFENDING TAIWAN

The impact of Taiwan's democratization on civil-military relations provides an important backdrop to the island's evolving national security strategy. Indeed, the contentious debates over Taiwan's current defense reforms owe much to the island's democratic consolidation. These debates have in turn uncovered difficult choices that the political and military leaderships will have to grapple with in the coming years. Consensus on critical defense policies and reforms, including how best to enhance Taipei's ability to wage modern war against an increasingly capable China, has remained elusive. Specifically, disputes over the level of China's threat to Taiwan, Taipei's evolving military strategy, and the direction of the revolution in military affairs have shaped and, in some cases, strained civil-military relations.

Debating the Security Environment: Identity Crisis and Threat Perceptions

The People's Republic of China's (PRC) military modernization of the past decade is the key driving force behind Taiwan's current defense reforms. Perpetual tensions in cross-strait relations—heightened by China's hardening stance toward the island's pro-independence movement—have made the Taiwan Strait one of the most dangerous flashpoints in Asia. China's economic ascendance has contributed to the double-digit growth of its defense budget over the past decade. As a result, Beijing has been able to make important strides to improve its war fighting capability for a Taiwan scenario. Indeed, the increasing sophistication and size of the Chinese military has raised fears in Taipei and Washington that the balance of forces may soon tilt in Beijing's favor. The potential inability of Taiwan to keep pace with the PRC has heightened the sense of urgency behind initiatives to bolster the island's defenses.

China appears poised to employ a variety of means to coerce Taiwan into early submission while preventing the intervention of U.S. forces for as long as possible. In terms of acquisition, the apparent preference for specific types of Russian-built and indigenous weaponry appears to conform to this coercive approach to a Taiwan contingency. Eschewing a potentially costly amphibious assault against the island, the Chinese have instead chosen to rely on politico-psychological and unconventional approaches to warfare. In addition to the array of advanced warships and fighter aircraft expected to enter service, Beijing has deployed short-range ballistic missiles and land-attack cruise missiles against strategic and politically symbolic targets on the island. Strikes against such sites are likely designed to rapidly undermine Taiwan's political will and military morale to fight and thus force Taipei to the negotiating table on Beijing's terms. At the same time, the People's Liberation Army has been arming itself with sea denial capabilities, such as antiship missiles that can be launched from the air, land, and sea as well as stealthy submarines, to deter possible U.S. military entry into waters near Taiwan. Given the multidimensional nature of the Chinese threat to Taiwan, Taipei faces mounting complications to its defense planning.

Yet, despite the clarity and singularity of Taipei's security challenges emanating from China, Taiwanese threat perceptions remain far from unanimous. As noted above, the injection of ethnicity into the political discourse has undermined the unity of the island. Taiwan's democratization combined with the DPP's drive to carve out a distinctive native identity has polarized the island sufficiently to impact Taiwan's defense over the long term. Without a national consensus on what Taiwan is and stands for, notions concerning the nature of the adversary have become murkier. As Denny Roy succinctly observes, "The ultimate goal is undefined: Is China the enemy or the mother country? With this question unanswered, a totally coherent grand strategy is perhaps impossible."[32] Michael Swaine concurs: "Taiwan's intensifying national identity crisis . . . prevents any agreement on issues relating to the scope and tenor of Taiwan's national security interests."[33] Given the chasms that divide the DPP, the KMT, and senior members of the armed forces over basic questions on Taiwan's future relationship vis-à-vis China, a civil-military consensus on threat perceptions has proved difficult.

In addition to fundamental disagreements over the nature of the Chinese threat, the civilian and military communities do not equally share the core assumptions that should underwrite Taipei's strategic responses to Beijing's military options. The Chen administration seems confident that the United States will commit itself to the defense of the island under almost any conceivable circumstance. Indeed, leading members of the DPP, such as the National Security Council's deputy secretary-general, Parris Chang, have declared that the island can count on American and Japanese intervention as reliable sources of the island's security.[34] In contrast, the military remains far less sanguine about the prospects of American help. The history of vacillating U.S. policy toward Taiwan combined with the strategic rise of China has dampened the military's faith that America's security guarantees are unshakable. The senior military leadership therefore believes that it needs to maintain the capacity to fight on its own across the entire spectrum of possible conflict scenarios. Differences over the extent to which Taiwan can count on external intervention clearly have implications for the island's war fighting strategy and options. Not surprisingly, the basic disputes over threat perceptions and strategic responses to China have spilled over to Taiwan's military strategy, highlighting another set of ingredients for continuing civil-military tensions.

The RMA Debate: An Uncertain Path to Modernization

Despite the ongoing disputes over basic questions and assumptions about Taiwan's defense, most Taiwanese agree that the island needs a modern military to cope with China's threat. Accordingly, over the past decade, Taipei has embarked on ambitious plans to modernize and streamline its armed forces. A major aspect of this modernization program has been the incorporation of RMA concepts and capabilities. There is recognition that the military's capacity to fulfill its more offensively oriented mission depends in part on the technologies, doctrines, and organizations inherent to an RMA. The ongoing debates and implementation of an RMA uniquely suited to Taiwan's conditions have in turn highlighted important aspects of civil-military relations that conform to and reinforce some of the features and problems noted above.

While the military began to examine the RMA in the mid-1990s, serious efforts to consider the benefits of information-based warfare did not occur until the civilian policy community entered the discourse.[35] The military was apparently deeply skeptical about the promise of the RMA. Indeed, there is evidence that defense planners rejected studies on the RMA conducted by civilians. Arthur Ding credits the assertion of civilian control during the democratic transition for the gradual shift in the debate.[36] The DPP's push to introduce potentially revolutionary concepts in the latter half of the 1990s in part reoriented the military's thinking. In addition, the passage of the two defense laws elaborated above had an important effect on how deliberations over the RMA evolved. The consolidation of civilian authority produced limited civil-military interactions that helped inject new ideas into the relatively insular defense community.

Given Taiwan's resource constraints and limited technological base, there is recognition that the island will not be able to replicate the kind of RMA envisioned by U.S. planners. Clearly, the island lacks the capacity to pursue the reconnaissance-precision strike complex that the United States already boasts. Taipei appears to have concluded that an RMA tailored to Taiwan's requirements would be primarily focused on "software" advances.[37] According to James Mulvenon, Taipei has settled on electronic warfare, C4I modernization, and information warfare as the key pillars of the island's military modernization to enhance the capabilities of existing hardware.[38] It is notable that the RMA debate in the 1990s and the associated capabilities envisioned by planners stand in sharp contrast to the high profile big-ticket defense items still mired in the political process.

Obstacles to Taiwan's RMA do persist and some pertain directly to civil-military relations. At the most basic level, the premise for Taiwan's military modernization is not universally accepted. One interpretation of Taiwan's security predicament views the emergence of identity politics as the key culprit behind the island's contentious relationship with China. For some, then, the nature of the cross-strait stalemate is an inherently political one rather than a military one. Therefore, these skeptics argue, military modernization will not only fail to address the core reason for the China-Taiwan dispute, but will actually heighten the rationale for conflict. This logic contributes to public disincentives for supporting Taiwan's armed forces.

To complicate matters, prevailing social attitudes among Taiwan's citizens toward the military will also impose constraints on Taipei's ability to leverage fully the promises of the RMA. The public is generally uninterested in military affairs and tends to gravitate to the more lucrative private sector. Given the demanding technological requirements of the RMA, the absence of active participation by well-educated, highly skilled personnel combined with the antiquated conscript system will hamper modernization efforts.

Finally, Taiwan's military culture, which still suffers from the legacy of the top-down, authoritarian past, stands in the way of implementing the RMA. Lower-ranking officers, those most likely to plant the seeds of change, lack the entrepreneurial spirit or are discouraged from promoting new ideas. At the institutional level, interservice rivalries prevent creative thinking on the RMA. High-ranking officers tend to be tied to their service allegiances and are thus less likely to champion new concepts that might infringe on their respective service turfs.[39] Indeed, Taiwan's defense ministers (invariably drawn from the chief of General Staff position) have often exhibited biases in favor of their own services. In particular, RMA developments most threaten the Army's equities and it will use its bureaucratic clout, as noted above, to continue to slow the pace of implementation.

IMPLICATIONS FOR TAIWAN'S CIVIL-MILITARY RELATIONS

This volume conceptually divides democratic civil-military relations into three components: civilian control, defense efficiency, and military effectiveness. These interrelated factors provide useful benchmarks for measuring the effectiveness of and the overall progress in defense reforms. For Taiwan, the aggregate of these measures produces a decidedly mixed and somewhat worrisome picture.

From the foregoing analysis, it is clear that civilian control made the most early and visible inroads during the democratic transition following Chen's presidential victory. The continuing dependence on and deference to the armed forces for leadership and expertise within the civilian sector, however, demonstrates that the extent of civilian control is largely artificial. Moreover, legislative activism poses another complicating factor. General inexperience and bitter partisan politics in the Legislative Yuan have made a mockery of an oversight process designed to enhance transparency and accountability. The often irresponsible assertion of legislative authority has harmed civil-military relations and stalled the long-awaited military modernization plans.

Genuine and effective civilian control will require several changes. First, the tensions and policy differences between the president's office and the senior echelons of the armed forces must be delinked from identity politics regardless of party affiliation. Second, and closely related, the political leadership must acquire sufficient confidence to place a competent and well-respected civilian leader at the head of the Ministry of Defense. Third, the president must be willing to expend the political capital to reform the military establishment. Genuine civilian presence at the Ministry of Defense will require a long-term sea change in social attitudes about the importance of defense, and reforms to educational and policy-related institutions. Finally, bipartisan consensus on defense issues and increased resources for establishing a sizable professional legislative staff on military affairs would go a long way to fulfilling the proper mandate of the Legislative Yuan.

In the context of Taiwan, defense efficiency can be defined in two ways. First, does political consensus over military strategy translate smoothly and in a timely manner into concrete acquisition processes and force structure development? Second, how productive and innovative is the defense industrial sector? Both pose daunting challenges to Taipei. As detailed above, political gridlock has prevented any modicum of agreement on a coherent national security strategy and the procurement of equipment necessary for the island's defense. As long as politics and associated muddled thinking about defense dominate the discourse, no amount of efficiency (in terms of resources to purchase from the United States or to produce on its own) would shore up Taiwan's defense capabilities.

On the latter question, the island suffers from two problems: An overdependence on the United States for arms and a relatively limited indigenous industrial-military complex. As the per unit cost of big ticket defense items skyrockets in the United States, Taiwan has become increasingly hard-pressed to afford equipment offered by Washington. Despite the messy politics in the Legislative Yuan, cost is a genuine concern within the body. Moreover, despite the impressive technological base on the island, Taiwan simply does not enjoy the necessary economics of scale to develop its own advanced capabilities (with the exception of certain niche areas such as missile technologies). The Pentagon rejected the Taiwanese shipbuilding industry's entreaties to build U.S.-designed conventional submarines on its own due in part to such considerations.

Over the long run, the persistence of governance problems, if permitted to go uncorrected, and the island's industrial limitations could gradually erode the effectiveness of Taiwan's military.[40] The inability to push forward reforms and to acquire key weapons systems, which would require substantially more time and energy for the island to absorb, will likely have cascading effects on the qualitative advantages that ROC forces have thus far enjoyed vis-à-vis the Mainland. China's steady military modernization will make even more apparent the potential corrosion of the island's fighting power. To what extent (and when) the anticipated cross-strait military imbalance will make conflict more likely—either as a result of Chinese overconfidence or Taiwanese miscalculation—remains unclear at the moment. What is certain is that the island's ability to defend itself will decline to unacceptable levels over the next decade as the balance of forces shifts in favor of China.

CONCLUSIONS

Taiwan should be credited for its democratic achievements and for establishing the basis for healthy civil-military relations. The assertion of civilian control over the military has not produced major setbacks that could have unraveled the democratic experiment. At the same time, however, the assertion of civilian supremacy still suffers from a high degree of artificiality. The basic rifts between the DPP and the military stemming from history and from basic differences over Taiwan's future have undermined President Chen's ability to govern with confidence. This sense of vulnerability has dissuaded him from investing the necessary political capital to reform an organization highly suspicious of his motives. Unruly legislative politics, which continue to strand important procurement plans, have increased resentment among military officers and raised doubts in Washington about the seriousness with which Taipei will seek to fulfill the island's defensive needs.

At the same time, the defense establishment has not fully accepted nor trusted the ruling party's national security agenda. The military is not inclined to share the DPP's pro-independence agenda, the apparently sanguine assessments of the imminence of China's military threat to Taiwan, and the ruling party's confidence in American security commitments. To exacerbate matters, the military considers DPP's enthusiasm for an offensive orientation as a potentially disastrous recipe for accelerating China's military modernization and undermining support from the United States. The DPP's positions have reinforced perceptions that the party is ill-equipped to govern and too inexperienced to determine the long-term course of Taiwan's defense. The DPP for its part remains deeply suspicious of the military, and many leaders perceive the armed forces as a secretive cabal dominated by Mainlanders.

Some of these obstacles to defense reforms have been cast in terms of an exclusively "DPP problem." A closer examination suggests, however, that the structural and systemic legacies inherited from the martial law era would have proved equally problematic for a KMT regime. Most notable, the military's continuing monopoly over security and defense expertise will not be reversed overnight. Only a long-term effort focused on incorporating civilians into professional military affairs and on changing social attitudes about the military will achieve genuine progress in civilianizing the defense sector. The authoritarian period also masked and even energized the emergence of identity politics following the democratic transition. As a result, political assumptions and public perceptions about Taiwan's security dilemma are often at odds with the military's stated priorities. While the Chen administration has been accused of placing political dimensions of arms procurement ahead of military considerations, it is not entirely clear that the KMT would have behaved differently. In other words, the political (rather than the war fighting) value of defense acquisition from the United States will remain a compelling motive regardless of party affiliation.[41]

Given the vagaries and messiness inherent to politics in a democracy, Taiwan may be excused for its indecision over its own defense. However, the security environment within which the island exists imposes costs that Taiwan may not be able to pay off. In reference to the political gridlock over defense matters, Denny Roy somberly concludes, "The phenomenon of politicians placing narrow partisanship ahead of national security is certainly not unique, but few other countries can less afford such risky behavior."[42] Shelley Rigger is equally grim in her assessment: "With the PRC so close at hand, Taiwan does not have the leisure to learn through its mistakes."[43] The burden on Taiwan is indeed formidable: The rise of China poses shorter-term security challenges that the expected long-term benefits of defense reforms will not be able to address in time.

NOTES

1. The terms "Taiwan" and the "Republic of China (ROC)" are used interchangeably in this paper.
2. This paper does not seek to explain why Taiwan's military has withdrawn from politics nor to predict whether the military's reentry into politics is a probable outcome. It assumes the permanence of the post-authoritarian phase as the starting point for analysis. In discussing the civil-military dynamics for South Korea and Taiwan, Muthiah Alagappa notes, "Force continues to be critical in safeguarding the international security of these states, but this has not led to an increase in the military's political influence because both countries now have widely acknowledged democratic governments, and public opinion is strongly against military involvement in domestic politics." Muthiah Alagappa, "Investigating and Explaining Change: An Analytical Framework," in Muthiah Alagappa, ed., *Coercion and Governance: The Declining Role of the Military in Asia* (Palo Alto: Stanford University Press, 2001), 60.
3. For example, in standard terms of military professionalism, the military's exit from domestic politics should in theory enhance its ability to sharpen its expertise on preparing for external threats.
4. For some of the unique features of Taiwan's democratization process, see Shelley Rigger, "Taiwan's Best-Case Democratization," *Orbis* 48, 2 (Spring 2004): 285–292.

5. Issues related to the evolving cross-strait military balance, Taiwan's current military capabilities and the specific procurement requirements to meet the island's defensive needs are already well documented elsewhere. This paper instead focuses primarily on the impact of defense reforms on the higher levels of Taiwan's political-military system and the island's broader national security agenda.
6. For details on Taiwan's democratic transition, see Cal Clark, "Successful Democratization in the ROC: Creating a Security Challenge," in Alexander C. Tan, Steven Chan, and Calvin Jillson, eds., *Taiwan's National Security: Dilemmas and Opportunities* (Burlington: Ashgate, 2001), 18–59.
7. For a historical narrative of the KMT's consolidation of power on Taiwan see, Denny Roy, *Taiwan: A Political History* (Cornell: Cornell University Press, 2003), 55–104.
8. Established in 1967, the National Security Council (NSC), headed by an active-duty general, served as a military advisory board to the president. Similarly, the notorious National Security Bureau, which functioned as the NSC's intelligence counterpart for domestic security, was a military domain.
9. For a detailed assessment of how such institutional arrangements persisted well into the late 1990s, see Michael D. Swaine, *Taiwan's National Security, Defense Policy, and Weapons Procurement Processes* (Santa Monica: RAND, 1999).
10. According to Chih-cheng Lo, "the primary danger to Taiwan's democracy and sound civil-military relations emanates from the military's 'conditional loyalty.'" Chih-cheng Lo, "Taiwan: The Remaining Challenges," in Alagappa, ed., *Coercion and Governance*, 144.
11. Through a series of deft maneuvers, President Lee eventually ousted Hau, a military strongman with political ambitions of his own.
12. Article 13 of the National Defense Law (NDL) states: "The MND has under it the General Staff Headquarters (GSH), serving as the staff organization of command system, and command mechanism of joint operations to the Minister. The GSH is headed by the CGS, who is in charge of military affairs of command system, and assumes the authority to command the ROC Armed Forces under the order of the Minister."
13. According to Article 6 of the NDL, "The ROC Armed Forces shall remain neutral from individual, regional and party affiliations in accordance with the Act. Active servicemen are forbidden to undertake the following activities: 1. Assume positions offered by political parties, political groups and electoral candidates; 2. Force active servicemen to join or help political parties, political groups, and electoral candidates; 3. Establish bodies within military units to promote partisan spheres, party platforms and other propaganda activities."

14. The remarkable absence of instability or setbacks during the democratic transition is documented by M. Taylor Fravel, "Towards Civilian Supremacy: Civil-Military Relations in Taiwan's Democratization," *Armed Forces & Society* 29, 1 (Fall 2002): 57–84.
15. Brian Hsu, "Tang Yao-ming to get defense post," *Taipei Times*, 10 January 2002.
16. Steve Chan, "Taiwan in 2004: Electoral Contests and Political Stasis," *Asian Survey* 45, 1 (January/February 2005): 55.
17. Lin Chieh-yu, "Coup? What Coup? MND official says," *Taipei Times*, 17 November 2004, 1.
18. For a sense of the emotional appeal of identity in Taiwan's electoral politics, see Chi Su, "Driving Forces Behind Taiwan's Mainland Policy," in Steve Tsang, ed., *Peace and Security Across the Taiwan Strait* (Oxford: Palgrave, 2004), 58–62.
19. The military distrust of the presidential office extends back to the Lee Tung-hui years. The top brass suspected that Lee rhetorically supported reunification but was in fact pursuing an independence agenda. Those suspicions deepened with the inauguration of Chen. See General Sun Chin-ming (ROC Army, retd.), "Taiwan: Toward a Higher Degree of Military Professionalism," in Muthiah Alagappa, ed., *Military Professionalism in Asia: Conceptual and Empirical Perspectives* (Honolulu: East-West Center, 2001), 69–70.
20. The current defense minister, Admiral Lee Jye, was chief of the general staff prior to his appointment in 2004. His predecessor, Army General Tang Yao-ming, also served as the chief of general from 1999–2002.
21. See John F. Copper, "Taiwan's Democracy Takes a New Step," *Far Eastern Economic Review* 168, 1 (December 2004): 12–14.
22. Taiwan's defense budgets have consistently declined in the past decade as a result of public demands for social services and an economic recession in 2000–2001. According to the Ministry of National Defense, defense spending as a percentage of GNP dropped from 4.1 percent in 1994 to 2.5 in 2003, or from 24.2 percent to 16.9 percent of the total government budget during the same period. ROC Government Information Office, *Taiwan Yearbook 2004* (Taipei: ROC GIO, 2004).
23. "Yu Defends Advanced Arms Procurement," *Central News Agency*, 22 September 2004.
24. Caroline Hong, "Pan-blue group rally against arms procurement plan," *Taipei Times*, 1 November 2004, 3.
25. "Warning on Arms Purchase Angers Taipei Opposition," *Reuters*, 7 October 2004.
26. Jimmy Chuang, "Cabinet Oks new budget for weapons," *Taipei Times*, 17 March 2005, 3.
27. "Changes in Defense Budget Seen as a 'Grueling Decision,'" *Taiwan News*, 31 August 2005.

28. "U.S. Official Warns of 'Repercussions' If Taiwan Fails to Approve Weapons Deal," *Associated Press*, 6 October 2004.
29. Charles Snyder and Debby Wu, "Taiwan urged to buy US weapons," *Taipei Times*, 23 June 2004, 1.
30. This point is raised in Michael S. Chase, "Defense Reform in Taiwan: Problems and Prospects," *Asian Survey* 45, 3 (January/February 2005), 380–381.
31. Michael Swaine, *Deterring Conflict in the Taiwan Strait: The Successes and Failures of Taiwan's Defense Reform and Modernization Program* (Washington, DC: Carnegie Endowment for International Peace, July 2004), 18.
32. Denny Roy, "Taiwan's Threat Perceptions: The Enemy Within," Asia-Pacific Center for Security Studies Occasional Paper Series, March 2003, 8.
33. Michael Swaine, "Taiwan's Defense Reforms and Military Modernization Program: Objectives, Achievements, and Obstacles," in Nancy Bernkopf Tucker, ed., *Dangerous Strait: The U.S.-Taiwan-China Crisis* (New York: Columbia University Press, 2005), 147.
34. "Parris Change Says the US, Japan Will Defend Taiwan," *Central News Agency*, 14 August 2005; and "Chen's Tripartite Call Against China," *Strait Times*, 5 August 2005.
35. In 1999, the Taiwan Research Institute (TRI), a partially government-funded think tank, spearheaded a high-profile project on the RMA concept. The TRI's Division of Strategic and International Studies sponsored several conferences and workshops and produced working papers on the RMA. The TRI's close connections with the government attracted substantial media attention, which in turn generated public pressure on the military to consider and adopt the RMA.
36. Arthur S. Ding, "Taiwan: From Integrated Missile Defense to RMA?" in Emily O. Goldman and Thomas G. Mahnken, eds., *The Information Revolution in Military Affairs in Asia* (New York: Palgrave, 2004), 177–178.
37. The imprint of U.S. influence on Taiwan's thinking is clearly visible. The most recent National Defense Report is filled with terminology and jargon that would be instantly recognizable to observers familiar with the Pentagon's lexicon.
38. See James Mulvenon, "Taiwan and the Revolution in Military Affairs," in Goldman and Mahnken, eds., *The Information Revolution in Military Affairs in Asia*, 150–160.
39. I thank Arthur Ding for his insights on this point.
40. The standard conditions for military professionalism (expertise, corporate identity, and social responsibility) are in place in Taiwan. Given the complexities of Taiwan's democratic transition, however, it is not at all

clear that the ROC armed forces will benefit from this shift in terms of military effectiveness.

41. See Michael D. Swaine and James C. Mulvenon, *Taiwan's Foreign and Defense Policies: Features and Determinants* (Santa Monica: RAND, 2001), 58–60.
42. Roy, *Taiwan's Threat Perceptions*, 4.
43. Rigger, "Taiwan's Best-Case Democratization," 292.

11

Democratization and the Challenge of Defense Reform in Indonesia

Michael Malley

Introduction

In 1998, more than three decades after General Soeharto[1] established the military-dominated New Order regime in Indonesia, massive protests brought it to an end. In the face of widespread opposition, Soeharto resigned and the military stood aside while civilian leaders crafted new, democratic political institutions. Since then, competitive elections have been conducted twice without military interference and today active-duty officers no longer hold political positions or staff the bureaucracy. Yet getting the military out of politics has been simpler than asserting civilian control over the military, and the unresolved character of civil-military relations hinders progress on the other key aspects of defense reform, namely military effectiveness and defense efficiency.

For Indonesians as well as their friends and neighbors, defense reform is an urgent matter. Although Indonesia is the world's largest archipelagic country, three-quarters of its military personnel are in the army, and most of these are assigned to "territorial commands" that parallel the civilian administration. Under Soeharto, their task was to enforce political stability, but a dispersed, largely immobile army, combined with the small and poorly equipped navy and air force, has been unable to respond effectively to recent challenges that include communal and separatist conflicts, terrorist attacks, and piracy in the sea-lanes that connect the Indian and Pacific Oceans.

Indonesia's military weakness was displayed prominently in the wake of the devastating tsunami in 2004, when Jakarta had to rely on foreign militaries to transport relief supplies to Aceh, even though thousands of its own troops were already deployed against an insurgency there.

Even as the need for defense reform has grown, there is broad agreement that after a period of rapid transformation between 1998 and 2000, the pace of change ground nearly to a halt. One of the leading opponents of American aid to Indonesia's armed forces, the East Timor Action Network, claimed in 2004 that "[m]ilitary reform in Indonesia is dead...the military has re-asserted itself in the areas it most cares about," and Indonesia's current defense minister seems to agree.[2] Just a few months before moving to the defense ministry from his post as ambassador to Great Britain in 2004, he wrote that "[s]ix years of civilian-based party politics has not resulted in any measurable degree of effective 'civilian supremacy,' much less 'civilian control,'" and as a result "seasoned politicians and political observers acknowledge that [military] influence, if not power, retains a strong hold over the entire polity."[3]

The main disputes today concern the reasons that defense reform has stalled and the steps that can be taken to revive, hasten, and strengthen it. Human rights groups and their supporters in the U.S. Congress contend that Indonesia's armed forces remain essentially unreformed because senior officers have not been held accountable for human rights abuses that occurred under their watch, whether before or since 1998. Consequently, the military leadership remains largely intact, and continues both to tolerate further human rights violations and to resist efforts to transform the armed services into a professional force accountable to civilian authority. This is a powerful position. Since 1992, it has underpinned the U.S. Congress's decision to impose tight limits on military assistance to Indonesia. New, more professional military leadership certainly is desirable. But the debate over whether assistance should be provided, as the Pentagon desires, or withheld, as Congress typically has decided, diverts attention from the broader question of why military professionalism, and defense reform more generally, has proven so difficult to achieve. To answer it, one must look beyond continuity in military leadership to underlying aspects of the Indonesian political and military landscape.

In this chapter, I will give greater explanatory weight to political and economic institutions than military culture and individual choice. Scholars who adopt this approach tend to highlight two variables that have slowed the process of defense reform: the weakness of democratic civilian political institutions and the financial autonomy of the military. For example, the most thorough recent study of civil-military relations in Indonesia concluded that "the prospects for…asserting civilian control still remain tenuous as the military has shown itself remarkably resilient in guarding its prerogatives in the post-Soeharto era. The weaknesses of the civilian political leadership in depoliticizing the military and of party politics in demilitarizing the political process have facilitated this scenario."[4] Again, Indonesia's defense minister, himself a scholar, seems to agree. Civilian politics, he argued in 2004, "is still largely disjointed, disorganized and often in disarray," and the military has maintained control over a "powerful independent financial base" that includes "a myriad of foundations, cooperatives and enterprises"[5] that provide more than two-thirds of the military's funding.

Democratization has brought major changes to civil-military relations, but the persistent weakness of civilian political institutions and the military's continuing reliance on independent sources of revenue have combined to limit the pace and scope of defense reform. The following sections describe how the military acquired political power and business interests; the process of democratization; and the main changes to civil-military relations that came as a result. The penultimate section considers alternative explanations for the slow pace of defense reform in Indonesia, and the concluding section sums up my argument that limited pressure has resulted in limited reforms.

The Military in Politics and Business

During the protests that drove Soeharto from office in 1998, demonstrators often called for the army to return to its barracks. The problem, as one close observer of Indonesia's military noted, was that this position "was based on the false assumption that [the military] would simply have to return to its original state of affairs," when in fact "there were no barracks to return to."[6] This was not, of course, literally true. But metaphorically, it accurately depicted a military that has never faced a serious foreign threat, never been focused primarily on national defense, and always been deeply involved in politics and business. In short, it characterizes a military whose past does not offer a template for a more professional future.

The revolutionary origins of Indonesia's armed forces and its political system help explain how civil-military relations became so heavily weighted in favor of the army.[7] Although an important actor in national politics since the end of Japanese occupation in 1945, the army finally asserted full control over Indonesia's political system in the mid-1960s, following an attempted coup in which several senior officers were killed. The most senior officer not targeted by the coup-makers was Major General Soeharto, and he organized a countercoup. The takeover was brutal yet gradual. With strong support from civilian groups, army units orchestrated the "annihilation" (*penumpasan*) of hundreds of thousands of communists and suspected leftists between 1965 and 1967. Sukarno, the country's founding father, was slowly stripped of his power until Soeharto himself assumed the presidency in 1968.[8]

During the late 1960s, Soeharto and his allies laid the foundation for the military-dominated New Order regime.[9] They established the dual function doctrine under which the armed forces had an obligation not just to defend the country, but to take an active sociopolitical role, as well. Although it merely codified actual political practice, it came to serve as an ideological (and, after 1982, a legal) justification for the military to monitor and interfere in the affairs of any social or political organization, anywhere in the country. Throughout its rule, the New Order justified this role by claiming that strong measures were needed to ensure political stability, which in turn was the key precondition for economic development.[10]

Concretely, the militarization of Indonesian politics under the New Order rested on two other main pillars. The first was the appointment of a large number of active-duty officers to political and bureaucratic positions throughout the country. Although this practice (known as *kekaryaan*) had begun in the late 1950s, it accelerated rapidly in the late 1960s and by the late 1970s, about three-quarters of all provincial governors and district executives were from the military, mainly the army. Moreover, the military was entitled to appoint officers to fill one-fifth of the seats in national, provincial, and district legislatures, and by the time the regime collapsed in the late 1990s, about 4,000 officers held political and bureaucratic positions.[11] The second pillar was the regime's political party, Golkar, which all territorial commands supported and to which all bureaucrats were required to belong. Elections were held in 1971, 1977, and then every five years until Soeharto resigned, and each time Golkar won from 60 to 75 percent of the votes.

The New Order brought about the longest period of economic growth since independence, and the military shared directly in the expanding pie. In the 1970s and early 1980s growth was fueled by rising global oil prices. The army had dominated the state-owned oil company since Colonel Ibnu Sutowo had taken control of foreign-run Sumatran oil fields during the Guided Democracy period. Under Soeharto, its revenues were used to fund the army along with a wide range of industrial and commercial ventures in which individual officers as well as military-linked foundations and cooperatives participated. When oil prices plummeted in the mid-1980s, the government no longer could afford the nationalist economic policies of the 1970s and began to pursue a course of economic liberalization, albeit an uneven one. The army continued to benefit from economic growth, but mainly, it seems, because of its control over land in rapidly industrializing urban areas and access to forest concessions in islands outside Java.

Despite Soeharto's commitment to modernize Indonesia, the result of fostering the military's involvement in business was to hinder its modernization and professionalization. Indeed, the regime's first serious crisis occurred in 1974, when conflicts between "professional" and "financial" generals contributed to widespread riots during a visit to Jakarta by Japan's prime minister. Public discontent focused especially on a general who had been Soeharto's financial adviser in the 1950s and who came to serve as the chief conduit for Japanese aid and investment in the late 1960s and 1970s. Soeharto sided with the financial generals, and the business practices of regional commanders in the 1950s and 1960s were increasingly institutionalized on a larger scale at the national level in the 1970s and 1980s.[12]

The reliance on off-budget sources of revenue allowed the government to devote an ever smaller proportion of the national budget to defense, and the military's share of national expenditures declined from more than one-quarter in the late 1960s to about 7 or 8 percent in the late 1990s. Since the beginning of the 1990s, the official defense budget has amounted to roughly 1.5 percent of gross domestic product, and often less.[13] The murkiness of off-budget accounts makes it impossible to know exactly how much money the armed forces spend, but it is generally believed that the government budget supplies no more than 30 percent of military expenditures. Under these conditions, official salaries were kept low and troops had to assign a high priority to fundraising simply to maintain their equipment and provide themselves and their families with adequate food and housing. Moreover, little was done to upgrade the facilities and equipment of the armed forces, with the exception of elite units.

Economic liberalization quickened the pace of social change and put pressure on the military to reconsider its approach to controlling society. The rapid growth of labor-intensive, export-oriented manufacturing spurred urbanization, gave rise to the first important labor unions since the army had crushed leftist groups in the late 1960s, and produced a growing stratum of middle-class urbanites whose children questioned the values of the regime.[14] These changes led to a wide range of responses from the military. On the one hand, it engaged in tortured efforts to adapt its ideological principles and doctrines to changes in society.[15] For instance, having divided the ideological spectrum into "extreme left," that is, communists, and "extreme right," that is, radical Muslims, it was at a loss over where to locate the increasing number of liberal student activists—until it hit upon the label "extreme center." Similarly, officers debated the merits of globalization, which they tended to equate with the influx of foreign capital and the spread of ideas about political freedom and democracy. In the view of leading hard-line officers, globalization posed a major threat to political stability (i.e., the military's political influence) and thus required greater "vigilance," which legitimated the continued involvement of the military in social and political affairs.[16]

On the other hand, however, many retired officers had become critical of Soeharto for concentrating power in his own hands at the expense of the military and straying, in their view, from original military doctrines such as the dual function. Some of these officers held seats in the national legislature, and took up the call made by departing U.S. ambassador Paul Wolfowitz in 1989 for more political "openness." Although they continued to believe that the armed forces had an obligation and a right to play a leading role in political life, these legislators held public hearings at which they broached a wide range of reforms, including the topic of presidential succession. Their pressure led Soeharto to endorse a policy of openness, which encouraged public debate about the nature of the political system. For his part, Soeharto agreed to increase the number of elective seats in the legislature from 400 to 425 (out of 500) beginning in 1997 by cutting the military's share of appointive seats by twenty-five, but otherwise these debates did not lead to any change in civil-military relations.

In sum, over a half-century of existence, Indonesia's armed forces had progressively deepened their involvement in non-military affairs and developed a force structure, doctrines, and system of funding that could not survive without such involvement. Globalization and economic liberalization contributed to debate about the nature of civil-military relations, but the result was mainly more repressive policies rather than progress on defense reform.

Democratization and the Weakness of Civilian Institutions

Indonesia's transition from authoritarianism began in May 1998 when Soeharto resigned amid a worsening economic crisis and increasingly violent protests against him and his regime. Just prior to the onset of the crisis in mid-1997, his government had resorted to heavy-handed tactics to obtain Golkar's largest electoral victory ever, and in March 1998 he had secured his uncontested reelection to his sixth presidential term. Over the next two months, protests spread to university campuses throughout the country, and gradually were joined by the public at large.

His opponents were able to force him from office, but they were too weak to gain control of the government or the process of reform. Instead, Soeharto turned power over to his vice president, B.J. Habibie, a German-educated civilian engineer who had served as minister of technology for two decades but had held the vice presidency for only two months. In his career, he frequently had been at loggerheads with the armed forces. As head of the government's Strategic Industry Development Agency, he controlled companies that produced ships, planes, and ammunition for the military. In the early 1990s, he arranged the purchase of thirty-nine former East German naval vessels, which would require expensive refurbishing and which the navy said it did not need, as part of an expensive plan to develop Indonesian ports and shipyards.[17] Indeed, it was reporting on these differences in 1994 that led the government to close down three of the country's best-known print media, thereby signaling the end of openness.

Soeharto's fall from power inevitably meant changing the role of the military in politics. But to explain the contemporary weakness of civilian political institutions, and the persistent strength of the military, requires attention to the conditions under which the New Order came to an end. In retrospect, three seem particularly important: intense repression of political opponents in the late 1980's until Soeharto's fall; the speed of the transition; and the emergence of sharp conflicts at the highest levels of military leadership.

The inability of opposition political parties quickly to replace Soeharto's Golkar reflects, in large part, the repression opposition groups and their leaders faced, especially during the period between 1994 and 1998.[18] The period of political openness during 1990–1994 had witnessed a flowering of advocacy groups and labor unions, and the revival of a moribund opposition party under the leadership of Megawati Sukarnoputri, the daughter of the man whom Soeharto had deposed a quarter-century earlier. Her party capitalized on a dramatic rise in labor unrest that accompanied the rapid expansion of labor-intensive manufacturing in the late 1980s and early 1990s. Moreover, even more threatening to a regime that had come to power by destroying the political left was her close relationship to Abdurrahman Wahid, the leader of the country's largest religious organization. Under Soeharto, the government had merged opposition parties into one that represented former Islamic parties, and another that included old Christian and nationalist parties, thus allowing its own political party to occupy the political center. Megawati's support from the new labor movement (left), Wahid's group (right), and nongovernmental organizations (extreme center), threatened the New Order's ideological and institutional construction of power. In the 1992 general election, Megawati's party doubled its share of the vote to 15 percent and appeared to be gaining momentum across the political spectrum.

From 1994 onward, the government increasingly resorted to the sort of harsh military tactics it had employed during its early years to control political opponents. In addition to closing down three major print media, it jailed labor activists, harassed Wahid's organization, and in 1996 organized a violent takeover of Megawati's party headquarters in order to allow government-selected leaders to run her party. At the next election in 1997, Wahid sought political cover by campaigning for the government's political party alongside Soeharto's daughter, and Megawati silently watched as the rump of her former party garnered only 3 percent of the votes. Shortly after Golkar's greatest electoral victory, however, the Asian economic crisis hit Indonesia. By March 1998, when Soeharto faced reelection, Indonesia's economy was in shambles. The currency had lost three-quarters of its value, major banks and industrial companies were bankrupt, and social unrest was mounting as prices and unemployment rose. Despite these conditions and Soeharto's vacillating economic policies, opposition and government party legislators elected the previous year, together with an even greater number of appointed delegates, "elected" Soeharto to his sixth consecutive term.

The public pressure that drove Soeharto to resign in May 1998 only began to build in March, and it failed to generate a leadership group capable of negotiating with the government, let alone actually replacing it. Indeed, until less than a month before Soeharto's resignation the movement was confined almost entirely to university campuses and few politically or socially prominent figures associated themselves with the demands for him to leave office. Only in late April and early May did protests even begin to spill off the campuses and gather broad public support. Consequently, Soeharto was able to resign in May without turning power over to the opposition or even agreeing to changes that would enable it to participate in government. And even though Habibie quickly appointed his own cabinet, minus Soeharto's daughter and other personal allies, control of the government was left largely in the hands of people who already served and had a stake in it. In short, regime defenders, not their challengers, gained control over the reform process.

Other than the hundreds of thousands of protesters who took to Jakarta's streets and occupied the national legislative complex in mid-May, the major drama of the transition came from deep splits between two Soeharto loyalists in the military. One was a former presidential adjutant, General Wiranto, who was serving as armed forces commander and defense minister; the other was Soeharto's son-in-law, General Prabowo Subianto, who was heading the army's Strategic Reserve Command, an elite force.[19] Both men vied for the president's attention and support, and each had his own supporters in the upper echelons of the military. During the anti-Soeharto protests, several generals who were aligned with Wiranto, some known as army intellectuals, met with the students and appeared sympathetic to their demands. (One of the leaders of this group was Susilo Bambang Yudhoyono, elected president of Indonesia in 2004.) Prabowo's troops, by contrast, turned out to be responsible for the abduction and probably the shooting of student protesters, and for instigating three days of rioting, burning, looting, raping, and other violence in Jakarta in mid-May, apparently in an effort to demonstrate Wiranto's inability to maintain civil order and thereby undermine his relationship to Soeharto.

This rivalry within the armed forces played a critical role in shaping the transition. Most immediately, it led to Soeharto's resignation. Wiranto was able to persuade Soeharto of Prabowo's culpability for the violence, and to assure him that the military would protect him even if he were no longer president. Combined with the last-minute defection of key civilian allies, Wiranto's intervention appears to have persuaded Soeharto to leave office. The rivalry and its resolution, however, had longer-lasting effects, too. Although Wiranto declared his loyalty to Habibie's government and transferred Prabowo and his associates to less important positions, the officer corps remained divided and lacked a common position on reform. Moreover, the activities of Prabowo's groups further discredited the army in the eyes of a public that had become increasingly critical of the army's involvement in political life. Consequently, at the time Indonesia embarked on its political transition, the military was less than firmly under the control of a Soeharto loyalist (Wiranto), and was too internally fragmented and publicly unpopular to influence decisions about the course of political reform.

PURSUING REFORM

The size and scale of the protests that drove Soeharto from power ensured that neither the civilian nor military leadership doubted the need for quick and substantial changes. But neither civilian nor military leaders were certain of their own grip on power, and they needed each other's support. Under these conditions, the armed forces turned inward to consider their own reform measures, while civilian leaders debated political reform.

Soon after assuming the presidency, Habibie announced a timetable for reforms that would create a new legal framework for free and fair legislative elections within a year, and presidential elections within eighteen months. Amid continuing protests, including those that challenged the constitutionality of his presidency, Habibie had little time to devote specifically to military reform, but he changed the country's political system in ways that directly challenged the country's armed forces. He released political prisoners, reversed Soeharto's policy of using the information ministry's 50,000 employees to monitor and control the flow of information, and freely issued publication licenses.[20] Long accustomed to respectful treatment in the press and other public fora, the military now faced "an onslaught of criticism in the media which soon turned into unrestrained condemnation."[21]

In this environment, military leaders quickly took steps to repair their public image and salvage a prominent role in politics. Wiranto convened a military tribunal that examined Prabowo's role in the May riots and then dismissed him and two associates from the army in August. The next month, the armed forces held a seminar at which they discussed and presented their own agenda for military reform, called the "New Paradigm." So-called intellectual generals (including the current president) had convened a seminar on reform in 1996, and after Soeharto fell they joined in a campaign to apologize for military abuses and articulate plans for reform. Still, the pledges made at the September seminar illustrated how reluctant even "reformist" leaders were to withdraw entirely from politics: They agreed that the military did not need to be at the "forefront of politics" or to exercise "control" over politics, but they insisted on sharing power with civilians and maintained a commitment to "influence" political decisions.[22]

These concessions marked a sharp break with previous military policy and doctrine, but they did not stem civilian pressure for further reform. Just after the New Paradigm was announced, the national human rights commission visited Aceh, where mass graves left from the military's counterinsurgency campaign between 1989 and 1992 were being unearthed. Shortly thereafter, as the House of Representatives (which still included seventy-five active-duty officers) began to consider bills that would establish a legal framework for democratic elections, civilians had a chance to put more pressure on the military. The result was a series of compromises in which the military committed itself to political neutrality, broke its formal ties to the governing party (Golkar), accepted the halving of its representatives to thirty-eight after the next election, and agreed that its members no longer would fill civilian political and bureaucratic positions (though currently serving officers could serve out their terms in office). Subsequently, Wiranto proposed removing the police from the armed forces and giving them the primary responsibility for internal security, in order to reduce friction between the army and society.

The Habibie government pursued a very specific agenda of political reform that involved rewriting laws on political parties, elections, and legislatures to prepare for elections. The rules that emerged from this process laid a foundation for the freest and fairest legislative elections since 1955 and the first competitive presidential election ever, but they also produced an outcome that virtually assured weak and unstable political leadership. To demonstrate its support for democratic reform and to avoid further antagonizing the opposition, which was excluded from the process of drafting the legal framework for democracy, the Habibie government adopted electoral rules that nearly guaranteed a House of Representatives in which no party controlled a majority. To this, it added an indirectly elected president chosen by an assembly composed of the 500-member House and 200 appointed delegates but accountable, in almost parliamentary fashion, to the House. Unlike a true parliamentary system, however, the fate of the legislature was not tied to that of the executive—it could quarrel with the president without worry that it would be dissolved and fresh elections called. The result was a unique combination of multiparty and executive power even more vulnerable to deadlock and instability that the sort against which Juan Linz and other Latin Americanists have warned so strongly.[23]

Instability and inaction did, in fact, characterize much of the period between 1999 and 2004. The military remained admirably neutral in the 1999 elections, but the polls predictably produced a House in which no party had a majority. Presidential electors chose Abdurrahman Wahid, leader of a party that won only 13 percent of the vote, rather than the leader of the largest party, Megawati Sukarnoputri, Sukarno's daughter. To compensate for this weakness, Wahid appointed a National Unity cabinet that included members of six political parties, but none received as many as positions as the armed forces, whose active and retired members, including Wiranto, filled six spots. Hobbled by these compromises, Wahid was unable to pursue programmatic reforms and attempted to promote change in the military mainly through personnel decisions: He appointed the first civilian defense minister (Juwono Sudarsono) since the 1950s, the first naval officer as armed forces commander, and then consistently intervened in the promotion process to favor reformist generals. These moves, however, tended to arouse resistance rather than broad military support for defense reform. Emblematic of the challenges Wahid faced was the behavior of the general he favored most. Once appointed to lead the elite army Strategic Command, Agus Wirahadikusumah hired PricewaterhouseCoopers to audit the command's foundation and announced that his immediate predecessor had misused and possibly embezzled more than $15 million in less than four months. Just a few months later, military headquarters retaliated against Wahid and Wirahadikusumah by reassigning the latter to another post.[24]

The most important security sector reform during Wahid's administration was the separation of the police from the armed forces and the rapid expansion of the police force's role in internal security. Of course, the military not only consented to this change, but had also initiated it; Wahid was able only to influence its implementation, which was troubled. Army and police units clashed repeatedly, mainly over control of resources. During 2002 alone, there were at least two dozen violent conflicts between units of the two forces, including one in which more than 100 soldiers staged attacks on police offices over nearly two days after the police arrested a civilian whose drug-trafficking apparently enjoyed army protection.[25]

After less than two years in office, Wahid was impeached for corruption and replaced by Megawati, his vice president. Military opposition was critical to his fall and her rise. Despite the armed forces' New Paradigm pledge of neutrality, Wahid's legislative opponents actively courted the armed forces bloc in the House of Representatives while Wahid tried to use the military to dissolve the House and enforce a state of emergency. Just days before Wahid was removed from office, the army chief of staff (Endriartono Sutarto) wrote in the country's leading newspaper that the military was not always obliged to follow presidential orders, and the commander of the army Strategic Reserves (Ryamizard Ryacudu) mobilized thousands of troops to protect legislators from Wahid supporters as they convened to impeach the president.[26]

Indebted to the army's conservative leadership and sympathetic to many of its views, Megawati facilitated its consolidation of control over the armed forces. Within a few months, "the legacy of... Wahid's intervention in military personnel matters was wiped out," and within a year the Megawati government had appointed Endriartono as commander of the armed forces and Ryamizard as army chief of staff, the two most important positions in the Indonesian military. Under these two officers, "reform measures have been effectively abandoned in the name of solidarity and institutional rejuvenation."[27] They paid little heed to the complaints of human rights groups and, in the interest of strengthening the military's ability to meet challenges to national security, favored officers with battlefield experience, including many who had served in East Timor. This was made especially clear with the appointment as chief military spokesman the general who had commanded the Jakarta garrison during the violence surrounding Soeharto's fall in 1998, and an army special forces unit at the time of a major massacre of East Timorese civilians in 1991. Megawati's lack of interest in strengthening civilian control of the military was further symbolized by her choice of a career politician with little grasp of military affairs to head the defense ministry, and her refusal to appoint a successor during her last year in office after her minister suffered a debilitating stroke.

The rapid succession of presidents continued in 2004, but under conditions that favored political stability as well as further defense reform. Following Wahid's short, turbulent administration, Indonesia adopted a constitutional amendment that strengthened the presidency by raising the bar for impeachment and making the position directly elected. Although legislative elections in 2004 returned another highly fragmented House of Representatives, a two-round presidential election saw the moderate military reformer Susilo Bambang Yudhoyono defeat Megawati by a large margin. If Yudhoyono manages to promote defense reform, it will be due less to the legacies of Habibie, Wahid, and Megawati than to the slow accumulation of reforms driven by civil society and written into law by legislators. Separation of the police from the armed forces required fresh legislation, and in 2002 the House passed two laws, on defense and on the police, to differentiate the functions of internal security and national defense. But the most important law is one passed in 2004, after Yudhoyono was elected but before he was inaugurated. Although it preserves the army's territorial command structure and still does not place the armed forces under the control of the defense ministry, it provides for civilian supremacy and requires the military to surrender its businesses to the government by 2009.

Alternative Explanations for Change

Democratization has been the chief determinant of the pace, scope, and content of Indonesia's defense reform, but in a comparative perspective it is important to ask why variables that have favored defense reform elsewhere have been less influential in Indonesia. This is especially true with respect to economic liberalization and globalization, which clearly have buffeted Indonesia in recent years.

Economic liberalization has played only a very indirect role in bringing about political and military reform in Indonesia, mainly because it was not a major factor during the country's period of regime change. Like so many other countries in the Third World, Indonesia liberalized its economy when it no longer could afford to finance its state-led industrialization strategy. The New Order regime initiated this shift in economic policy, however, more than a decade before economic crisis and popular protests prompted its collapse and opened the door to defense reform. It is certainly true, as described above, that liberalization planted some of the seeds of the regime's destruction, but it also pulled the country out of an economic crisis and brought about a sustained period of economic growth that enabled the regime to survive. Moreover, the principal source of the New Order's weakness in the months before its collapse was the president's unwillingness to adopt further liberalizing reforms, chiefly those that would have eliminated protection for sectors and industries dominated by Soeharto's children and political supporters.[28]

It is just as clear that globalization, treated here as the spread more of ideas and knowledge rather than economic and technological processes, has affected Indonesia. Since the late 1980s, military leaders and other pillars of the New Order correctly identified the spread of ideas about democracy and political liberalization as a threat to the regime, and they adopted tactics to accommodate, contain, or repress Indonesian groups that espoused these ideas. There is little evidence, however, that contemporaneous ideas about defense restructuring gained traction in Indonesia, testimony to the military's overwhelming focus on maintaining domestic security rather than meeting foreign threats. Indeed, the Indonesian army's lack of concern about foreign threats has made it less susceptible to pressure from Western countries on human rights: In the absence of obvious external threats that would require military modernization, Western restrictions on military sales have amounted to only the smallest of admonitory sticks.

Global defense norms have acquired greater influence during the post-Soeharto era, mainly because Western donor agencies, and a small group of Indonesian activists, have sought ideas they can use in their struggle to establish civilian control over the military and consolidate democracy. In the military-dominated New Order, very few civilians acquired expertise in military affairs, and most proponents of political reform developed strongly anti-military positions. In the wake of the transition, however, a small group of scholars and activists interested in defense reform built networks that linked them to sympathetic military and political leaders in Jakarta as well as to foreign donors and academics. One group, a loose network called ProPatria, stands out for its role in drafting alternatives to military-sponsored legislation on defense-related issues. In 2003, it helped to stall a bill on the armed forces that had been drafted by the military leadership and presented to the House by Megawati's government. The bill contained a provision that came to be known as the "coup clause" because it allowed the military to deploy its forces without presidential approval for up to twenty-four hours. This sparked a public outcry, as did a revised bill, again drafted by the military that continued to limit civilian authority. Behind the scenes, however, ProPatria activists worked quietly and successfully to gain legislative support for language that would strengthen civilian control over the military.[29] Morever, because of their expertise and commitment to further reform, Yudhoyono's defense minister, Juwono Sudarsono, regularly seeks their input.[30]

As in most countries, the revolution in military affairs (RMA), with its emphasis on expensive and sophisticated technology, has had little impact in Indonesia.[31] In Asia, only a small number of countries have the resources and the strategic interest to pursue the sort of defense transformation that the RMA calls for, and even they have made little progress.[32] During the early and mid-1990s, when the RMA was first described and popularized, Indonesia enjoyed economic growth but did not face any significant foreign threats. Since the onset of political and economic crises in the late 1990s, the government's official view is that the country does not face the threat of invasion or attack, and in any case the government has been in no condition to fund major improvements in the armed forces.[33] Moreover, in the absence of any alliance with major military powers, Indonesia faces no pressure to adopt the RMA in order to enhance interoperability.

Limited Pressures, Limited Outcomes

Apart from the burst of reform that occurred between 1998 and 2000, progress toward defense reform in Indonesia has been slow. Civilian politicians have concentrated more on gaining and retaining power than seeking to reform the defense sector. Indeed, their failure to remove the military entirely from politics at the time of transition created incentives for civilian leaders to place a higher priority on winning the military's political support than on asserting their own control over the military. Particularly under Megawati, the longest-serving president since Soeharto, the military faced almost no significant external pressure to undertake reform and was able to reestablish internal unity. As a result, many critical issues remain unresolved. The army's territorial command structure remains in place, and the military's economic interests remain essentially untouched.

Since civilian control over the military exists more in law than in practice, it is not yet possible to speak meaningfully about progress toward greater military effectiveness and defense efficiency. In the terms defined by the editors, military effectiveness is "understood as [the] ability of defense and security forces to successfully carry out the roles and missions assigned to them by elected leaders." In Indonesia, no government has conducted a defense review in more than two decades, and the politicians elected since 1999 have shown little interest in doing so. Likewise, defense efficiency remains a distant goal in Indonesia. Civilian and military leaders have not reached any agreement on the military's appropriate roles and missions, and consequently it is impossible to assess whether and how these can be accomplished at the least possible cost to society.

In sum, the limited nature of defense reform reflects the limited number and strength of the forces behind it. Democratization has brought changes that were nearly unimaginable a decade ago, but the conditions under which regime change occurred favored the rise of weak civilian governments that have proven unable and occasionally unwilling to assert control over the military. Forces that have contributed to defense reform in other countries, such as liberalization, globalization, and the RMA, have had little or no impact on Indonesia, further diminishing the prospects for rapid, far-reaching defense reform.

NOTES

1. Many Indonesians use a single name.
2. East Timor Action Network, "'Military Has Already Won' Indonesian Election, Says East Timor Action Network/U.S," press release, 18 September 2004, available at http://www.etan.org/news/2004/09elect.htm; accessed 28 September 2007.
3. Juwono Sudarsono, "Real Military Reform Depends on Civilians," *Jakarta Post*, published in two parts on 23 and 24 June 2004.
4. Jun Honna, *Military Politics and Democratization in Indonesia* (London: RoutledgeCurzon, 2003), 209.
5. Sudarsono, "Real Military Reform."
6. Marcus Mietzner, "Politics of Engagement: The Indonesian Armed Forces, Islamic Extremism, and the 'War on Terror,'" *Brown Journal of World Affairs* 9, 1 (Spring 2002): 75.
7. On the revolutionary period, see Salim Said, *Genesis of Power: General Soedirman and the Indonesian Military in Politics, 1945–49* (Singapore: Institute of Southeast Asian Studies, 1991); and Ulf Sundhaussen, *The Road to Power: Indonesian Military Politics, 1945–1967* (Kuala Lumpur: Oxford University Press, 1982).
8. The conspiracy that led to the generals' murders remains poorly understood, but the military's ensuing assault on the Communist Party and its supporters is much better documented. The best account remains Harold Crouch, *The Army and Politics in Indonesia* (Ithaca, NY: Cornell University Press, 1978). On the killings, see Robert Cribb, ed., *The Indonesian Killings, 1965–66: Studies from Java and Bali* (Clayton, Australia.: Monash University, 1990); and Geoffrey Robinson, *The Dark Side of Paradise: Political Violence in Bali* (Ithaca, NY: Cornell University Press, 1995).
9. The best description of events during this period is found in Crouch, *Army and Politics.*

10. One of Soeharto's closest army associates, Ali Moertopo, described the regime's thinking in Ali Moertopo, *Dasar-dasar Pemikiran tentang Akselerasi Modernisasi Pembangunan 25 Tahun* [Some Basic Thoughts on the Acceleration and Modernization of 25 Years' Development] (Jakarta: Center for Strategic and International Studies, 1973).
11. International Crisis Group, "Indonesia: Keeping the Military under Control," *ICG Asia Report* 9 (5 September 2000): 4; and Geoffrey Robinson, "Indonesia: On a New Course?" in Muthiah Alagappa, ed., *Coercion and Governance: The Declining Political Role of the Military in Asia* (Stanford: Stanford University Press, 2001), 234–235.
12. Michael Malley, "Soedjono Hoemardani and Indonesian-Japanese Relations, 1966–1974," *Indonesia* 48 (October 1989): 47–64.
13. For percentages, see Angel Rabasa and John Haseman, *The Military and Democracy in Indonesia* (Santa Monica: RAND, 2002), 70; and Danang Widoyoko, Irfan Muktiono, Adnan Topan Husodo, Barly Harliem Noe, and Agung Wijaya, *Bisnis Militer Mencari Legitimasi* (Jakarta: Indonesia Corruption Watch, 2005), 33. For share of GDP, see SIPRI, Military Expenditure Database, available at http://www.sipri.org/contents/milap/milex/mex_database1.html; accessed 28 September 2007.
14. On the rise of political opposition, see Edward Aspinall, *Opposing Soeharto: Compromise, Resistance, and Regime Change in Indonesia* (Stanford: Stanford University Press, 2005).
15. These are examined in Jun Honna, "Military Ideology in Response to Democratic Pressure during the Late Soeharto Era: Political and Institutional Contexts," *Indonesia* 67 (April 1999): 77–126.
16. See Honna, *Military Politics*, ch. 5, "Creating New Threats: Ideological Dogmatization," especially 113–116.
17. Adam Schwarz, *Nation in Waiting: Indonesia's Search for Stability* (Boulder, CO: Westview Press, 2000), 313.
18. On the struggles of the opposition, see Aspinall, *Opposing Soeharto*; and ch. 5, "Disorganising Civil Society," in Richard Robison and Vedi Hadiz, eds., *Reorganising Power in Indonesia: The Politics of Oligarchy in an Age of Markets* (London: Routledge Curzon, 2004), 120–144.
19. Their rivalry is well-described in Honna, *Military Politics*, 159–164.
20. Kevin O'Rourke, *Reformasi: The Struggle for Power in Post-Soeharto Indonesia* (Crow's Nest, New South Wales: Allen & Unwin, 2002), 146.
21. "Indonesia: Keeping the Military under Control," 2.
22. Honna, *Military Politics*, 164–167; and Rizal Sukma and Edy Prasetyono, "Security Sector Reform in Indonesia: The Military and the Police," Working Paper no. 9, Netherlands Institute of International Relations, February 2003, 22–23.
23. See, for example, Juan J. Linz and Arturo Valenzuela, eds., *The Failure of Presidential Democracy* (Baltimore, MD: Johns Hopkins University Press, 1994).

24. Sukardi Rinakit, *The Indonesian Military after the New Order* (Singapore: Institute of Southeast Asian Studies, 2005), 176–177.
25. Michael S. Malley, "Indonesia in 2002: The Rising Cost of Inaction," *Asian Survey* 43, 1 (January/February 2003): 141–142.
26. On the military's role in the transition from Wahid to Megawati, The Editors, "Current Data on the Indonesian Military Elite," *Indonesia* 75 (April 2003): 14–18.
27. Ibid., first quotation, 12, second, 21.
28. Michael S. Malley, "Indonesia: The Erosion of State Capacity," in Robert I. Rotberg, ed., *State Failure and State Weakness in a Time of Terror* (Washington, DC: Brookings, 2003), 186–188.
29. International Crisis Group, "Indonesia: Rethinking Internal Security Strategy," *Asia Report* 90 (20 December 2004): 9–12.
30. John Haseman and Eduardo Lachica, *Toward a Stronger U.S.-Indonesia Security Relationship* (Washington DC: US-Indonesia Society, 2005), 65–69.
31. Ahmed S. Hashim, "The Revolution in Military Affairs outside the West," *Journal of International Affairs* 51, 2 (Spring 1998): 431–445.
32. Richard A. Bitzinger, "Come the Revolution: Transforming the Asia-Pacific's Militaries," *Naval War College Review* 58 (Autumn 2005): 39–60.
33. The Defense Department White Paper stating that the country faces no external threat is available at http://www.dephan.go.id/buku_putih/bukuputih.pdf; accessed 28 September 2007.

12

The Challenge to Reform Defense

David Pion-Berlin

Introduction

Why should we ever expect states to reform their civil-military relations or their defense forces? Reform is hard, and harder still for military bureaucracies. As Stephen Rosen said, "almost everything we know in theory about large bureaucracies suggests not only that they are hard to change, but that they are designed not to change.... Military bureaucracies, moreover are especially resistant to change."[1] Once bureaucracies stumble upon a successful formula for survival, they stick to it. Routine and repetition become the names of the game. More of the same is better, because it has worked in the past. Those within the bureaucracy who owe their career successes to the organization have a vested interest in seeing the successful formulae repeated ad infinitum. And it is they who will oversee promotions and thus instill in aspiring careerists for generations to come, an appreciation for the status quo.

Militaries are not just bureaucracies; they are also political organizations with a stake in preserving their quota of power. In many Third World countries, that quota is sizeable, and militaries have through the years, accrued decision-making autonomy, generous budgets, numerous perks and privileges, and even immunity from prosecution. These are advantages they would rather not give up and thus they attempt to fend off efforts by civilians to rein them in. Newly democratizing countries cannot hope to ever consolidate their rule without gaining some measure of control over their armed forces.

Certainly there have been heretofore politicized military organizations that finally submit to civilian rule. And militaries do innovate now and then. The common notion is that an organization is more prone to change in response to a challenging environment. For the military, this could mean a defeat in war in the not so distant past, a threatening security environment in the present, or a prospective security challenge in the near future. Even then, innovation is no sure bet. There have been many examples of defeated armies who then lost again for having failed to reform.[2]

Innovation is a tough sell, because it is asking the military to do something it has not done before. It is unfamiliar, and thus for many inside the organization, it is risky. It is also threatening to those accustomed to organizational power, perks, and privileges. Those in positions of authority must often be convinced that a change is a win-win situation; that it will mean the creation of a more effective fighting force without a loss of resources, manpower, units, or positions. For that reason, innovation via downsizing is a very difficult concept to accept. Even if there are efficiency gains to be had, the prospect of fewer troops, installations, and units, means someone will be losing position and benefits. Effectiveness and cost-cutting efficiency are often on a collision course with each other in a military torn by service rivalries.

For these reasons, it has been argued that the innovators must come from the outside. Only those with no vested interests—who can stand above the interservice feuds—can see how the whole institution may benefit from change.[3] And only those with authority can impose a solution on those who would resist it. These two sets of individuals are usually not the same. For example, innovators may be found in what Kimberly Zisk calls, a defense policy community.[4] But those policy entrepreneurs must find civilian elites who are on good terms with military commanders who in turn are receptive to their ideas and who can use their authority to set the innovations in motion down through the chain of command; who can promote young officers more open minded to change; and who can remove the old guard who stand in the way. Power, problem, and policy streams must converge for reforms to succeed.[5]

Under favorable circumstances, defense reform is still a chance occurrence; it depends on many variables falling into place at the right time. But even if the opportunity for reform presents itself, what motivations do states and their leaders have to seize upon them? Many states have other pressing priorities, and place defense reform lower down their agendas. Outside of the United States and a few other developed nations, it is hard if not impossible for political leaders to find an electoral advantage in reforming defense, let alone even paying attention to it.[6] Besides, many states have little confidence that they could actually achieve the goal of reform, assuming they wanted to. As James Wirtz explains in Chapter 4, most countries do not develop public national security strategies because they would rather not call attention to the issue, for fear that they would have to make good on their declared goals.

If we begin with the reasonable assumption that most states would rather leave well enough alone, then it becomes essential to identify those factors that roust some nations out of their lethargy to actually engage in defense reform. The fact that a few states *do* change all or part of what Bruneau and Trinkunas describe as the trinity of civil-military relations—civilian control, defense effectiveness, and efficiency—is inherently interesting. What causes them to do so? What causes most others not to bother?

Global Influences on Defense Reform

Most scholars look for causes within the confines of a given nation state. Those who do look beyond the borders of the nation consider regional threat environments, or more specifically, threatening adversaries. This volume is unusual in that it has focused on global factors that are rarely associated with civil-military affairs. It finds that democratization, diffusion of new norms associated with military professionalism, economic liberalism, and revolutions in military technology have each played a role in promoting reform. But it also discovers the limits to global influences, and how reform efforts and results vary greatly from country to country. What follows is a review of the book's central findings and its implications.

Let us begin with democratization. If the authoritarian interlude preceding the third democratic wave taught politicians anything, it was just how dangerous a politically aggressive military could be to the survival of their competitive systems. Democratic promoters of defense reform understood all too clearly that the first order of business must be to help newly democratized states devise ways of subordinating their militaries to civilian control. It would make little sense to change defense missions, doctrines, strategies, and efficiencies in the absence of a prior agreement as to who the principals and who the agents would be in a civil-military relationship. Were there to be lingering doubts about the right of elected civilians to be the ultimate decision makers, and the obligation of soldiers to be decision takers, then the funding of defense projects could play into the hands of power-greedy generals who fancy themselves the principals and civilians their agents. It is not surprising then that externally based defense reform promoters placed so much emphasis on fostering civilian control in the host countries. But how would that control be achieved?

In countries with traditions of military praetorianism, it would be difficult to talk politicians out of a seductive idea: exert power over the military by weakening it. Deny the military its customary budget shares, downsize it, deplete it of resources, personnel, and facilities, and thus render it a smaller, less potent force. Governments with limited resources and defense expertise, facing no serious threats at their borders, are most tempted to employ precisely such a strategy, because they would rather invest their limited funds into projects that have greater urgency and popular or electoral appeal. The problem with this approach, however, is that it works at cross purposes with the goal of fulfilling the other components of the trinity: military effectiveness and efficiency. It is impossible to sensibly reconfigure defense forces to undertake assigned roles in an effective, cost-efficient manner when the military is being stripped down for political purposes, without any regard for strategic consequences.

Democratic leaders are often wary of building military capacity back up because they fear it will simply restore political power to the armed forces. The challenge for democratic promoters of reform is to overcome that fear, to convince political leaders that they can, in fact, achieve the twin goals of greater civilian control and greater military capacity at the same time. It would seem doable, if for no other reason than it calls attention to the time-tested strategy of carrots and sticks: suppress the military's autonomous instincts but then reward it professionally by enhancing its ability to conduct missions. And yet, success stories are few and far between, because as Bruneau and Trinkunas point out, it is hard to find the right mix of incentives to get *civilian* leaders to care. Where are the carrots for them?

The one place in the world where the right incentives do exist is in the Central European states. Here, the prospect of joining NATO or the Partnership for Peace spurs full democratization, and motivates civilians to both control and more efficiently equip their militaries so that they can be integrated with allied forces. The returns on this investment are sizeable, and come in the form of shared costs, greater security, prestige, and domestic political support. Unfortunately, the NATO model may be the exception that proves the rule: that elsewhere it is very hard indeed to fulfill the trinity.

The second global force affecting almost all cases considered in this volume is the transnational diffusion of values, and specifically norms of professionalism, international law, and human rights. As this volume has shown, normative changes in recent decades can potentially have beneficial effects on the military. Norms "entrepreneurs" have had success at both legitimizing international, humanitarian interventions into the domestic affairs of sovereign states, and of linking human rights, peace, and security. Meanwhile, the locus of conflict has shifted from between to within states. States are traumatized internally by genocide, civil wars, ethnic tensions, and countless other humanitarian disasters that have set back the cause of internal peace and nation-building efforts. As a result, there are now powerful security rationales for multilateral military interventions—via invitation or not—into sovereign states to help avert atrocities, protect human rights, maintain a fragile peace, or rebuild war-torn societies. Many militaries have taken up these challenges as they accept new definitions about legitimate roles, joining in on U.N. sanctioned, nontraditional missions. But because there is heightened sensitivity toward human rights, these very militaries fall under closer scrutiny. They can hardly be praised as human rights protectors while violating those rights.

Scandalous information about military misdeeds now finds its way rapidly onto the pages of newspapers and television and computer screens with increasing ease. It is next to impossible for security units to conceal wrongdoing for very long. As Anne Clunan has argued in Chapter 2, norms diffusers can use this information to stoke public outrage, and thus compel states to "change the ends to which militaries are put and the means they use..." This would augur well for the reform of certain military practices. In theory, civilians could more easily exert oversight, arguing that military self-monitoring in an age of human rights awareness will not suffice. Moreover, there would be solid rationales to build in various doctrinal, tactical, and operational safeguards against immoral conduct in the prosecution of warranted missions, or the elimination of unwarranted missions altogether.

In practice, not all armies agree to humanitarian assignments, nor are all equally subject to the same levels of ethical scrutiny. Normative pressures succeed unevenly for various reasons. As will be emphasized later, some states are less vulnerable to all sorts of external pressures, because they are larger and more powerful. They cannot be easily coerced or shamed into compliance with new international standards, because the international community has less effective leverage over them. Others are less powerful but more hostile to what are perceived as Western beliefs. They will take umbrage at any effort by outsiders to induce reforms that conform to what they view to be a set of biased values. Finally, there are states that are situated in tranquil security environments. They face no imminent threats from abroad or within, do not see themselves in a competitive situation with other states or non-state actors, and thus calculate the costs of ignoring normative trends to be low.

A third global force considered in this volume is economic liberalization, although it tends to constrain reform rather than initiate it. With the move toward free market economies comes the refrain that defense expenditures are a drag on economic growth. It is a refrain that has been widely accepted by international financial institutions like the IMF, resulting in calls for drastic cuts in defense spending in order to promote development. If, as the IMF maintains, defense spending is wasteful, that a dollar spent on the military generates fewer jobs or useful products than a dollar spent elsewhere, then reducing it could be thought of as means of gaining greater overall efficiencies. But what is efficient to the economy could not be more injurious to national security. Zealot finance ministers determined to limit deficit spending slash away at the defense budget until the military is hollowed out, leaving it unprepared to fulfill its professional obligations. From a security point of view, this is misguided policy. Instead, the objective would be to achieve greater *defense* efficiencies by salvaging missions deemed vital to security in a way that reduces their costs.

Politics invites many tradeoffs. Countries are finding that too much adherence to neoliberalism can be a bad thing, because it exposes vulnerable groups to the ravages of the market without adequate protection, causing widespread voter dissatisfaction among the poor and lower middle classes. With electoral consequences in mind, politicians from many developing nations have recently retreated incrementally from free market formulas, embracing redistributive policies, government transfers, and a more aggressive role for the state. But what if defense spending were to persist at the same rate in countries that move away from economic liberalism? For those nations in challenging threat environments, where it is essential to maintain enhanced military preparedness, there may be no alternative other then to accept a tradeoff between better security and poorer economic growth. Those countries with fewer security threats could reap a peace dividend, as transfers of funds out of defense could be used for redistributive ends, or to help generate growth. Consequently, we would predict different outcomes to the guns versus butter dilemma, with the threat environment being a critical intervening variable.

The fourth and final global driver is the Revolution in Military Affairs (RMA). The price tag for importation of RMA is too high, the learning curve to catch up is too steep to make it worthwhile for most other countries to pursue. However that does not mean that the RMA is not without influence. The very fact that the defense gap between the United States and others has grown so large has meant that those without RMA, realizing they could never compete with the United States on the conventional battlefield, have had to make innovative adjustments of their own.

These adjustments lead nations away from symmetric warfare scenarios to asymmetric ones. For adversaries of the United States, this can mean one of two strategies. The first would be to go nuclear, assuming that technology was within their grasp. Having nuclear weapons would serve as a deterrent to invasion. It could also deter the United States or its allies from even threatening the nuclear state by arming its neighbors with conventional weapons. The second would be to develop people's war strategies. The use of guerrilla-style operations that blend with and depend on support from civilian populations, or the use of irregular forces as adjuncts to large-scale armies—ones that are small, rapid, agile, and lightly armed—will be strategies of choice to offset the U.S. advantage. Other strategies might include the use of paramilitary forces, militia, or terrorists.

These responses to RMA may have harmful repercussions for democratic civilian control. Asymmetric warfare is often conducted by armed units that do not easily answer to the central government. They may be renegade forces, or they may profess greater loyalties to an ethnic or religious group, a movement, or an ideological cause. They may also be more adept than the official military at protecting their constituents while striking back against the United States and its allies. If that is so, then the central authorities will have no power over them, and no legitimacy with the citizens for whom they cannot provide protection.

In the political world, there are no global forces that uniformly influence the internal affairs of all countries. Within the cases considered in this volume, it is clear that democratization and the globalization of new norms of military professionalism have had a significant impact on civil-military relations. Economic liberalization has played a constraining role in a couple of important cases, such as Indonesia and Colombia, but it does not appear to precipitate defense reform.

The RMA appears to drive defense reform only in the United States and India, although Taiwan does show that thinking about the RMA has played a role in the conceptualization of defense reform, if not its implementation.

It should come as no surprise that the four global defense reform drivers reviewed here impact nations unevenly. But what accounts for this variation? This is the subject to which we now turn.

Accounting for Variations in Defense Reform

The first observation would be that state power matters. Those states in the global system that are, by dint of population size, GPD, and/or military might, significantly more powerful than others, have the means to either shape the global drivers (United States) or to dull, deflect, or ignore their impact. Certainly the United States is primarily responsible for generating the RMA. Nearly all the cutting edge technological innovations that have transformed modern weaponry, operational capabilities, and battlefield tactics have occurred with the U.S. military industrial complex. The other global drivers have been influenced by the United States but not as decisively.

The United States is also one of those countries that has achieved genuine defense reform in the area of command and control. The reasons for the innovations designed by the Goldwater-Nichols act have more to do with domestic assessments of military shortcomings and less to do with international forces. U.S.-based think tanks and presidentially appointed commissions made recommendations and key congressmen with strong defense credentials pushed the reforms through.

As Rajesh Basrur points out in Chapter 9, new global forces have had an impact on India, opening up its markets and shaping its strategic environment. The nation has become a nuclear power—as has its neighbor, Pakistan—and by no coincidence has also become more vulnerable to unconventional, globally inspired, terrorism. But in the end, domestic variables are more important in determining whether or not reform will succeed. India is an old democracy, one that predates the new democratic wave, the Third Wave, by many decades. In theory, it should have had ample time to hone its system of democratic civilian control. And yet it demonstrates many shortcomings: civilians cede bureaucratic power to the military, give in to misguided military views on nuclear strategy, and fail to stem army-led counterinsurgency and counterterror missions that have proven disastrous. The problem can be traced to a deficit of civilian will and expertise, the result of which is that civilians fail to exercise the formal power they enjoy. India is a cautionary tale about democracy: having the legal instruments, the institutions and bureaucracies is not enough; they must be properly empowered, or else militaries will fill the void that is left.

Smaller and less developed states like Taiwan, Colombia, Romania, and to some extent Indonesia demonstrate higher vulnerabilities to the international system. These countries cannot impose barriers to external influence at will. Some are financially dependent on foreign donors and would suffer huge economic setbacks were they to openly defy global actors. Others (Colombia, Romania) desire military aid to complete missions or enhance security, and wish to curry favor with major suppliers of hardware, technology, and knowledge. Yet others like Indonesia have been at times subject to international human rights pressures, and have had to make cosmetic adjustments to escape the scrutinizing glare of world opinion.

Each of these nations has taken up some reforms in response to outside pressures. Taiwan got caught up in the third democratic wave and started its transition to a competitive system in 1987 with the lifting of martial law. As has been the case elsewhere, democratization in Taiwan had a stronger influence over civilian control than it did over military efficiency or effectiveness. The United States controls the purse strings of Plan Colombia, and has used that leverage to induce greater military effectiveness in combating the FARC and the narco-terrorists. Eager to fulfill the conditions for entrance into NATO and the European Union, Romania has made progress on all three fronts: democratic civilian control, military effectiveness, and efficiency.

At the same time this volume has shown prudence in not overstating the positive influences of global forces. There is a long road to be traveled between the emergence of global defense reform drivers on the one hand and the successful completion of reform on the other. External influences must be effectively transmitted; they must be timed to coincide and synergize with other forces; and perhaps most importantly, they depend on the will and capacity of domestic actors to see the reforms through. Many elements can turn that road into a veritable obstacle course.

As Bruneau and Trinkunas argued in Chapter 3, unless there are agents, agencies, and explicit mechanisms in place to transfer lessons about defense reform from the developed to lesser developed nations, then democratization in and of itself will not induce reform, whether it be via contagion, demonstration effects, or osmosis. Where mechanisms are in place, they do not impact all countries evenly, and their emphasis seems to be predominately on the civilian control part of the trinity, not the other two elements.

Timing is of critical importance. The tide of economic liberalism may actually undermine moves toward democratization, civilian control, effectiveness, and efficiency if it washes ashore before regime change to democracy occurs. Free market principles made their way to Indonesia and Chile when Suharto and Pinochet respectively first came to power. The influx of capital helped to fortify these dictatorships, keep control of the armed forces in the hands of generals, and delay the transitions to democracy. Like so many other military regimes, those in Indonesia and Chile were notorious for ignoring the efficiency criteria they imposed on others. In the absence of countervailing checks and balances, they could spend lavishly, unwisely, and indefinitely on their own pet projects, or profit from illicit gains. Ironically, it was the crash of capitalism throughout Asia in 1997 that helped weaken Suharto by unraveling the credibility of his economic policies. It left Suharto vulnerable to his international creditors who by that time, favored a turn toward democracy. In Chile, economic liberalism only had a positive effect once accompanied by the reemergence there and throughout the Southern Cone of democratic governments—all of whom were anxious to promote economic integration, defense transparency, and cooperation. Economic liberalization does not appear to have a decisive influence in initiation defense reform, but it may provide a background constraint (in countries that are in the midst of economic crisis) or enabler for successfully completing reforms.

In the final analysis, what goes on inside each of these less powerful countries matters critically to the success or failure of defense reform, even though they are more vulnerable to external influences. Here, reform meets face to face with unwilling leaders, veto groups, or systemic impediments. Sometimes resistance is blunt, as when the Indonesian military makes it clear to the courts that it will not tolerate seeing its officers put in the dock for human rights violations. On the surface it appears as if civilian control has been enhanced. Below the surface, there has been a proliferation of para-military units that operate outside the chain of command. A closer look reveals that the very laws it passes are designed to place key powers in the hands of the president, or to reserve more power for the armed forces themselves.

Speaking of presidents, oftentimes obstacles to reform lie precisely in the executive office. Having replaced Indonesian president Abdurrahman Wahid who was impeached in 2001, Megawati

Sukarnoputri showed complete disdain for reform efforts. As Michael Malley reveals in Chapter 11, she appointed as commander of all the armed forces, an officer who had publicly taken issue with the principle of civilian control; she hired a defense minister with no understanding of military issues; and she abandoned all efforts to bring military human rights violators to trial and in fact appointed to high positions generals who had been implicated in the massacres of East Timorese. President Uribe of Colombia has harmed his own defense ministry by personally interacting with top commanders, encouraging them to go directly to him with their problems rather than through the defense minister. Accordingly, as Douglas Porch demonstrates, the military shows little respect for the civilian ministerial staff and for the ministry in general, despite the fact that the MOD is in the chain of command, and has actually done some admirable work, including having drafted the nation's first National Security Strategy.

If chief executives do not stand in the way of reform, others may. Veto groups are those in a political system with enough power to overturn policies or to prevent them from being realized. As suggested at the beginning of this chapter, the most formidable veto group may be the armed forces themselves. In Indonesia, the military has for decades enriched themselves off the books through control of enterprises given to them by the state. Now the state wants them back, but the military show no signs of cooperating, despite legislation that says it must. In Colombia, all bets have been placed with a military solution to the country's civil-war. This means greater power for the military whose lobbyists usually have their way with obliging legislators. And in Taiwan, as elsewhere, the military use their monopoly over security expertise as a veto weapon. Less knowledgeable parliamentarians feel pressured to defer to military points of view, and civilian defense ministry officials seem reluctant to make their presence known.

The Taiwanese case also suggests that democracy itself can yield veto opportunities or better put, bottlenecks. The move from a Leninist-styled system dominated by the KMT to a democratic one replete with partisan clashes over questions of identity and threat assessment has often obstructed reform efforts. Arms procurement legislation has been tied up for years in the parliament. Partisanship has resulted in gridlock over whether China is the mother country or the enemy, which prevents agreement on what the nation's defense strategy should be. Some want a tamer defense, others a more forward looking, deterrent capacity. Splits occur not only between parties but within the armed forces itself, with the army most opposed to an aggressive defense, and the air force and navy viewing it more favorably.

Likewise, in Indonesia, democracy's new electoral rules devised after the transition proved to be a hindrance to presidential-legislative cooperation on defense. The rules increased the number of political parties past the point where working majorities could be forged, and at the same time denied the president the right to dissolve the parliament in order to call for new elections. In short, democratization has spawned spirited debates about defense, but has also hampered progress in realizing reform.

If democratic systems can create their own obstacles, they can also create their own opportunities. In Chile, the logic of electoral competition has caused conservative political parties to distance themselves from the Pinochet legacy so that they may better compete for the politically centrist voter. As a result, they have joined the other parties in congress to pass historic legislation that has enhanced civilian control. The military itself has gradually accepted the center-left administration as fully capable of setting defense priorities, in consultation with officers. The armed forces went so far as to renounce their veto power in the Chilean system. As institutional spaces for dialogue between erstwhile antagonists have emerged, each side has acquired a greater understanding of, respect for, and trust in the other.

Why then is a democracy like Chile's able to advance the cause of defense reform while others languish? It would be too facile to chalk it up to a culture of consensus in a country that has had its share of polarizing, violent conflict. Certainly political opportunity has to be factored in. The arrest of Pinochet in England in 1998, gave great momentum to the human rights cause, and to the process of civil-military dialogue, best represented by the Mesa del Diálogo that was initiated in 1999.

Opportunities arise, but it depends on leaders to seize them. Thus, the final consideration is whether differences in strategic leadership abilities might account for some of the variation between cases. In Chile, it took strong initiative on the part of Presidents Eduardo Frei and Ricardo Lagos to push for change. Frei's 1995 proclamation that civilians had the right to make defense policy followed by the creation of that nation's first white book on defense in 1997, were examples of leadership. President Lagos' approval of the first national strategic and defense plans in 2003, followed in 2004 by his successful bid to win congressional approval of a package of constitutional reforms that in Marcos Robledo's words, set the "institutional basis for democratic civil military relations," were important strategic moves.

These actions were that much more vital in a country like Chile where the institutional setting that was bequeathed to the new democracy and that persisted for a decade or more thereafter was designed to perpetuate military autonomy while weakening civilian control. Strategic leadership is most needed precisely when reform opponents who are in a position to preserve the power and privileges they acquired during authoritarian rule can cement into place conditions, laws, and agreements that institutionalize constraints and seemingly foreclose reform options later on.

By this measure, strategic failure would be best demonstrated in those countries where transitions or the systemic environment open up ample opportunities, but where politicians fail to exploit them. One example would be Indonesia, where Suharto's sudden, stunning fall from power in 1998 precipitated by protests and widening divisions within the military seemingly left authoritarians with a much weakened hand and democratic opponents with the clear advantage. The post-transitional government of Habibie had good intentions, but made strategic errors by setting up new electoral rules that as Michael Malley relates "assured weak and unstable political leadership" by multiplying legislative factions while ensuring deadlock with the executive branch. Presidents that followed were unable (Wahid) and unwilling (Megawati) to push for serious defense reform. This gave the military time to heal its wounds, reunify, and reassert its historic power.

India is another example of strategic missteps. It is an age-old democracy that has had many decades to fine tune its bureaucratic instruments of civilian control. Politicians are *structurally* invulnerable to undue military influence. In this ideal setting, civilians should have subjected the defense sector to their own strategic vision. Instead, they have made what Rajesh Basrur describes as excessive use of military approaches. Rather than implement their own ideas, civilian leaders consistently defer to military judgments where they need not have, on failed counterinsurgency campaigns, nuclear weapons policy, and defense doctrine.

SUMMING UP

In this globalized world, states are supposedly more susceptible then ever to foreign influences. Sovereignty is under siege, as countries struggle to shape their own destinies in the face of an international environment that seems to impinge ever more on their policymaking efforts. No policy realm is more tied to state sovereignty than defense. A nation cannot claim to be sovereign if it loses control over its territory, fails to safeguard its borders, or deter foreign aggressors—all central elements of defense preparedness. It follows that if a nation has lost some measure of autonomy to the outside world, then so too has defense. In this respect, we would have expected the global drivers for reform studied in this volume to have exerted a substantial influence on defense policy in nations that are now more vulnerable than ever to globalization.

Instead, what we found is that full-fledged defense reform continues to elude most countries, notwithstanding some evidence of progress here and there. Achieving the trinity of civilian control, military effectiveness, and efficiency is difficult under any circumstances. Many elements must fall into place at the same time, and seldom do. History can conspire against it, institutions can stymie it, militaries will resist it, and politicians who are not properly motivated often fail to act.

Many promoters of defense reform have invested considerable time, energy, and resources to make democratic civil-military relations a reality. Their efforts should be applauded, and hopefully continued. This volume has demonstrated what they are up against—the head winds of reform antagonists that make progress painfully slow. But it has also shown that at times, global forces can be the tail winds that speed the process up, allowing democrats to realize the defense reforms they have long sought.

Notes

1. Stephen Peter Rosen, *Winning the Next War: Innovation and the Modern Military* (Ithaca, NY: Cornell University Press, 1991), 2.
2. Ibid., 9.
3. Kimberly Zisk, *Engaging the Enemy: Organizational Theory and Soviet Military Innovation, 1955–1991* (Princeton, NJ: Princeton University Press, 1993).
4. Ibid., 21.
5. John W. Kingdon, *Agendas, Alternatives and Public Policies* (Boston: Little Brown and Co., 1984).
6. David Pion-Berlin and Harold Trinkunas, "Attention Deficits: Why Politicians Ignore Defense Policy in Latin America," *Latin American Research Review* 42, 3 (October 2007): 76–100.

Index